Medicine Power

by Brad Steiger

Medicine Power

*The American Indian's Revival
of his Spiritual Heritage
and Its Relevance for Modern Man*

BRAD STEIGER

DOUBLEDAY & COMPANY, INC.   GARDEN CITY, NEW YORK
1974

ISBN: 0-385-02607-2 Trade
0-385-00925-9 Paperbound
Library of Congress Catalog Card Number 73–82248

Acknowledgments

I would like to express my sincere thanks to those who gave so generously of their time and their patience as I went about gathering material for this book. There will be some who granted interviews who will not find their comments included in the text of this book. Others who gave their permission to use valuable research papers may be disappointed when they find that I have not quoted their material. Although the limitations of words and pages demanded that certain input be excluded, I hope that those interviewees and contributors whose comments and material I could not use will understand that their shared insights were very important to me in the weaving of the diverse threads that make up the fabric of this volume. Among those who assisted in the gathering of thoughts, ideas, and good medicine were the following:

Ann Underwood, Beckley, West Virginia; Sun Bear, *Many Smokes,* P.O. Box 5895, Reno, Nevada 89503; Rarihokwats, *Akwesasne Notes,* Mohawk Nation, via Rooseveltown, New York 13683; Iron Eyes Cody, Los Angeles; Bill La Gana, Los Angeles; Twylah Nitsch, Irving, New York; Naomi and White Bear, Oraibi, Arizona; Tom Laughlin and Billy Jack Productions, Culver City; Dallas Chief Eagle, Pierre, South Dakota; Nada-Yolanda, Mark-Age MetaCenter, Inc., Miami; Minnesota Historical Society, St. Paul; Dr. E. Mansell Pattison, Department of Psychiatry and Human Behavior, University of California, Irvine; Don Wilkerson,

Director, Arizona Indian Centers, Phoenix; Norman Paulson, Brotherhood of the Sun, Santa Barbara; Father John Hascall, Baraga, Michigan; Wanda Sue Parrott, Los Angeles *Herald Examiner;* Gordon Alexander, Mystic, Connecticut; Donald W. Wanatee, Tama, Iowa; Dr. Walter Houston Clark, Professor Emeritus, Andover Newton Theological Seminary; Dr. Robert L. Bergman, Chief, Mental Health Program, Indian Health Service; Bertie Catchings, Dallas, Texas; Dr. Leo Louis Martello, Hero Press, New York; Gavin Frost, School and Church of Wicca, St. Charles, Missouri; Irene Hughes, The Golden Path, Chicago; R. Clark Mallam, Luther College, Decorah, Iowa; Bevy Jaegers, Psychical Research & Training Center, St. Louis; Ed and Lorraine Warren, Monroe, Connecticut; F. J. Houle, Jr., Tribal Secretary, Confederated Salish and Kootenai Tribes, Flathead Reservation, Montana; John Catchings, Austin, Texas; Col. Arthur J. Burks, Paradise, Pennsylvania; Heard Museum, Phoenix; Deon Frey, Chicago; Bess Krigel, Chicago; Al G. Manning, ESP Lab, Los Angeles; Tenny Hale, Beaverton, Oregon; Komar, Wooster, Ohio; Jeanyne B. Slettom, Minneapolis; Evangelist Julia Ratliff, Washington, D.C.

Contents

Introduction

There is only one Great Spirit, but because of cultural differences man may apprehend Him in various ways and may receive the sacred transfer of His secret name in different symbols. Because there is only one Great Spirit, all men are brothers, all women are sisters, and all those who achieve an attitude of humility, a respect for all living things, a sense of harmony with their environment, a balance between the sacred and the mundane, may reach out and touch the Great Spirit and receive His strength.

Although there is but one Great Spirit, there may be prescribed methods of communicating with Him that function better in one area than another. There may be unique modes of enlightenment which have been bestowed upon certain peoples and places in order to accomplish a more vital and meaningful realization of Divine Energy within the confines of certain spiritually delineated borders. When the European invaded North America, he may well have upset the continent's cosmological, as well as its biological, ecology.

Because of the European's haste to conquer, to civilize, to capitalize, and to convert, he did not take the time to understand the native people's social and spiritual customs, nor did he slacken the pace of plow and Progress long enough to consider the possibility that the native people may have taught him essential lessons on how best to survive in spirit, as well as in body, on the North American continent.

The Great Spirit's 2,000-year-old message to the Europeans had
become so distorted by dogma, eroded by ecclesiastical edicts, and
battered by bloody reformations and counter-reformations that the
storm-lashed soul of the whiteman had developed a spiritual anes-
thetic that numbed his sensitivity to any religious expression that
had not been pressed in the familiar cross-shaped mold cherished
by his fathers.

The sacred words given to the whiteman by the Great Spirit
had long since been adapted to justify an insatiable greed for gold
and the establishment of earthly kingdoms. When black-robed missionaries sought to convert the Amerindians, they too often were
able to hear only the self-righteous echo of their own sermons,
which had become as standardized as any other product of the In-
dustrial Revolution. Centuries of rationalization for crimes against
brothers had produced a new gospel of the Great Spirit for the
whiteman—a gospel that preached a Manifest Destiny which must
be realized at any price. Tragically, the redman became a sacrificial
offering on the gore-stained altar of Progress.

In order to quiet the troubled consciences of the more sensitive
homesteaders, soldiers, and traders, it was widely taught that the
redmen worshiped a Great Spirit different from that of the whiteman's God. The redman's Great Spirit was said to be inferior,
bloody, savage, dark, a pagan god that must die along with any
claim which the redmen might have on the land.

Although many historians and anthropologists believe that the
native people buried their god as well as their hearts at Wounded
Knee and that the contest between the whiteman's religion and
the redman's medicine was decided along with the issues of ter-
ritories and treaties, the last decade has seen a dramatic rebirth
of the strength and spirit of Amerindian magic. The old ways and
traditions have always been carefully nurtured and quietly cherished, but medicine power has returned in a manner that reveals
our Amerindian heritage as laden with spiritual insights fraught
with special meaning for our new age of ever-rising awareness.

The sacrificial blood that was spilled has begun to dry. Collective guilt and expanding consciousness has produced a generation who may at last be willing to give peace and love a chance. The essential self within each human may be explored without apology. Thoughtful men and women can see that the psycho-religious system of the various Amerindian people was centuries ahead of the whiteman's psychology, and that the shamans, the sacred doctors, had explored inner space to an extent not yet dreamed of by the invaders who crushed the redmen with technological tools of death and debasement.

The return of medicine power has fostered New Age Amerindian prophets who are speaking to contemporary youth. Ancient Amerindian metaphysics are influencing everything from our young people's popular music, their hair styles and manner of dress, to their personal spiritual philosophies. Contemporary Amerindian mystics are demonstrating that the medicine of the Great Spirit can soar beyond science to present modern man with a system of relevant spiritual guidance for anyone who will learn to walk in balance, to live in harmony with Nature and with the Cosmos.

May we be granted the wisdom and the vision to comprehend the spiritual gifts which our red brothers have to bestow upon those of us who share their land and those of us who wish to share their world.

Medicine Power

1. Quetzalcoatl's Promise

According to legend, long ago there lived a wise and powerful prophet-king of the Toltec Indians of southern Mexico named Quetzalcoatl, the Feathered Serpent. Quetzalcoatl, often described as being white or fair of skin and bearded, brought the Toltecs a spiritual philosophy of love and kindness, and he taught them to raise better crops, to construct more material things, and to fashion a rather sophisticated scientific structure. Quetzalcoatl shaped the Toltecs into the greatest nation in Mexico; and by the time the Toltecs were supplanted by the Aztecs, the Feathered Serpent had been elevated to the position where prophet became nearly indistinguishable from deity.

It is said that when Quetzalcoatl left the Toltecs to travel to a faraway place beyond their knowing, he provided them with a last prophecy.

He told his people that in time whitemen, who would resemble him only in appearance, not philosophy, would come from the eastern sea in great canoes with massive white wings. These whitemen would, in turn, be like birds with two kinds of talons. On one foot would be the gentle, soft talons of a dove. The other foot would bear the hard, powerful talons of an eagle. One set of talons would seek to hold the Indians in love and kindness, while the other set would be prepared to claw them and grip them fast in slavery.

A few hundred years after the arrival of these first whitemen, Quetzalcoatl promised, other whitemen would appear who would bear only the talons of the peaceful dove. At this time, Quetzalcoatl, or the spirit that was in him, would also return. The Indians would once again have pride in their ancestors, and they would earnestly seek to regain both the spirit and the wisdom of the ancient people. The Indians and the whitemen who bore the feet of doves, would work together to build a new and better world of peace, love, and brotherhood.

The Aztecs, who inherited their culture from the Toltecs, corrupted the teachings of goodness bequeathed to them by Quetzalcoatl and introduced the dark and bloody elements of human sacrifice and the subjugation of other nations. When the Spaniards came from the eastern sea in their great canoes with the billowing sails that appeared to be massive white wings, Emperor Montezuma and his people delighted in what they suspected might be protracted intercourse with a race of men as wise and as kind as the great Quetzalcoatl. But Cortez and his soldiers and priests soon revealed themselves as man-greedy rather than god-generous. In one hand the Spaniards held the cross of the gentle Jesus, but with the other hand their eagle's talons wielded the sword and touched off the cannon.

In desperation, Montezuma turned to the true teachings of Quetzalcoatl, but he was too late to assist his people in anything other than their destruction and enslavement. Mortally wounded by one of his own people, Montezuma was given a vision of the future, which he told to Tula, his favorite daughter.

Montezuma saw the Aztec crushed, defeated. He saw the whiteman striding powerfully across the land, conquering and killing all who rose up against him. He saw the Indians suffering ages of wrong committed against them, but he also foresaw a day of splendor when they would once again become one of the deathless nations of the earth. This day would not occur, however, until there evolved a generation of men and women who respected sacred traditions and who understood correctly the concepts of God and freedom. With this understanding would come a new birth of brotherhood in which the cross of the whiteman's religion would remain, but its priesthood would vanish.

In their *Warriors of the Rainbow,* William Willoya and Vinson Brown have a young Indian boy ask a wise old woman of the tribe why the Great Spirit permitted the whiteman to take away the Indian's lands. The old woman, remembering the words of the old wise ones, tells the lad why the whitemen were sent to the North American continent:

> . . . the white men come from a land where only white men lived, and it was necessary for them to come to this place where they would learn about other races and learn to live with them, and that one day, when the Indians got the old spirit back again, they would teach the white men how to really love one another and how to love all mankind. Now, because the Indians were humbled and made poor by the white man's conquest, they have been cleansed of all selfish pride. They are ready for a great awakening, and they will awaken others.

Has Quetzalcoatl's promise been fulfilled? Has his spirit returned to give the Amerindians pride in their ancestry so that they might once again demonstrate the power and the wisdom of the sacred traditions and lead us all to a new and better world of peace, love, and brotherhood?

Sun Bear, a Chippewa medicine man, who publishes *Many Smokes* magazine in Reno, Nevada, told me: "This is happening now, because it is in harmony with our prophecies that foretold a time when there would be a return to our medicine and our ways on this continent.

"We feel that we are the traditional keepers and protectors of the Earth Mother, and we feel that there is coming a time when there is going to be a major cleansing and changing of things. At this time, according to our prophecies, there would be people returning to our philosophy and our direction.

"There are a lot of young people in the country today who are interested, and they are taking on the outer surfaces of Indian things, but they don't fully comprehend it yet. There are a great many of them who are going only part way in terms of our metaphysics, but they don't really understand the true significance of our philosophy, and they haven't really made a full commitment.

"One of the big problems with white youth, of course, is their whole cultural background. They grew up under a different type of culture, so that for many of them, getting into the Indian thing is like reading another book. They hover over it for a while, and maybe a bit of it hangs onto them, but they don't really make any full commitment.

"To the traditional Indian people, medicine is a life-long thing and it has a really strong significance.¯ To really appreciate and benefit from Indian medicine power, one has to have this conviction and feeling. You have to really be involved in it."

"This involvement extends beyond putting on a headband, a beaded belt, and some moccasins," I said.

"Right," Sun Bear agreed emphatically. "A lot of people come to me and say that they want to learn about medicine power. They say they want to get into the spiritual thing. I tell them that the start of it is that they must first learn to walk on the earth with a good balance. That means you have to learn to relate to each other and to the Earth Mother and learn to live in real harmony with her.

"That's where the first problem comes in. Ever since the whiteman came to this country, he has operated on a basis that he wants to get to heaven, but he doesn't want to bother to take any real responsibility for the Earth Mother and for the things around her.

"If the whitemen can't find a balance and work in harmony with the land and each other and show real love here, we traditional Indians wonder what the Great Spirit would want with such a bunch of ding-a-lings. We feel that the first step is to learn to walk in balance on the Earth Mother, then seek the medicine power that comes with the Great Spirit."

The well-known actor Iron Eyes Cody admitted that he had to relearn many of the old traditions in order to be better prepared for the return of medicine power.

Iron Eyes: I have always been a traditional man. I was a champion dancer, and I made easy money going around following pow-wows. I got into the movies as a technical director. In 1949, Cecil B. De Mille made an actor out of me in the Gary Cooper picture *The Unconquered.*

I am fifty-six years old, and I and a lot of other people had got away from the old traditions. But then about eight years ago, our young people wanted to learn the old ways. We older Indians began to think then that the circle is going to come back. Our dream is coming true. We are all going to get back in the Great Circle of Life.

I went into scouting work to teach the Indian boys to dance and sing—they even won merit badges, besides! The boys got merit badges, but the singing and dancing was taking me back to my tradition. I went right back into the old ways.

"So you, like so many Amerindians, had to relearn many of the old ways that had nearly become lost to you."

Iron Eyes: That is right. Many of us have forgotten our own Indian traditions. We say, "Oh, well, now I am a Catholic. Why should I join the Native American Church?"

I have come to the point where I have faith in all churches. I have a son who was an altar boy at a Catholic church. He was so devout, he even taught Latin to younger boys. Today he is living on the Ute reservation, working with a medicine man. That doesn't mean he is going to give up Christianity altogether, because he believes in all religion the way I do. I won't criticize anyone else, but I believe that now we've got to go with our Indian beliefs, our ways, and we must stick together.

I was in one Sun Dance where a young boy of about eight or nine was participating in his first big dance. I was the Receiver of the Pipe, who brings in the pipe, the altar, and the skulls.

This little boy's grandfather is a medicine man, but at his age, the boy was not pierced like the other dancers. Instead, they tied a rope around his shoulder. He pulled with the rest of the men, who were trying to break the flesh around the skewers in their chests and the rope attached to the Sun Dance pole. I know that little boy will one day be a medicine man.

My son is a traditional Indian. He sings the Sun Dance song while I serve as the Receiver of the Pipe. I also sing with the Sun Dance singers. A Sioux by the name of Jackson Tail is the lead drummer. Eagle Feather is the conductor of the Sun Dance. He is a spiritual man, a medicine man, a Yuwipi man.

I belong to the Yuwipi. We pray to heal people. We go into the sweat lodge to pray. Then we go into a building, and in one hour of light, we go through all kinds of ceremonials and put the altar up and pray to the tobacco sacks and pray for the people who are there. After one hour, the light goes out, and the room is in total darkness.

In the darkness, the medicine man, whom I myself have tied up, wrapped him with rawhide, lies before the altar. When the light comes on, the altar of a hundred and fifty sacks of tobacco tied by women are all rolled up. Nobody has moved. I know that nobody moved in the dark, because my son and I were singing in the darkness by the altar, and we didn't feel anybody go up in that area. So we have what you would call a spiritual happening!

Our younger generation is picking up the old traditions, learning the languages, learning the songs, learning the mysteries of the Great Spirit.

Right here in Los Angeles, we have about sixty thousand Indians. For many years I was on the Board of Directors of the Indian Center. I was forced to resign because I had to go to Spain to make a movie. But my point is that we have as much tradition right here in this city as you will find on several reservations, because we old-timers believe in teaching our children the languages, the songs, and the Indian way.

I taught my sons my language songs, and my wife taught them

her songs. My older boy is the champion fast-Oklahoma-style dancer. Here in Los Angeles, we have an Indian get-together where we sing and do the tribal dances every Saturday night.

We must all please the Great Spirit. We must go back to protecting this country like we did once before—all of us, not just the Indians! We must not destroy; for when we start destroying our environment, we begin to destroy ourselves. What we have in our medicine is strong, you know that; and our medicine does a lot of things.

We must please the Great Spirit!

Don Wanatee is proud of his Mesquakie people, because he feels that they have pleased the Great Spirit by remaining as true to the old traditions as possible, while living near Tama, Iowa, the very center of the Midwest Bible Belt.

Don Wanatee: I think that at least 70 per cent of all Indians living today have lost their basic beliefs, but I believe that most of them want to go back to the old ways. The trouble is, they have had no ways or means of going back. We believe once an Indian loses touch with the old way, he can regain it; but he must be shown the way.

There are a few pockets of Indians throughout the country that have maintained basically the same type of religion that their tribes have practiced for hundreds of years. The Mesquakie is one of these people who have held on to their old ways.

Of course we have had many inroads of conversionary types of religion, including Indians from the West, some from the North, who contributed the peyote and drum societies, which are held in high esteem by some of the Mesquakie because they reflect some of the old religious ways of their forefathers. The Native American peyote church, of course, combines the old ways with Christianity, and the Drum Society combines with a Chippewa belief, to which some of the Objibwa up North in Minnesota still adhere. To expect things to be exactly as they were three hundred years ago is not realistic. The Mesquakie have changed their methods of practicing their beliefs, but the basic ingredients of those beliefs remain the same as they were four or five hundred years ago. That is why I tend to believe them.

"So you have always been a traditionalist?"

Wanatee: Yes. There have been times, especially in my younger days in grade school, that the missionaries of the Presbyterian Mission used to ride out to the settlement and try to convert us. They taught us verses and hymns and told us how bad our religion was and how good theirs was. I have had moments like those, but they have reaffirmed my belief in the Mesquakie way.

"But now Indian metaphysics are spreading out from those pockets of traditional practitioners of the old ways to affect our entire nation. Do you think there is a reason for this to be happening now?"

Wanatee: Yes. I think it is happening because this land itself is Indian, and the ancestors of the many tribes are still on this earth, only in a different state. The Mesquakie believe that the thin veil between life and death is so slim that the dead may influence the living.

In my estimation, the younger generation perceives the faults and the incongruities of Christianity, which is supposed to be one of the better of the great religions of the world. Some of the practices and shenanigans that go on by professed Christians is not the Indian way. The Indian way is that you maintain your religious beliefs as part of the life that comes to you from the earth. Life comes from the earth. You don't give earth its life; it gives life to you. I think the Indian can show the younger generation—whether they be white or black or whatever—the proper way of treating life. Life is not a commodity. Life is a process.

What non-Indian people need to do is to look at themselves and then develop a basic philosophy that will enable them to come into an understanding of what the earth holds for them. They should create a new religion. Some of their old religion is good, too; but remember, it came from the Old Country.

The young people are beginning to understand. I can see it in their life-styles. I remember about twenty years ago, Great White America was making fun of the Indian because of his dress style, the cut of his hair, the color of his skin, the way he lived in old huts, shacks, and tents—everything about the Indian was put down. But now I see many of the young people living that same way, and nobody really cares, because most of the predominant society—I did not say the dominant society, but the *predominant* society— think they are a lost cause, much the same as they thought the Indian was a lost cause fifty years ago. The younger generation is accepting more and more of the Indian ways.

I asked Dr. Walter Houston Clark, Professor Emeritus of Andover Newton Theological Seminary, to respond to the question of why we might be witnessing a return of the spirit of Indian medicine at this time.

"I think our civilization has overemphasized the rational faculties of man," Dr. Clark said. "Our ideas of science have been so restrictive that the essential nature of human beings is being starved. Unconsciously, modern man is reaching out for something that goes beyond the purely rational, the purely scientific. Our young people are ready for an expression of the intuitive side of their natures. The psychedelic drugs have been perhaps as important a catalyst as any in disclosing to these young people their essential natures, and I am sure that this is one of the reasons for the amazing concern about meditation and religion of many kinds among the young people.

"In the American Indian, our youth find a person who has expressed a simpler kind of existence that coincides with their desire to get away from the cities and to associate themselves with nature in order to live a life sufficiently simple in its essential needs so that there is a little more time for thought and consideration of what it is that makes life worthwhile."

Twylah Nitsch, a granddaughter of the last great Seneca medicine man, observed that whenever she attended an Indian get-together, she noticed a spiritual aura connected with each Indian present. "It is always there whenever we are together," she said. "You don't even have to mention it, for it is there."

"The rebirth of Indian medicine power will also bring with it an emphasis on *humanhood*," Dallas Chief Eagle, a Sioux, the author of *Winter Count,* told me. "I must tell you a little story about how, back in 1947, I came to have a better understanding of the two major rules of life.

"I had returned from the Marines, and I used to visit an old-timer to bring him a piece of roast, coffee, and bread so he would sit and talk with me in Indian. I could imagine that during his long lifetime, ministers and all kinds of missionaries had come to visit him. I used to tell him what I had observed in the outside world and tell him about the things I read.

"Once we got on the subject of religion, and I said, 'Grandpa (we refer to all our elders in the tribe as grandfather and grandmother), the whitemen have Ten Commandments to serve as their major guideline in life. Do we, as Indians, have any major rules or commands in life?'

"The old man said, 'Grandson, we have only two: First, we love the Great Spirit and we always pay homage to Him. Second, we love *humanhood* (you cannot even find the word humanhood in the whiteman's dictionary). And I think, grandson, this is why we lost the country, because we were believers in humanhood and in these two major rules of life.

" 'But the Great Spirit is everything and everywhere, and because he is everything, he is also a humorist. He likes to laugh. I'll bet he laughs every day because he gave the whiteman eight more rules to confuse him!' "

I have long observed that mystics always get along famously, regardless of their ancestral or cultural backgrounds. Dogmatic differences in religions mean nothing to them, because they operate in a spiritual sphere that concerns itself with the dynamics of the Cosmos, rather than the details of ecclesiasticisms. In the course of gathering material for this book, I asked a number of psychic sensitives for their impressions regarding Amerindian mysticism and the Resurrection of the Great Spirit.

Irene Hughes, the internationally known Seeress of Chicago, is one quarter Cherokee, and she has many fond memories of her maternal grandmother's wisdom and of her knowledge of herbs and healing. "Grandmother wasn't very tall, but she was slender and she had very dark hair and very black eyes. She was a woman of deep perception," Irene recalled as she reflected on her childhood in Tennessee.

"There is a tremendous interest growing in our Indian heritage," she continued. "I feel that the government will take a greater interest in the rights of the Indian and assist in preserving some of the benefits that come from their wisdom."

"Do you think that the fact that you were able to discuss openly your dreams and visions as a child may have been due to your mother's acceptance of her own mother's ability to use her dreams to guide her life?" I asked.

Irene Hughes: Yes, I think my family had a greater tolerance of my abilities because of our Indian heritage. "Knowing" could be regarded as a natural way of life.

"I recall that many times you have mentioned that you were never made to feel odd or peculiar when you told your father to get the crop harvested in a hurry because a storm was on its way."

Mrs. Hughes: That is true. I was absolutely never made to feel odd. My predictions were followed as a natural way of life.

"Do you see any special insights which our Amerindian heritage may offer us today?"

Mrs. Hughes: I feel that one of the very distinctive things is going to be the intense interest in herbs that Indians use and the medicinal advantages of them.

I feel that we are truly evolving to a higher spiritual vibration. I feel that even the marijuana that our young people have been smoking may somehow be aligned with some of the hallucinogenic substances which some of the ancient people smoked in order to place themselves into an altered state of consciousness. Unfortunately, too many of our youth have prostituted the use of marijuana, and I feel much better about their going into meditation. It is wonderful that kids today are taking the time to meditate and to tune in.

The fight against pollution is yet another way by which we may reach the Spirit of God.

Indeed, we are having an evolution of spiritual growth in many different ways.

I see that small groups will replace the organized church and that these powerful little groups will be filled with the Holy Spirit and with divine fire. I see that we will go into different types of rituals and develop once again a worshipful attitude toward Nature.

I feel that we will take a step higher in our spiritual evolution when we begin to realize that some of the ancient teachings were far better than so much of our modern philosophy. I see that we will perhaps go even deeper into those ancient teachings with a new understanding.

Those metaphysicians who believe that an acceptance of the doctrine of reincarnation can provide us with answers to many otherwise imponderable questions have stated that many of the slaughtered Indians, who were killed before their time by the encroaching whites, are being reborn today as white youth. This is the reason, these metaphysicians say, that coincident with the restoration of Indian magic we are witnessing large numbers of white young people affecting both the manner of dress and the life-style of the Amerindian. I asked a number of my interviewees to respond to the question of reincarnation and karma in regard to the Resurrection of the Great Spirit:

Don Wanatee: I do not believe that our ancestors could be reborn as whites, but I think there is that possibility among the Indians. Some of us probably have gone to the other side and have come back again in the form of another person, yet we are still in the same tribe. But as far as the white children are concerned— no, I cannot believe it. If they find a way to communicate with their own ancestors, I imagine they could come up with a new type of religion whereby they might be able to do it, but it would be difficult.

Don Wilkerson, Director, Arizona Indian Centers, Phoenix: I tend to think that there is a strong possibility this may be happening, but I don't know. I don't fight the Unknown. I accept it. I don't personally believe in that form of reincarnation, although my people [Creek-Cherokee] have a form of reincarnation and so do many other tribes. I won't deny that there are some strong elements of proof in the world that reincarnation exists. Whether it happens to us or not, I don't know. I do know that in some tribes belief in reincarnation is so strong that they will even point to someone and say that he was living before and say who he was.

Deon, Psychic Sensitive, Chicago: Rather than reincarnation, this phenomenon seems to me to be more of an evolutionary thing. I think the children of today are more in tune with the universe, and they are reverting to a more simple life-style. The vibratory forces of the Indian, Indian awareness, may be influencing them without their knowing it. Now it is possible that this awareness may come from a past life, but it could also be due to the fact that someone in spirit with an Indian background may be guiding them. These young people want to live close to the earth; they want to grow their own things; they want to eat right; they want to be where the air is clean and pure. They are searching, yet being led, by an inner awareness of spiritual customs of which the great majority of people are not aware.

"Do you feel this Indian awareness could be an example of the dead influencing the living?"

Deon: At present, this awareness is emanating from an unknown quantity, but it is an inner awareness, a feeling, to which we are now closer than we have ever been. Even in the crowded city of Chicago, you can begin to feel the vibrations changing. You can even feel it in your bodies. It is as if a vibratory force is attempting to raise us higher spiritually so that we might attune ourselves to hear the cosmic forces. Many people are receiving these vibrations and interpreting them as feelings of nervousness. They feel as if they are out of place, and they can't quite keep their minds on things that are happening in the material world. I think someone is really trying to get through to us and make us more aware. I am sure there are many entities watching over us at this time.

While traveling near Albuquerque on January 30, 1962, Yolanda, who channels "interdimensional communications" for Mark-Age MetaCenter, Inc., of Miami, Florida, received a communication from a higher plane that told of her previous incarnation as Princess Lobo-Tan of the Tanoan tribe.

According to her vision, the young Indian maid had been trained in the mystic arts and had been accepted as the prophesied woman-child who would lead the Tanoans back to the Great Spirit. However, when she demonstrated friendliness to the Christian missionaries, the princess was declared a traitor and made an outcast. The Spaniards called her Lobo-Tan—Lobo for wolf, Tan for the Tanoan tribe. Left to wander, Lobo-Tan was captured and tortured by a band of marauders, who eventually took her to the Grand Canyon and threw her into the chasm to test her powers. Although they searched for her corpse, they never found it. Thus Lobo-Tan came and left the earth plane under mysterious circumstances.

On January 31, Yolanda was directed in a meditation to go to the Sandia Mountains . . . at the eastern edge of Albuquerque. She was told that spiritual initiations have taken place in these ranges for centuries, and that the Indian astral forces . . . were they to be united, would meet them there. This would result in Yolanda receiving the powers she had as Lobo-Tan, so she would be able to charge the mountain with divine power and love, thus aiding the devic forces to eliminate the dangers inherent in the area resulting from atomic experimentations. . . .[1]

At the foot of the Sandia Mountains, Yolanda made contact with Black Cloud, an Indian spirit guide, and performed an "inner plane ceremony" that brought forward many messages, among them, the following prayer-statement:

We are all brothers. As brothers, we must come together under the Great Father Spirit which created us all. With this pledge, all powers of accumulation will be given for these deeds. All forgivenesses are sealed in the heart of each man and each leader, who is responsible to his many lives and to his many pasts. With this understanding, we carve new paths into the future, that all men can walk the one path and discover the one goodness and become the one heart.

Love is the key. We understand this and we shall live this. All is in readiness. Many moons will pass across the Earth's sphere before we know all the good that shall come to pass because of this time together and dedication. We kneel to the Spirit in each thing that exists. In this way we recognize the Great Spirit which is in all things.

So let us love one another and hunt for the future that the Great Father has created, and for which we still hunger. Our thirst is for righteousness and truth. We call upon the rain clouds to show us we are true sons of the Great Spirit and to nourish our bodies and our minds and our souls and to cleanse us as well as to feed us.

We understand the depths of these things and the symbols which we perform, because we are true Indians. An Indian is a son of the Great Spirit which exists and is not seen. This is the meaning of the Indian brotherhood. All men, then, are Indians as we are, from our birth and unto the end of time.

We acknowledge all that has taken place and we accept it peacefully; peacefully and for the good of all things, that they may become true brothers and Indians, in the sense of the Father who created

[1] From *Linking of Lights,* Vol. 6, *New Paths with AmerIndians* (Miami, Fla., Mark-Age MetaCenter).

us to care for the land, to protect the land, and to pass the land on to the next generation who follows our footsteps. Amen. I speak in the name of all brothers in all lands, because the land of all is one land.

It did not occur to me to ask Tom Laughlin if he felt that he might have lived a previous life as an Indian, but in his film *Billy Jack,* the actor-writer-director has provided the moviegoer with the unforgettable study of a half-breed Vietnam veteran who drops out of white culture in order to study ancient Indian lore.

The modestly budgeted film has become a counterculture classic, playing some cities in nine-week cycles, then returning to the same full-house engagements. Regrettably, *Billy Jack*'s initial distributor, Warner Brothers, was slow to realize the youth market potential of the film, and released the story of the young mystic-warrior who leaves his seclusion only to protect the students at an interracial Freedom School primarily to porno houses and drive-ins. *Billy Jack* won the Grand Prize at the Festival of the Nations in Taormina, Sicily (1971), as well as Best Screenplay ("Frank and Teresa Christina" are really Tom and his wife, actress Delores Taylor), and a NAACP Image Award.

When I interviewed Laughlin in May 1972, he was immersed in court battles which had been undertaken in an attempt to settle some of their distribution problems. I found him to be not only a very aware exponent of Amerindian medicine, but an individual who had learned the validity of its power through firsthand experience.

Tom Laughlin: I believe very strongly in dreams, and I do think the dream is telling me something about myself I don't already know. If I knew, I wouldn't need the dream to help me understand. I also know that it takes me sometimes as much as a year or two after a dream before I fully understand it.

"What was the reaction of the Native Americans to *Billy Jack,* Tom?"

Laughlin: Let me put it this way. There were an awful lot of Native Americans who descended upon us in the making of the picture. Some of them had had dreams and things of that nature which they felt should be in the film. We have had Native Americans come to us since the picture and ask us to do some rather heavy things. They meet with us in our home, and we are involved in a lot of work that they are doing. These are some very powerful medicine-type people.

One guy who is very heavy in this field brought a group of Native Americans who were more militant than mystical, and they told me that they did not like the Black Power-type salute at the end of the picture. Then about a month later they were busted in Los Angeles because they did a sit-down on the museum that had the dead baby's bones. As they were being taken away in paddy wagons, all of the same guys who were upset about that salute, put their fists up in the air. They sent me a picture of it afterwards and said, "I don't know who your inspiration was, but you knew something we didn't know!"

The reaction by and large has been very strong from the Native Americans and from Medicine people. Rolling Thunder, the Shoshone medicine man, said that he considered it the first true Indian movie ever made. But we do have our detractors as well.

"I was very impressed with the manner in which you presented Billy Jack's use of clairvoyance throughout the film."

Laughlin: I wouldn't intellectualize it, but certainly, I think we indicate that Billy has a way of knowing that goes beyond what we are used to at this time. I think the Indian is in tune with what we might call the unobstructed universe. I think Billy Jack is clearly in touch with some source of communication that most of us don't know about.

"What inspired you to submit to that dramatic rattlesnake ceremony?"

Laughlin: Again, that was the Shoshone medicine man Rolling Thunder, who is a very big force in both the Native American political and religious movement. He came to us and said that he had been told that we were supposed to have that ceremony in the picture. He told me about it, and he went through it. He had previously taken some apprentices through it, but, to my knowledge, no whiteman had ever seen that ceremony before.

Indians and people I trust told me that Rolling Thunder can walk down a road in the Nevada desert, walk a quarter of a mile inland, and there, under a rock, will be a rattlesnake. Rolling Thunder will talk to the snake, then come back on the road and go on his way.

So Rolling Thunder not only told us to put the ceremony in the movie, which we had not intended to do until he appeared, but he remained there throughout the entire filming. The morning we shot the scene, we went through a special ceremony. Rolling Thunder was there with a seven-foot rattlesnake. I wouldn't have submitted to the ceremony without Rolling Thunder being there.

[*From a studio press release:* "Since no known white men have been introduced to the snake ceremony, Laughlin's indoctrination was in itself deemed a precedent. Rolling Thunder, impressed with the star's sympathetic understanding of the mystical ways of the red man, explained: 'Being an Indian is not a matter of blood; it is a way of life.'

["In the actual ceremony, the candidate, after thorough purification and preparation, goes high on a mountain top and permits himself to be bitten over and over by a rattlesnake. According to the Indian, if the candidate has power and has been properly prepared, he will recover, absorbing the mana of the snake and thus become a 'brother to the snake.' Shoshone . . . means snake. . . .

[" 'The relationship between man and reptile in the Indian belief is highly spiritual, very personal and not transferable.' Thus even Rolling Thunder could not command the snake in the way that a trainer controls a dog. The only help Laughlin had was a helicopter which was an hour's flight from Santa Fe.

["While crew and cast marvelled at Laughlin's courage, Rolling Thunder was not surprised: 'It's why he's playing Billy Jack,' he said. 'In his heart he is Indian.'"]

"Tom, I'm certain you've noticed that we are now witnessing a resurgence of Amerindian magic and mysticism."

Laughlin: Yes, I think the drug movement was a colossal movement into the spiritual realm. The kids knew that there was something more inside of themselves than they had been led to believe. All of a sudden they realized they had a soul, and that there were things in the soul beyond a little ego structure. There were powers that could be stirred up—both good and bad—and experienced.

The unfortunate problem with the standard religions in America is that they don't believe in the soul anymore. Orthodox religion has become an ego trip. You identify your ego with Christ, and you have that kind of super power. It doesn't seem to occur to them that there is really a mystical, transcendental experience inside everyone.

So I think that is what the drug thing was about. I think that is what the Maharishi was about. And as you know, the Maharishi came into power only because the Hopi closed their gates to the kids. The moment the Hopi re-opened them a year later, the Maharishi came over and his tour fell absolutely flat.

Brad, you know better than I that when the Indian approaches the drug, the peyote, or whatever, they really prepare and they know that God is there. They know that if they don't prepare, they can be taken away.

The kids are beginning to realize that there is something more than a kick in drugs. They are gravitating toward the Indian, who has, in my opinion, kept this country together with his spiritual life.

I think the center of the religious power structure is Taos Pueblo, which is the one place you can't find out their secrets no matter who you are. I believe it is because if they let their secrets out and that religious grace that is being held there were dissipated, our country would go totally down.

We had Andy Vidovitch, Wovoka's [the Paiute Peace Messiah, originator of the Ghost Dance] spiritual heir, on location. Vidovitch is a very spiritual person. His wife, who is Wovoka's daughter, and his son had died a couple of years ago. Just before we started making *Billy Jack,* Andy was preparing to die. A water heater had blown up and had burned 80 per cent of his body. He was lying there, wanting to go, when his wife appeared and sat on the bed and told him he couldn't die and permit Wovoka's message to die with him. He had to stay alive until we got the Ghost Dance part in the movie. [Vidovitch passed away in April 1972.]

But Andy wouldn't help me write the speech for that Ghost Dance scene. Every day he kept telling me not to worry about it. Finally it was time to shoot it, and he still wouldn't help me write it—so I wouldn't shoot it.

The last day, I had to shoot something, and Andy said, "You just go in there and that little fellow, that Holy Spirit, he will tell you what to say."

I went in there, and it was the most embarrassing time of my life. Honest to God, until I got back and saw the rushes, I had no idea what the hell came out of my mouth.

"In other words, it was a spontaneous possession type of thing."

Laughlin: Totally. Before I saw the rushes, I told Andy that we would have to leave the scene out of the movie. I told him that I couldn't think of a thing to say.

He smiled, and said that I would love the scene. "Wovoka spoke," he said. "You didn't speak."

I was amazed when I saw the rushes. There was a speech about how the spiritual life in America had failed the kids and how they had gone to drugs and that now they are looking for something more substantial. I was very stunned to hear all that.

If Andy Vidovitch, Wovoka's son-in-law, had not been there when we did the Ghost Dance, there would have been heavy trouble. The Taos Indians were shocked to see that we knew the dance correctly. It has always been taken as a circle dance, which is totally different from the way we did it—not totally, but there are a couple fundamental things that make it quite a different dance from the spiritual point of view.

If you go back and see the picture, you will see a man in khaki pants and khaki shirt and a hat standing outside of the old *kiva* that we're in. That is Andy Vidovitch. I did not want him out of the picture. I wanted everything right. I didn't want to fool with that dance.

I went into trance during that scene. I have a rule when I'm acting that no one else can say cut, because maybe I am going to go back and start the scene over, so no one can say cut. There are ten minutes of film in a camera's magazine. We started doing that dance, and when I finally said cut, I was shocked to find that twenty minutes had gone by. The camera had run out. Everyone was just standing there. No one dared to say cut.

I thought it had only been a minute or two. The colors just got so incredibly beautiful, I got fascinated with them. After a while, I thought, well, we've got enough film shot now; and I was stunned to find it was twenty minutes later. So if you did that dance properly all night long, I know what would happen!

Tom Laughlin has tested the validity of Amerindian medicine for himself, and he has found that it does have a power and a relevance for the non-Indian. He has also learned that, as Rolling Thunder said, "Being an Indian is not a matter of blood; it is a way of life."

Billy Jack could not have been made fifteen, even ten, years ago. Indian medicine power had not yet been restored. Quetzalcoatl had not yet fulfilled his promise to restore his spirit to the continent.

2. The Invisible Dead of Many Tribes

In the Los Angeles *Herald Examiner*'s CALIFORNIA LIVING for October 13, 1968, I read an article by Wanda Sue Parrott that found a special place in my memory bank. According to Wanda, the bulk of ghost reports received by the *Herald Examiner* consisted of incidents involving the spectral manifestation of American Indians.

In one of the cases Wanda recounted, a Mrs. W. was told by the ghost of an Indian man that he would leave her apartment only if she disposed of the Amerindian artifact which she had recently acquired. Mrs. W. did so, and even though the ghost was true to his word and departed with the artifact, she found herself so unnerved by the eerie experience that she consulted a psychiatrist. The psychiatrist consoled her with the astonishing statement that there was nothing wrong with her; many of his patients had had similar experiences with the ghosts of American Indians.

"A number of San Gabriel Valley residents have shared in the Indian experience," Ms. Parrott wrote. "Men, women and children alike have reported seeing a male Indian appear in their yards, bedrooms and living rooms at all hours of the day and night.

"Most of the witnesses agree, 'He seems friendly enough. He stays for a moment or two, then fades . . .'"

As I interviewed Medicine people from many different tribes in the process of gathering data for this book, I recalled Wanda's article. I had long become convinced that our new age of ever-rising awareness was experiencing a return of the power and spirit of Amerindian magic, but as I listened to an impressive number of well-documented accounts of Indian ghosts from both Amerindians and Anglos, I began to wonder what elements in addition to the rebirth of Medicine power might be summoning these specters from other dimensions of being.

I believe that I may have found a clue to these continuing and increasing manifestations of Amerindian phantoms in the prophetic warning of Chief Seathe (Seattle) to the whitemen who cheated his people out of their lands with the Treaty of Point Elliott in 1855:

> . . . Our religion is the traditions of our ancestors, the dreams of our old men, given them by the Great Spirit, and the visions of our sachems, and is written in the hearts of our people. . . .
>
> Every part of this country is sacred to my people. Every hillside, every valley, every plain and grove has been hallowed by some fond memory or some sad experience of my tribe. . . .
>
> The braves, fond mothers, glad-hearted maidens, and even little children, who lived here . . . still love these solitudes. Their deep fastnesses at eventide grow shadowy with the presence of dusty spirits. When the last red man shall have perished from the earth and his memory among the white men shall have become a myth, these shores shall swarm with the invisible dead of my tribe. . . .
>
> At night when the streets of your cities and villages shall be silent, and you think them deserted, they will throng with the returning hosts that once filled and still love this beautiful land.
>
> The white man will never be alone. Let him be just and deal kindly with my people, for the dead are not altogether powerless. Dead, did I say? There is no death, only a change of worlds.

Did the whiteman, imbued with the rationalization for greed which he called Manifest Destiny, convert Chief Seattle's warning into a malediction?

While the redman hallowed "every hillside, every valley, every plain and grove," the whiteman yearned to possess them.

While the redman believed that the Great Spirit had decreed that man must learn to live with the Earth Mother, the whiteman was convinced that Almighty Providence had hidden wealth and riches in the soil and in the mountains to "reward the brave spirits whose lot it is to compose the advance-guard of civilization."[1]

While the redman knew that the Earth Mother could cradle all men to her fertile bosom, the whiteman's revelation told him that ". . . the Indians must stand aside or be overwhelmed by the ever-advancing tide of emigration. The destiny of the aborigines is written in characters not to be mistaken. The same inscrutable Arbiter that decreed the downfall of Rome has pronounced the doom of extinction upon the red men of America."[2]

And so the whiteman ignored Chief Seattle's plea to be "just and deal kindly" with his people. And they laughed away his admonition that "the dead are not altogether powerless." In an era of bloody madness that has been mythologized as glorious, the West was won and the Amerindian nations were nearly decimated.

"For a mighty nation like us to be carrying on a war with a few straggling nomads . . . is a spectacle most humiliating, an injustice unparalleled, a national crime most revolting, that must, sooner or later, bring down upon us or our posterity the judgment of Heaven," observed a conscientious John B. Sanborn, who bore the role of a peace commissioner with what dignity such an ironic title might provide.

These shores shall swarm with the invisible dead of my tribe.

"[The ghost] looks like an Indian," Mrs. [Gale] Sokol says, "and it makes more sense if it's an Indian because my house is on an old Indian burial ground . . ." She disappears, reappears with three Indian artifacts. "I found these Indian carvings in my backyard."

[1] Cheyenne (Wyoming) *Daily Leader,* March 3, 1870.
[2] Ibid.

[John Pascal, "Long Island Diary," *Newsday,* Garden City, New York, August 4, 1972]

At night when the streets of your cities and villages shall be silent, and you think them deserted, they will throng with the returning hosts that once filled and still love this beautiful land.

[Edward] Amberman said he did not receive a strong impression from the man with a cloak but . . . while on one side of Harland Street there was the impression of a group of Indians. . . .

. . . The Indian, Mingo, died in 1763 and in 1898 when Mingo Street was cut in off of Canton Avenue the graves of five Indians were discovered by excavators. . . .

. . . The man in the cape, [Jacklyn Berman] said, appeared to have piercing red eyes and [she] guessed that an Indian in the Colonial period would wear the type of clothing such as a cape. It was her guess that this ghost was that of the Indian, Mingo. [Richard Kent, *Patriot Ledger,* Quincy, Massachusetts, August 28, 1972]

The white man will never be alone. . . . for the dead are not altogether powerless. . . . There is no death, only a change of worlds.

Mrs. Potter said her husband had many encounters with the Indian before their marriage. After marriage, Mrs. Potter had her first encounter with the Indian in 1961, before a serious illness.

"He came to warn us of danger ahead," she said, "and he protected me." [Wanda Sue Parrott, CALIFORNIA LIVING, Los Angeles *Herald Examiner,* October 13, 1968]

Does the fact that increasing numbers of white Americans believe themselves to be haunted by Indian specters provide yet additional evidence of the rebirth of Amerindian medicine power? Or are such phantoms the inevitable result of the guilt that the collective unconscious of the United States is experiencing as a more sensitive and aware nation comes to grips with the question of whether we are the posterity upon whom the Indian Wars and avaricious Manifest Destiny have brought down the judgment of Heaven?

Since Wanda Sue Parrott had written her article on Indian ghosts in California four years before I began my research on *Medicine Power,* I thought that I must contact her in order to learn whether she had received any additional reports of encounters with Amerindian ghosts who were "not altogether powerless."

Wanda frequently appears on radio, television, or before groups to speak on her experiences with psychic phenomena. Despite a life filled with paranormal experiences, she remains an objective and often skeptical person about planes beyond the physical.

"About four years ago I was given an assignment to interview people in Los Angeles who claimed to have seen or encountered the 'spirits' of American Indians," Wanda recalled.

"One woman, who said an Indian burned her foot in bed, knew I didn't believe her story. She said, 'You'll believe it after an Indian has come into your room. Then, nobody will believe *you!*'

"I was nearly finished writing my story when I went to bed at about 11 P.M. one night in June. I fell into a very deep sleep. As I drifted off, I had been wondering how an Indian would manifest if one should come to my room. Would I be scared? Would I be able to see or hear him?

"Suddenly a loud banging sound awakened me. Someone or something was knocking loudly on the center of the door. It was full moon; I could see the door's middle shaking in the moonlight.

"Then the banging stopped and the gold-colored knob started turning. First it turned one way, then the other. It was so noisy, such a rattling sound, that I knew my husband would wake up. If he could witness this phenomenon, he might not be the world's Number One psychical skeptic any longer.

"I had the very strong feeling that someone was trying to reach me, desperately trying to alert me to something or get a message to me.

"I was not frightened. I watched the doorknob in fascination. But when my husband did not wake up, and when the door did not open, I decided to open it myself. I did. I peered into an empty hallway, as I knew would happen.

"I then went to my five-year-old son's room. He was fast asleep, as I knew he would be. He could not have been pounding on the door or trying to turn the knob.

"Nothing gave me a hotfoot, and I saw no chief with feathers, so I went back to bed. Next morning I told my husband of the experience—which lasted fully ninety seconds. Of course he said my imagination was overactive.

"All that day I had the strong feeling someone was desperately trying to contact me. And when I got home and read my mail I knew I had been right. A cousin, whom I had not heard from since 1962, had sent an airmail letter. She was holed up in a motel in Iowa, suicidally depressed over her husband's leaving her. 'You are the last person in the world to turn to for help,' she wrote.

"I made a long-distance call immediately. Suddenly I seemed to know exactly the right words to say—and said them in about three minutes' time. My cousin did not kill herself, nor have I ever heard from her again, by letter or phone. She is apparently quite alive and busy in her new life.

"And I was entering a new phase of my professional life. I was suddenly writing quite a few Indian stories and meeting many Indians from various reservations. I even spent a whole day at the Bureau of Indian Affairs, a most depressingly sterile, non-spiritual suite of technological cubicles lit with that modern-day artificial sunlight, the fluorescent tube.

"And I met Len Fairchuk, a Salteaux Indian. Rather, Len met me. He had founded an Indian workshop where Indians in Los Angeles could create fashioned products for money, while making the transition from the reservation to the city. I did a story about Len, and met many Indians, ranging from Sioux to Pawnee.

"They made me an honorary chief of the White Buffalo, crowning me with a huge beautiful paper feather headdressing made at their workshop. The White Buffalo is a symbolic spiritual group embodying the Indian spirit of all surviving tribes.

"I began receiving many invitations to become an advisor to one Indian group, a counselor with another, and a volunteer worker with yet another Indian organization which was trying to help Indians establish new lives in the city. But I had neither time nor enough energy to get involved in all these activities. My involvement remained in spirit only.

"And it seems that once a whiteman—or woman—is involved with the Indian spirit, it does become part of one's life on a true spiritual level.

"In 1970 while trying to buy a fishing license in a drugstore in the Ozarks, I felt an intuitive urge to go browse through a comic book stand. I quit reading comics in 1948! But I went to this rack, suddenly to find myself facing a twenty-five-cent copy of Henry Wadsworth Longfellow's *Hiawatha* in comic strip form.

"I opened it a few days later, after boarding a Los Angeles-bound plane at Kansas City. And I had an experience so profound I shall never forget it. I was not looking at printed pages—suddenly I was in Longfellow's land of laughing waters—smelling the crisp leaf-scented air, tasting the clear cold waters, hearing the singing, ringing musical silence, feeling the invisible, invincible civilization that *was* the Indian spirit.

"When my plane landed in Los Angeles, I looked around at the smog, the airplanes, the sea of cars, and sad, mad, tense people at International Airport. It was all familiar, yet strangely unfamiliar. Where were the trees, the rushing waters, the invisible air one could smell because it had a perfume of its own? I felt like an Indian transplanted into a strange city of the future, a city actively alive but spiritually dead.

"And for a few moments I felt a presence near my shoulder, almost strong enough to reach out and touch. It was the presence of a naked man with only a few feathers woven into leather thongs that were draped on a few areas of his body.

"I have never seen an Indian guide. But I do believe that in some way I have attuned with the Indian spirit."

In addition to her own experiences with Amerindian ghosts, Wanda shared the following accounts from her personal research files with me:

David St. Clair, author of *The Psychic World of California,* was researching his book in Los Angeles in 1971. On the day he was due to interview Mae West about her true psychic experiences, he was down to his last thirty-five cents, only enough money to pay his four-mile, one-way bus fare.

"I had been waiting for days for a check that was supposed to arrive," the author recalls. "But the check didn't come and it didn't come. Everybody had been telling me the spirits were supposed to be guiding me, but I was wondering just how, if the spirits were guiding me, I was going to pay my motel bill."

St. Clair went to Brazil in the 1950s. A reporter, he was skeptical of spiritism and related occult phenomena. After approximately fifteen years of living in Brazil, he came back to the United States as a believer in spirits.

"But I also believe that if there are spirit guides, it's good to talk to them aloud once in a while," the good-natured Ohio-born writer says. He admits he not only talks to the spirits, but when the spirit moves him to do so, he shouts. And that is what he did the day he was down to his last few cents.

"I started cursing out the spirits. 'Goddamn you, spirits,' I said. 'This is the last time! I have had it! I didn't want to write this book. I wanted to get a nice job and settle down like other people do, but you people kept pushing me to write this book.

"'Now everybody says you're supposed to be guiding me. How am I supposed to pay my rent?'"

St. Clair was combing his hair in front of the bathroom mirror as he was cursing his spirit guides. "All of a sudden this snow white feather appeared out of nowhere. It fell, right in front of me.

"My first reaction was to look up and see if there was a pigeon stuck to my ceiling. It did shake me up.

"I had been in the motel three months and hadn't seen any feathers. I took a razor blade and slit open my pillows, but they were stuffed with bits of plastic foam.

"And it was ridiculous to think a feather had been stuck to the ceiling just waiting to fall for all that time.

"The windows had screens. So I took it as a sign the spirits were saying, 'Calm down, David. We're still with you. We're working on it for you.' I went on the interview with Mae West. I walked home."

The next day St. Clair showed astrologist Doris Doane the white feather. She said, "That is an apport. It's probably a sign that you have an Indian guide, and he is showing you he is with you and not to be discouraged."

St. Clair later showed the feather to Jerry Quintero, who has charge of a group of metaphysical people who hold prayer groups in the San Jose, California, area. The representative of Universal Receivers Association held the feather and, not knowing Doris Doane had done the same, said:

"I get this is from an Indian, one of your guides, who is trying to tell you not to despair."

St. Clair adds: "Two days after I cursed at the spirits, my long overdue check arrived." He felt humbled. "I knew I didn't walk alone."

Clarisa and Russ Bernhardt, residents of Hollywood's famous Gingerbread House, are known during the month of December as Mr. and Mrs. Scrooge. Bernhardt has played the Dickens character in one-man shows, raising monies for charity, during the holiday season for the past thirty years.

Clarisa Bernhardt is an actress and scriptwriter; her most recent filmscript, *Subject to Change Without Notice,* has been made into a soon-to-be-released picture.

The Bernhardts' lives involve a lot of fantasy on a business level, but they are actually down-to-earth, realistic people. Therefore, it came as a surprise when they both came face to face with non-physical Indians on the estate of a friend. Clarisa Bernhardt tells it this way:

"We went to Ojai to visit a friend, Flo Cates, who owns the house that once belonged to Libby of Libby Glass, and later to the attorney for Henry Ford. It is on about five acres. It was deserted and in ruins when she bought it."

"After the house was restored she had strange things happen. No woman could spend the night there without waking up in the morning with red places on her fingers and without feeling burning sensations.

"This house had been built next to, and over, a Shumash Indian graveyard. These Indians were of the early, early Americans.

"It is said that Ojai is a very unusual place. There are a few descendants of these original Indians in this area living there. Mrs. Cates met the Indian chief . . . she got the hotfoot, but finally she made peace with him and things settled down.

"You can go in that house, and immediately you feel a presence. When I went there, suddenly I stopped because I got a little bit cold. There was this strange feeling that came over me.

"I had the privilege of seeing people on the other plane. I met the chief. He was in the hallway. He was in feathers. There was a very high vibration there. The Shumash were apparently very highly evolved people."

Bernhardt tells about his experience with the "vortex" on this land. "It's an energy, like a whirlpool under water; and you actually feel an energy swirling around on the ground. It comes up through your feet, legs, and arms."

He says an elderly friend who had rheumatic fever stood on the property for a short time. "She was in particular pain. We stood her on the spot. She started tingling. For two months afterward she had no pain at all."

Did the Indians center around this vortex because of its magnetic healing properties? The Bernhardts are not sure.

They are sure, however, that the ghost of the Indian chief exists. "He comes around, it seems," says Bernhardt, "to make sure that nobody's going to do anything to violate the tribe."

"At first he was hostile," says Clarisa Bernhardt, "but after we went back a couple of times he was all right."

"He doesn't like ladies," says Bernhardt, laughing. "But he was very nice to me. He squeezed me gently."

Following their "meeting" with the chief, Clarisa had the intuitive awareness, "there is oil on this land." She told Mrs. Cates of the "message" and subsequent tests were run on the land. Oil was found.

"Mrs. Cates is now concerned about drilling. She does not want to disturb these 'people,' but I feel that if she does drill and some of the money goes to help the Indians now living, everything will be all right," says Clarisa.

"I'm half Cherokee," says Clarisa Bernhardt. "My grandfather was Chief John Muskrat, buried in Tahlequah, Oklahoma."

Which raises the question: do Indians, as well as whitemen, have Indian guides?

Ed and Lorraine Warren, a husband and wife team of ghost hunters from Monroe, Connecticut, discovered that whether or not Amerindians have red spirit guides, they can certainly be the percipients of haunting phenomena. On February 15, 1972, while lecturing at the University of Maine campus in Bangor, the Warrens took time from their schedule to appear on local television and radio talk shows. In response to their broadcasted conversations about ghosts and hauntings, a Cherokee woman, who lived with her husband, a Pequot, on the reservation, telephoned the Warrens to seek their assistance in dealing with a series of manifestations in her home.

Through the courtesy of Ed and Lorraine, who provided me with a tape recording of the session, the reader will be able to experience vicariously the investigation in the midnight seance held on the reservation.

Ed and Lorraine Warren, a husband and wife team of ghost Mrs. S., you told me many interesting things. Could you tell us some of these now?

Mrs. S.: A few months ago, I went out on the porch to pray during a summer rain storm. It was thundering and lightning. I saw a vision in the sky, and a strong feeling came with the vision. I saw a huge Indian, a false face, a bear, and a wolf. The bear denotes good, because he has always been food for the Indian. The bear is a sign of plenty, of survival. The wolf is a bad omen, because he is a sly and crafty creature. The false face is used in our religion, and it could have meant something about me or another person.

The vision repeated itself two nights in a row. On the second night, about three o'clock in the morning, I saw a dark image standing in my front yard, beckoning to me. Fear came over me.

Warren: It was beckoning to you?

Mrs. S.: To me. The old Indian burial ground is in our front yard and down over the hill you just came up, and it seemed to me that the image was beckoning to me and pointing toward the graveyard.

Warren: What did you take this sign to mean?

Mrs. S.: I didn't know. I got in touch with the chief of the Mohawks, and he said it could mean several different things, but he wasn't sure. Now he was gone to Hopi country, and he will ask the chiefs there, who keep up with these things.

On the third night, this huge Indian appeared. He was kneeling, and there was a fire at his knees. I couldn't see his face clearly, but the muscles in his body stood out so that I could see them just perfect.

Then that . . . other thing happened to me.

My husband had been at Eastport for over a week, and I was here by myself. I was sitting on the couch when this feeling hit me in the stomach. My stomach twisted, just like when you are carrying a baby—but it was on my outside. I looked down and there was nothing near me. No book. Nothing that could have put any pressure on me. A kind of silliness, a kind of trance came over me, and I went to lie down on the bed.

That same night I woke up with something pounding on the bottom of my feet. I wasn't dreaming, and I don't take any pills stronger than aspirin. I was so afraid that I couldn't move. I had heard and seen other things in the house, but they didn't bother me. This time, I was scared.

Then a . . . feeling—it is hard to explain—a feeling came over me, and there was a pressure between my legs. I was afraid to move. It wasn't a dream. It wasn't a dream. It was like what you were talking about on the program.

Warren: I was talking about a demon called an incubus that can sexually attack a woman, or a succubus that can attack a man.

Mrs. S.: Well, this really happened. I haven't told my husband completely. I have been afraid to tell people all of what happened. But the memory of the feeling that came over me has nearly faded.

Lorraine Warren: You are lucky that you can erase it from your mind.

Mrs. S.: The grave incident is fading, too. But the footsteps keep sounding, and they are not the result of the house settling. My husband has even nailed the door shut to the one room, but we still find the door standing open.

This is why I asked you to come here; I want you to tell me if there is something evil in this house. If it is not evil, I want it to stay, because I think the spirit of the huge Indian is trying to tell us something. The tribes are coming together. The Indians really do have powers, but they don't always know the meaning of what they do. I am afraid that because you are white people the Indian spirits here may resent you.

Lorraine Warren: There is resentment here.

Warren: Lorraine, you told me when you first came in here that you felt as if you would be forced to your knees. Why did you say that?

Lorraine Warren: When I came in the door, I felt depressed. I didn't even want to sit down. I felt as if I wanted to drop to my knees. [To Mrs. S.] Can I get to that bedroom through here?

Mrs. S.: No.

Lorraine Warren: Could you ever?

Mrs. S.: Yes, at one time that was a dining room and this was a serving door in through here, but it is all closed off now.

I forgot to tell you that after my vision in the thunderstorm, a ball of red light appeared. I was depressed that night, too, and I had been praying. I do not go to Catholic church any more. I do my praying and my tobacco burning by myself.

Warren: How old is the young man who has experienced different things in the house?

Mrs. S.: He will be twenty in August. He is bothered by these things, and he will tell you about them.

Warren: Do you think that he might have brought something in the house here when he came to live with you?

Mrs. S.: No, this place has been this way for a long time. There are people on the island who won't even come into my house.

This house was really a mansion at one time. The governor even lived here. No one knows how long this house has been here. There is no record. The old people don't remember.

One time a whiteman who is married to an Indian came here and told me that he would sleep upstairs. He has been to some of the religious ceremonies and he understands a good deal of them. He lay down, but he soon came down. He said he heard things, and he knew that he wasn't wanted.

Lorraine Warren: There is someone here now who resents our being here. The reason I say that is because here on this part of my hand there is a lot of pressure, *a lot of pressure,* and that feeling of wanting to go down on my knees! It is as if something wants to force me down.

[At this point, W.M., the young Indian who had boarded with the S. family before his marriage, arrived to answer questions for the Warrens.]

W.M.: I was just about brought up in this house. My great-great-uncle used to own this house about fifty years ago. This house is one of the oldest on the island. It is over two hundred years old. This used to be one of the most beautiful homes on the island until a certain family moved in here, and they just wrecked it. When the S.'s moved in, they fixed it up surprisingly well for the condition it was in when they came.

Warren: What were some of the things that happened to you in this house?

W.M.: I used to stay in the front room, and I used to lie in bed and watch the stairway door open. Mrs. S. had a huge box filled with baskets that was really heavy to move, and there was a rack of clothes there. I used to watch that door open and the box and everything move.

These things didn't really bother me, because I have had such experiences ever since I was a kid. [W.M. told the Warrens that he is able to predict death on the island with a regular and a high degree of accuracy.]

Warren: That is interesting, because since you have a certain degree of clairvoyance, you might be able to get things in this house that others would not.

W.M.: One day I was sitting here reading the paper, and I was talking to my girl friend—now my wife—on the telephone. The television wasn't on, but I was watching the screen. All of a sudden, the dogs started barking, and they came running out here. I could see the doorway reflected in the screen, and I could see the figure of a man standing there.

Warren: Was the figure white . . . black . . . ?

W.M.: It was a dark figure. I was more intrigued than frightened, but the figure stood there for several seconds.

Mrs. S.: Several times you were awakened by a punch on the shoulder. You would wake up, find no one in the room, then come out and ask me if anybody had been in your room.

W.M.: Yeah. Everytime the stairway door opened, things would go on for five or six minutes. Sometimes the clothes on the rack would spread apart, and I could feel a cold breeze go right by me. It was that strong. I wondered sometimes if it would blow the curtains down as it went by.

Mrs. S.: The same thing has happened to me in this corner, and it is completely blocked off. But several times I have felt the cold touch either my legs or my arms in that corner.

Now it was midnight, and Lorraine, who is a light trance medium, indicated that her sensitivity told her it was time to hold a seance.

Ed recalls that it was a very cold, windy, bleak night, just the kind of evening that people would visualize as being ideal for a seance. Although their visit to the S. home was to have been a secret, more than twenty curious Indians had arrived to kibitz the white medicine people. Ed pleaded too many people for an effective seance and managed to thin the ranks. A skeptical reporter and a photographer doggedly insisted upon staying to observe the proceedings.

"I was uncomfortable because of the persistent sensation that something wanted to force me to the floor," Lorraine said, "but I went into a light trance in spite of this psychic harassment.

"I got the name Priscilla, and she made herself so very clear to me," Lorraine told me. "Again, I felt as if I were actually being forced to the floor. I felt as though she were married to a man who was a very dominating person, a very cruel person.

"I saw a cemetery. A small white building with little diamond-shaped latticework. A short white fence around a number of graves. I knew that Priscilla had been buried inside that fenced-in area," Lorraine said.

"Priscilla was so clear to me. Then I saw her husband, a tall, blond man, who stood on a rock with his arms folded."

Ed Warren said, "Now, of course Lorraine had no way of knowing names, Brad, but the Indians told me that a young Indian girl named Priscilla had married a whiteman, who had treated her in a cruel manner. They had lived in this home, and he used to stand on a big rock out back with his arms folded. I was surprised that Lorraine would pick up a whiteman living on an Indian reservation, but I was told that he had filled some official capacity. When I said that I had not seen the big rock in back of the house, the Indians said that it had been blasted away long ago.

"He is buried just a couple of blocks away in a small cemetery. Priscilla, according to Mrs. S., is buried in a fenced-in area. There is also a small white building with diamond-shaped latticework near her grave.

"The sensation Lorraine experienced of being pushed down is one of great negativity, often found in cases where demonology is concerned. The older Indians testified that the husband had been very cruel to his young Indian wife. Perhaps this domineering personality lives on in this old mansion. Right after the seance, the photographer shot what appears to be a whitish figure in a window."

If one wishes to accept the spiritistic hypothesis, it would appear that the same personality who sought to abuse and to possess completely his Indian wife, may now be seeking to torment the Indian woman who occupies his home. Mrs. S.'s vision of the bear, the wolf, the mask, and the huge, muscular Indian man may be interpreted as either evidence of the protective element within her medicine summoning her own guide from the spirit world, or as an example of the symbology of the Amerindian unconscious seeking to inform Mrs. S. of some external or internal threat to her psychic or physical well-being. There is no way of knowing how much Mrs. S. knew of the story of Priscilla and her abusive white husband and whether or not domestic turmoil may have caused Mrs. S. to identify with a tortured wife. Neither is there any clue whether the alleged incubus attack may have been an example of sexual psychopathology or actual demonic invasion.

With the information available, we can but conclude with the Warrens that some psychic presence maintains a hold on that eerie mansion on a Maine Indian reservation.

Gordon Alexander, a photographer from Mystic, Connecticut, told me of a woman whose family had constructed a new home in the immediate proximity of an Indian burial ground.

According to Gordon, Louise Abel (not her real name), her husband, and children had learned just how thin the line can be between the living and the dead, especially if one chooses to build his house on sacred ground. The Abels wish no publicity, and Louise consented to an interview on my promise that her real name and the name of their village would be kept secret.

Louise Abel: Down and back behind my house and in our area, a great many Indians were slaughtered, and their land was taken away from them. There is a mass burial site where many of these poor, tricked Indians were piled in and covered up.

"What kind of manifestations have you observed, Louise?"

Mrs. Abel: All sorts. Every kind of visitation and poltergeistic manifestations. Even the non-believers can see the images projecting themselves.

"Has there been any communication at all?"

Mrs. Abel: Yes, but the problem is that we have been getting a lot of Indian words, and we have no idea how to interpret them.

"Have there been any communications in English?"

Mrs. Abel: Yes, there have been some who have come through and tried to give us the English translations. Since the manifestations, I have begun to work quietly with some groups interested in psychic matters, and we have just been waiting for someone to come along who might break through and be able to understand what is happening.

"And your home is not some three-hundred-year-old New England mansion?"

Mrs. Abel: Ours is a new house, only three years old; but we built it near the burial ground. You know, it is impossible for the kids to play drums or certain music without bringing on manifestations. That song "Cherokee Nation" used to bring about a really strange reaction. Before I realized what was happening, the kids would play it, and then everybody would kind of slump over and begin to walk differently. I had to stop them from playing it, because it was just getting too powerful. It was drawing too much from us.

"Did anyone in the area ever report such manifestations before you built your home there?"

Mrs. Abel: It seems these things have been happening for years. Perhaps some kind of psychic vortex was created here because of the way the Indians were tricked out of their land and the way their lives were cut short. I feel the whole area here has been saturated with negative vibrations. In our case, our home often receives violent slams during the night, and we can often hear drums beating. Other people here have also heard them.

Once we were drawn to a particular spot on the lawn, and when we looked back at the house, we saw projections all over. They were the most fantastic and beautiful things I have ever seen in my life. We saw Indians, early settlers. It was one of the most fascinating experiences I think I have ever been through in my life.

"Did that occur at night or in daylight?"

Mrs. Abel: That happened in broad daylight. Now, of course, when the moon is full—especially in August, September, and October—you are more apt to hear the drums, although we are certainly not devoid of them at other times. On some nights, you can see what looks like masses of Indians carrying torches. They seem to be gathering for some kind of ceremony.

"Since you seem to have some degree of psychic sensitivity, do you think that these spirits may be gathering in your home in an effort to use you as a channel to get some particular message out to the people of today?"

Mrs. Abel: I do feel that this may be the case. Those of us in our psychic study group feel that they are desperately asking for help so that they might stop some of the ecological destruction that is taking place in the area.

One word that we have received quite often—and I am attempting to trace its meaning—sounds something like *Naw-has-ee*. I don't know if that is a name, a greeting, some kind of plea for help, or what it could be. It is difficult to understand these things unless you have someone helping you from a higher spiritual vibration.

If the Amerindian Medicine people whom I have interviewed during the past year are correct in their interpretation of the signs which have begun to proliferate in the last decade, then we are at this time receiving a great deal of help from a higher spiritual plane.

Not everyone may be sensitive enough to perceive spectral members of vanished Amerindian tribes, but all men and women who want to learn to achieve harmony in their lives may gain spiritual strength from the Resurrection of the Great Spirit. If the manifestation of Indian ghosts that throng our cities and villages in the silence of night offers dramatic evidence that the line of demarcation between worlds of being is growing ever thinner and less strictly defined, then one has but to attune himself to Amerindian prophets and teachers to learn that the power, richness, and relevance of Amerindian magic is being restored. The teachings tell us that the Great Spirit will once again be recognized as the primal mystery that permeates every hillside, every valley, every plain and grove, every part of this country. If we permit a commitment to the Great Spirit to fashion our dreams and our visions, then not only will we change our lives, but our world, and despair and defeat will give way to joy and freedom.

3. Chief Joseph's Skull Is an Ashtray: Archaeology and Anguish

CLARKSTON, Wash. (UPI)—Thieves invaded a 100-year-old Nez Perce Indian burial ground near here, stealing skulls and jewelry, anthropologists reported.

Authorities said human skulls were worth $25 each and more in a bizarre underground market centered in California.

"It makes me mad to just be around the place and see what has been done," said Richard Halfmoon of Lapwai, Idaho, chairman of the Nez Tribal Council. "They don't let our Indians rest in peace whether they are dead or alive.

"We know the name of the dentist who has Chief Joseph's skull and uses it for an ashtray."

Chief Joseph, the Nez Perce's greatest chief, was pursued by the U.S. Cavalry in the late 1800s when he led part of his tribe on a 1,500-mile escape to Canada.

"The time has come when we are wanting museums and everyone to return these [skeletal remains] so we can put them back in the proper place where they belong," commented Rolling Thunder, a Shoshone medicine man, who is regarded as one of the most influential of today's medicine people.

Cautious and respectful archaeologists and anthropologists are arranging ceremonies to be held over the excavation sites before a single shovel begins to turn over sacred soil.

Although technical supervision was provided by John Sigstead, curator of anthropology at the University of South Dakota, Vermillion, all of the work on the burial mound recently found west of Wilmot was done by Indians under the direction of the Sisseton-Wahpeton Sioux Tribal Council. In addition, according to Ed Red Owl of the Tribal Office, a medicine man performed a ceremony at the mound site in order to protect the workers and to maintain the dignity of the dead who were buried there. "We didn't want the excavation to be a sacrilege to the people buried there," Red Owl said.

Even though ceremonies and dead feasts are being conducted over sites where archaeological students are preparing to dig for skeletal clues to the Amerindian's past, there still remains the principal point of contention in many a serious Native American's mind that sacred ground is being desecrated. How complete must a ceremony be to compensate the grandfathers and grandmothers for defilement? Anthropological and archaeological violation of the final resting places of countless Amerindian men, women, and children has not only set an ethnic pot to boiling, but scholarly shovels may have set in motion a series of psychic disturbances totally beyond their scientific ken.

"To us, the ashes of our ancestors are sacred and their resting place is hallowed ground," Chief Seattle told Governor Isaac Stevens when he surrendered his land in 1855.

Chief Joseph of the Nez Perce, that same noble warrior whose skull now serves as an ashtray in a dentist's office, was told by his own father: "My son, never forget my dying words. This country holds your father's body. Never sell the bones of your father and your mother."

Chief Joseph observed with fervor that, "a man who would not love his father's grave is worse than a wild animal."

Museums, archaeologists, and anthropologists throughout the United States are discovering that there are numerous very vocal Amerindians who do, indeed, love their fathers' graves.

Charles Ellenbaum, an anthropologist in charge of a dig at St. Charles, Illinois, conducted by the College of DuPage, resisted the arguments of the American Indian Center to cease his excavations. Mrs. Pat Rensch of the Indian Center told him, "If you people want to dig graves, dig up your own."

Ellenbaum countered by stating that the remains belonged to the owner of the dig site and that his studies would yield valuable information about the early Amerindians of the Fox River Valley.

Susan Powers, Chairman of the Board of Directors of the Indian Center, replied that Ellenbaum knew it was wrong to continue with the excavation. "The white man better start studying [himself]," she said. "Your world is falling apart. Your children are running away from you. You are a confused people."

Matthew War Bonnet, a Sioux and an instructor in Native American history at the Circle campus of the University of Illinois, led a protest group to the Field Museum of Natural History when spokesmen for the museum announced their recent acquisition of the skeletal remains of nine Miami Indians, circa late seventeenth century. In response to War Bonnet's objections, curator Dr. Donald Collier issued a statement pointing out that the museum had always endeavored to treat the ancient dead with respect. The Field Museum would, Dr. Collier said, replace the bones and pay for any costs incurred. After an evening ceremonial fire officiated over by a medicine man, the museum delivered the remains to a Winnebago burial ground near the Wisconsin Dells.

When Mohawk Chief Lawrence Lazore learned that an archaeology professor and eighteen of his students had disinterred six skeletons from a burial ground near the St. Lawrence River in July 1972, he denounced the field trip as "plain grave robbery." Lazore, who presides over the St. Regis Reservation and who has an archaeology degree of his own, said that if archaeologists ". . . want to use cemeteries as laboratories for their students, they should use their own cemeteries."

On October 1972, Cherokee leaders protested against what they termed the plundering of ancestral graves by artifact-hunting archaeologists.

The archaeologists defended their position by stating that they were rushing to uncover and preserve relics that will be lost forever when a Tennessee Valley Authority dam floods them in a few years.

Vice Chief John Crowe of the eastern band of Cherokees said that the TVA was going to flood ". . . a whole race of people's history and heritage off the map."

A TVA spokesman issued a statement declaring that they were funding the digging of Dr. Alfred K. Guthe, Director of the McClung Museum at the University of Tennessee at Knoxville, so that the heritage to be found in the old Cherokee village and fort near Tellico Plains would not be destroyed.

The essential issue of to dig or not to dig can be evaded by pointing a desperate finger toward the insatiable god named Progress. "Why not excavate Indian graves?" the archaeologist can shrug. "If we don't get the bones, the bulldozers and housing developments will."

It is amusing to visualize the inevitable day when an Amerindian archaeologist descends upon some forgotten pioneer cemetery with his students and announces his plans to excavate. "We wish to make an analysis of pioneer pathology," he will tell the press. "We are curious to see what diseases the early Anglos suffered in this area and how their pathology fits in with the larger frontier pattern. We are also curious to discover what artifacts these settlers buried with their dead, and we shall seek to determine what we can about the Anglo historical process from these relics."

How will the shoe fit when it is on the other foot? What hue and cry will white America raise over such desecration? Or are the two situations analogous? The white settlers kept written records, an anthropologist could protest. We really know more about early white America than we do about early red America. Even the question of the origin of the Amerindian is far from resolved. There is certainly no such thing as a unified Amerindian race, and European physical traits are as strongly represented among the aboriginal tribes as Mongolian.

Just a few decades ago, the majority of textbooks taught that man did not arrive in the Americas until some adventurous Asiatics trudged across the Bering land bridge at about the time of Christ. Certain anthropologists were prepared to state that man may have been in the New World by 3000 B.C., but only a few academic anthropologists and archaeologists were foolhardy enough to suggest that man may have been in the Americas as early as 8000 B.C. Then, in 1952, Dr. Paul Sears of Yale University dug up some maize pollen grain from about 240 feet below the surface of the dried lake bed on which Mexico City is built.

Maize is the most highly developed agricultural plant in the world, so highly developed that scientists have never been able to trace it back to its original ancestors. According to radiocarbon testing, the pollen grains from the Mexican lake bed are at least 25,000 years old.

In 1960, Dr. Juan Armente Comacho, Director of the Department of Anthropology at the University of Puebla in Mexico, dug a piece of a mastodon's pelvic bone out of the desert soil at Balsequello, sixty miles southeast of Mexico City. On the bone's surface some ancient artist had engraved the images of a horse, a camel, a reptile, and a type of mastodon thought to have been extinct for 100,000 years.

Dr. H. Marie Wormington, Curator of Archaeology at the Denver Museum of Natural History stated that the artwork and the bone were contemporary. The carving could only have been done on fresh bone, Dr. Wormington said, not fossil bone.

Certain authorities believe that the earliest immigrants to arrive in the Americas via the Bering Strait were definitely Europid-Caucasian in type. In their opinion, the Mongol migrations probably did not occur until 2000 B.C., and then from the Pacific as well as Siberia.

"It is because of this very late admixture of yellow blood that the various tribes of America create a Mongoloid impression which has given rise to their erroneous classification in the Mongol race," states the German ethnologist Ivar Lissner. "For many tens of thousands of years, the early inhabitants of America were the descendents of paleo-Europid peoples who had also occupied Siberia."

When the Europeans began their invasion of North America early in the sixteenth century there were about three hundred different tribes with a combined population of over one million. Today, with a population of about 800,000, the Amerindian is far from a "Vanishing Race," and although some tribes have been totally decimated, others, such as the Navajo, the Sioux, and the Cherokee have grown in numbers.

The serious anthropologist does not regard himself as a grave robber. Quite the contrary, he conceptualizes himself as a guardian of Amerindian culture who is working in basically the same direction as the Indian. At the same time, he recognizes the fact that he must walk a thin line between two cultures and deal with a situation in which the anthropologist and the archaeologist are conceived of as the enemy. Anthropologist R. Clark Mallam, currently on the teaching staff of Luther College, Decorah, Iowa, agreed to talk with me about how it feels to have the shoe of prejudice now on the other foot.

R. Clark Mallam: The American Indian today is an individual who is becoming aware of his heritage; and as he becomes aware of his heritage, he also becomes aware of his identity. Since he is an individual who possesses a distinct identity, it is logical, then, that anything that is held in a museum is considered denigrative to that identity. If I were curator of a museum, I would state that the displays of artifacts are not denigrative to the Indian people. The displays are there for the purpose of preserving that particular cultural aspect which would be lost, given the location of most of these burial grounds.

By and large, judging from where most of these Indian cemeteries or mounds have been located in the past, it is logical to assume that, as some archaeologists have suggested, within the next fifty years there is hardly going to be an Indian site in America that will be worth studying, because of our rapid mobility in terms of building urban and suburban areas. In areas where Indian burial grounds are not located on reservations, the graves are open to vandalism and to commercial exploitation of the grossest sort. At the same time, they are open to real estate dealers who can sell the land and permit the artifacts to be simply bulldozed away and scattered.

I think we are dealing with a situation in which there are levels of denigration. These so-called artifacts—especially human artifacts —are of immense value in reconstructing a prehistoric cultural history of the American Indian. From these skeletal remains, we can learn how long the Indian has lived, what diseases he was susceptible to, and a variety of other important populational and demographic factors.

"How can such information be important and helpful to the Amerindian of today?"

Mallam: I think in some cases the Indian does not realize the potentiality of how he can be helped by this information. At the same time, many anthropologists and archaeologists have reduced this information to an inner circle of discussion, and they have not been taking this information and disseminating it to the American public so that some of the stereotypes and myths that are so rampant in white culture regarding the Indian might be eliminated.

In my opinion, we in American archaeology are, in terms of our dealing with the American Indians, at an impasse, an impasse that has been prompted by the archaeologist's inability to accept the fact that his information is of sufficient use that it can be disseminated to the public and have a practical value associated with it. The archaeologist's failure to recognize this has resulted in the Indian stating that his services are derogatory to Indian identity.

If the artifacts are to be kept within a closed circle of academicians, then I favor their being restored to the rightful owners.

I would say that we are dealing with a series of social processes in which individuals of different identities are motivated and actuated by different things. The archaeologist makes his bread and his name by discovering a site, working it, publishing it, and ultimately having artifacts from it displayed somewhere. From that type of research, the archaeologist will achieve a certain degree of fame and, at the same time, will be recognized by his college and by his particular department, thereby giving him rank, perhaps tenure, and greater accessibility to funds for future work. Indian artifacts are, in this sense, a prime means for an individual in the field of archaeology to achieve status in his society.

Now, this system is completely antithetical to the Indian concept of obtaining status, because the artifacts are limited and there is competition for the obtaining of the artifacts. Competition is a term that is not really known to the American Indian. If you were to draw a very generalized picture of the world view of American Indians, it would be one of co-operation and harmony. The Indian cannot see what moves the white archaeologists, and the white archaeologists cannot see what moves the Indian, so we are at an impasse.

What we need is compromise, and the compromise has to be worked out within the context of the situation in which it occurs. I don't believe we can legislate anything dealing with artifacts. I don't think it is possible to legislate a morality borne between two cultures. We will have to have people of understanding on both sides.

"What if a process of understanding with a living culture had started one hundred and fifty years ago?"

Mallam: It did almost start one hundred and fifty years ago with Thomas Jefferson directing the archaeological excavation of some mounds.

"But then Progress and Manifest Destiny and the Westward Movement would not be denied."

Mallam: Right. I have been doing some research on the history of the mound-builder myth. Because of the assumptions that whites had about this New World, the mounds were not really ascribed to Indian creation until about 1890. It is interesting that the actual death of the mound-builder myth tends to coincide in a general fashion with the Massacre at Wounded Knee in 1892, which was the last major confrontation between whites and Indians. And 1890 is also the official closing of the frontier for the U. S. Bureau of Census. What we are saying is that it was impossible one hundred and fifty, or even one hundred years ago, for the whiteman to have had this type of interest in the Indian, because people were acting upon sets of cultural assumptions that were logical and positive to them at that time.

"What if there had been a controlled immigration program that slowed up the western movement considerably. Could this have encouraged greater interaction and understanding between the two cultures?"

Mallam: It might have worked; but, you see, the Indian never had a chance once white contact was made, because white contact spread so rapidly that there was a great deal of acculturation going on between Indians and whites from the very onset. Indians recognized that whites had certain cultural traits that were of value to them, so they took them and incorporated them into their own society. Whites did the same thing. In fact, almost any meal we eat today is largely derived from Indian foods that were produced independently on this continent.

But if there had been no pressure to settle the New World, and if there had been controlled immigration to the New World, then the situation might have changed so that the Indians would have at least achieved a status of parity in the interaction with whites. The Indians did have that status at the very beginning of colonization, even though there were basic cultural assumptions about their inferiority.

Once the seaboard was occupied, however, and the penetrations had begun into the interior, a process was started whereby one Indian tribe was being moved out until it came into contact with another Indian tribe, and a snowball effect was created. There was constant pressure on the Indian to preserve his own life-style in the face of an encroaching civilization.

Under circumstances of acculturation whereby two sides view themselves as complete, politically autonomous units, there is an excellent chance for understanding. But the political autonomy of the Indian soon began to disappear, and he became the victim of a whole series of programs directed toward the very base of his existence, which is his identity.

"Once you have obtained the proper legal permissions, do you feel any qualms in unearthing bones from a burial mound? Would you feel that you were desecrating sacred ground?"

Mallam: Specifically, I, as an individual, would be fully aware that the mound was a sacred place, but I am faced with a situation where it is almost an either-or situation in the sense that either someone who is trained and knowledgeable about Indian mythology and history can handle these artifacts with discretion, or the relics can be left alone and eventually be rooted out by vandals. I cannot think of one mound in the state of Iowa—with the exception of the Effigy Mounds National Monument—that has not been potted by vandals. These are the artifacts that find their way into private collections and are displayed on mantelpieces.

"You advise making pragmatic use of a deplorable situation."

Mallam: I think you can say I advise making pragmatic use of a deplorable situation in the hope that, ultimately, the end result will be aesthetic and that there will be a new understanding created.

What I am trying to do here in northeast Iowa is to write a history of Indians from prehistoric times to the present which can be utilized in the classrooms of grades one through six. The idea is that the archaeological work that we conduct in northeast Iowa will be used for illustrating Indian identity and will be disseminated directly to the elementary school as a specific part of social studies units which deal with American Indians.

I feel that if factual and valid information is presented to children at the elementary level, proper Indian-white structural relationships can be created. From what I have seen, most of the material that comes out of the American public school system, at least in the elementary grades, is so ethnocentric and degrading that the child builds up a set of cultural assumptions that will permit him to see no wrong in destroying Indian sites, because Indians are a thing of the past and are gone. If we are not pragmatic, we are going to watch a whole series of Indian sites and sacred places be destroyed.

Two Navajos and a Hopi recently filed suit in Coconino County Superior Court in an effort to halt a zoning decision that would permit a ski village to be constructed on the San Francisco Peaks north of Flagstaff, Arizona. According to the Indians, Navajo, Apache, Hopi, Camp Verde Yavapai, Havasupai, Walpi, and Pueblo people regard the area as holy.

Robert Lomadafkie, Jr., warned that the high winds and the continuing drought in the area were no accident. "The spirits are angry," he said, regarding the plans of Summit Properties, a Flagstaff development firm, to fashion ski jumps and chalets on the Sacred Western Mountain. To Lomadafkie, Jr., a Hopi, the Holy Mountain is the home of the Kachina spirit people.

Bill Beavor, operator of Sacred Mountain Trading Post, saw the central issue as being one that pitted skiers and business against Indians and religion. "You wouldn't ski through the Vatican," he said. "You wouldn't throw snowballs in the Tabernacle in Salt Lake City. That's basically what it boils down to."

For the traditional Amerindian, there is a very thin line of demarcation between the living and the dead. As Chief Seattle remarked, "There is no death, only a change of worlds." A major portion of any traditional Indian's medicine is his deep and abiding belief in personal contact with the unseen world of his grandmothers and grandfathers. His medicine tells him that direct communication with this invisible world is possible, that the dead and the living depend upon one another in countless ways which fashion and uphold the world.

Don Wanatee, a Mesquakie, told me: "We have maintained the basic ways of our ancestors, so therefore we are in direct contact with them every day. As a matter of fact, the beliefs that we practice today are basically for them, because we believe that the dead take care of the living, as the living take care of the dead."

4. Medicine Power and the Cosmos

In an old book entitled *The Fourteen Ioway Indians* (London, 1844), an account is given in which a packet ship was becalmed for several days near the English coast. A group of Amerindians were on board, and the captain decided to call upon their medicine man to "try the efficacy of his magical powers with the endeavor to raise the wind."

> After the usual ceremony of a mystery feast and various invocations to the spirit of the wind and ocean, both were conciliated by the sacrifice of many plugs of tobacco thrown into the sea; and in a little time the wind began to blow, the sails were filled, and the vessel soon wafted into port.

During the summer of 1865, the great warrior Roman Nose undertook many medicine fasts in order to receive protection from enemies. Under the tutelage of White Bull, an elderly Cheyenne medicine man, Roman Nose lay on a raft for four days in the midst of a medicine lake, partaking of neither food nor water, suffering a relentless sun by day and pouring rain by night. Spiritually equipped with the visions obtained during the fasts and solemnly bearing the protective eagle feather war bonnet that White Bull had fashioned for him, Roman Nose requested the honor of leading a charge against the Blue Coats who were invading the Powder River.

On the day of battle, Roman Nose mounted his white pony and called to the assembled warriors. He asked them not to fight that day for single honors, but to fight in a unit as the Blue Coats did. Then, to prove his medicine power, he told the warriors not to charge until he had ridden before the whites and caused them all to empty their guns.

Roman Nose broke away from the war party, urged his pony into a run toward the ranks of white soldiers standing before their wagons. When he was near enough to see the Blue Coats' faces, he wheeled his mount and rode parallel to their ranks and their rifles.

Roman Nose had completed three or four passes before a ball from a Springfield musket smashed his pony from under him. Roman Nose rose, unscratched, and the massed Cheyenne and Sioux shouted their war cries and attacked the Blue Coats' lines.

In September 1867, Roman Nose was asked by the Sioux to join them in an attack against a group of white scouts who had been sent by General Sheridan to search out Indian encampments for winter attacks. Roman Nose agreed to join the Cheyennes' allies; but first, he said, he must undergo a purification ceremony. One of the women had inadvertently used an iron fork to prepare his food, and since his medicine vision had told him that his power to turn away Blue Coat bullets would be destroyed if any metal contaminated his food, he must have time to restore his magic.

Although the Cheyennes respected their great warrior's wish, their impatient allies exerted pressure upon Roman Nose to abbreviate his purification rites. Roman Nose was not a chief, but he was the warrior-mystic who had inspired his people to continue to fight to protect their lands and their way of life. Courageous charges, brave deeds, and acts of honor would be sparked by Roman Nose's presence on the field.

Realizing that his medicine had been destroyed and that he would surely be killed that day, Roman Nose yielded to the Sioux's demands, painted his face, and placed his war bonnet on his head. He was cut down that day by Forsyth's Scouts in the fight the whitemen called the Battle of Beecher's Island and the redmen called the Fight When Roman Nose Was Killed.

In the modern classic *Black Elk Speaks,* John G. Neihardt tells of accompanying the aged holy man of the Oglala Sioux to Harney Peak, the same place where the spirits had taken Black Elk in a vision when he had been young. The old man painted himself as he had seen himself in his great vision and called out to the Great Spirit to hear his prayer that the Indian people might once again find their way back into the sacred hoop, the Great Circle.

Neihardt writes that as those who stood by watched, thin clouds began to gather out of a clear sky. "A scant chill rain began to fall and there was low, muttering thunder without lightning. With tears running down [his] cheeks, [Black Elk] raised his voice to a thin high wail, and chanted: 'In sorrow I am sending a feeble voice, O Six Powers of the World. Hear me in my sorrow, for I may never call again. O make my people live!' "

According to Neihardt, Black Elk stood for a few minutes in silence, his face uplifted, weeping in the rain. Soon, the sky was once again cloudless.

What makes Amerindian medicine power work? How can sacred doctors summon wind, ward off bullets, squeeze rain out of cloudless skies?

Sun Bear, Chippewa medicine man: Some people would think of these things as magic. We think of them as simply using forces that have been here for all time for our benefit or our needs. Magic is not "magic" if you understand it. It is something that works. It is when you will something into existence because you have need of it.

Rarihokwats, Mohawk, Editor of *Akwesasne Notes:* I'm not certain it is possible to respond to the question of what is the power evident in Amerindian magic. You see, the Power is the power of creation. Whatever that power is, it causes the grass to grow, the Earth to rotate, and all the things that happen in all of creation. This is a tremendous power. It is the power to create life. And the more that Indian people or other people become acquainted with that power, the more they are able to internalize and utilize and flow with that power.

"Is part of it the recognition that man is a part of nature and everything is part of one whole?"

Rarihokwats: Yes, and the whole is contained in each part. It has to have both of those aspects. You are not only part of the whole, but the whole is part of you.

"Man is individual, and at the same time, man is part of all men. Man is part of the Cosmos, and the Cosmos is part of man."

Rarihokwats: Right, and in indistinguishable kinds of ways. If you just say, "I am part of the Universe," then it is possible for you to withdraw from the Universe at some point and set up your own separate shop. On the other hand, if the Universe is part of you, and not only just a part that can be amputated, but a part upon which you are dependent, then you cannot separate yourself, you cannot withdraw.

Although we shall attempt to define the more subtle and sacred aspects of medicine power and the methods by which we might acquire those "indistinguishable kinds of ways" that will enable us to become one with the Cosmos and acknowledge that the Cosmos is one with us, we might be well advised to offer additional physical proofs of the efficacy of medicine power before we define the abstract elements inherent in Amerindian magic.

Perhaps the best-known demonstration of medicine power is the rain dance. The imagery of dancing Indians bedecked in colorful costumes, chanting prayers to the Great Spirit for life-giving moisture is firmly implanted in the white consciousness as the single most representative act of Amerindian magic.

There is no reason for the more knowledgeable students or practitioners of medicine power to be offended that such a ceremony has become stereotypical of a vast and serious cosmology. Man is no less dependent upon the harvest of his crops today than he was one hundred years ago. An adequate supply of food will never lose its impact as a basic issue in man's survival as a species. There is not a farmer today so sophisticated that he has not asked himself if the medicine of an Indian rain dance really works.

There seems little question that the ceremony, properly practiced, does most certainly provoke the fall of rain.

The northeastern section of the United States suffered its worst drought in recorded history when New York City was host to the World's Fair in the summer of 1965. As a promotion for the Niagara Falls' Maid of the Mist Festival in July and in order to alleviate the drought conditions, a seventy-five-year-old Tuscarora chief named Black Cloud performed a rainmaking ceremony on June 30.

Attired in full regalia, Black Cloud began the ritual at 10:25 A.M. Just a few moments before 11:00 A.M., raindrops began to splatter the fair grounds. Within an hour, Manhattan was experiencing what the weather bureau described as a "good rain shower."

Lorraine Carr, writing in the Albuquerque *Tribune* (June 5, 1972), states that the rain dances held at the Tesuque Indian Pueblo on May 28 brought a gentle five-hour rain that "soaked the thirsty mother earth."

Ms. Carr went on to recall the June day when she attended a dance at Santo Domingo Pueblo accompanied by two skeptical Texas friends. Although the blue sky was cloudless when they left Taos at 10 A.M., Ms. Carr brought her raincoat and umbrella. Her doubting friends were amused by her faith in a bunch of stomping Indians' ability to produce rain.

> The Indians, dressed in their impressive regalia, danced rhythmically in the hot sun. They never missed a beat.
> About 4 in the afternoon the thunderheads had built up and here came the rain. I put on my raincoat and stretched my umbrella, while my friends and other spectators sought shelter.

The rain came in torrents. As we started for Taos, we found the arroyos filled.

As my host maneuvered the car through the swirling water he glanced at the sky still heavy with rain clouds and all he said was, "I'll be damned."

I have attended many Indian dances for rain and the rains never fail to come. Someone asked, "Why not hire Indians to do rain dances rather than hire cloudseeders?"

The Indians put little faith in such a rainmaker dance. It would anger the Great Spirit. The Indian has always been a partaker of nature, not a destroyer.

Snow, as well as rain, apparently can be "danced" into falling. When Calgary Productions, a subsidiary of Walt Disney Studios, was filming the million-dollar movie *Nomads of the North* in 1959, the movie company found itself in an ideal location in the Kananaskis Forest near Banff, Alberta, Canada—ideal, except for the lack of snow. The ground was spotted with nothing more than a light film, and the seventy members of the company, together with 100 extras, stood about waiting for snow to fall at a daily cost of thousands of dollars to Calgary Productions.

After five days of financial anguish, the moviemakers held a conference to discuss the problem. The use of artificial snow was rejected, because the cost of covering several acres with the stuff would have been prohibitive. Then someone mentioned Chief Johnny Bearspaw and his Stony tribe, who had become well known for their successful rain dance at the Calgary Stampede.

Although Chief Bearspaw admitted that the Stony tribe had never before danced for snow, he saw no reason why it could not be done. He asked a fee of ten dollars per dancer, told thirty-two members of his tribe to turn out in full ceremonial costume, and the ceremony was performed.

Shortly after the dance had been concluded, seven inches of beautiful snow blanketed the Kananaskis Forest.

It would also seem that Amerindian medicine people have the

Iron Eyes Cody has appeared in countless motion pictures depicting Amerindian life. Although he considered many of these portrayals denigrative to his people, he did perform the sacred song *Wakan Tanka* in an authentic manner for *A Man Called Horse*. Iron Eyes is a member of the Sioux Yuwipi Society and is active in many American Indian groups. He is very serious about his practice of the medicine tradition.

Twylah Nitsch is the granddaughter of Moses Shongo, the last great Seneca medicine man. Well tutored in the medicine ways of her people, Twylah teaches a course in "Seneca Wisdom" for Human Dimensions Institute in Buffalo, New York. *Credit: Robert J. Koch*

Norman Paulson has patterned his Brotherhood of the Sun upon the mystical teachings of the Hopis and the principles of Essenic Christianity. Taking only what they consider the non-poisonous, non-pollutant artifacts of contemporary culture with them to their communal farm outside of Santa Barbara, the Brotherhood of the Sun draws upon the spiritual guidance of White Bear, the well-known Hopi prophet and teacher.

Deon Frey, former Spiritualist minister and well-known Chicago sensitive, has materialized Amerindian spirit entities and is a great friend of the Hopis, who call her "Little Pumpkin."

Bertie Catchings, popular Texas psychic sensitive, has received both guidance and physical assistance by a manifesting Amerindian spirit.

Irene Hughes has become one of the most renowned of the United States contemporary seers. Mrs. Hughes is one quarter Cherokee and attributes much of her sensitivity to the example set by her mother, Easter Bell Finger.

These photographs by Iron Eyes Cody capture a contemporary performance of the ritual Sun Dance, which was held in Wounded Knee, South Dakota, in 1970. Eagle Feather, the medicine man, sees to the skewering of a participant (nine), then has his own flesh pierced so that he may offer a prayer. Iron Eyes participated as Pipe Man and as a singer, as did his son, Robert Cody.

Dallas Chief Eagle was made a chief of the Sioux during a ceremony overseen by two descendants of the great chief Red Cloud. He is the author of *Winter Count,* a novel rich in authentic detail of Amerindian life before the tragic Massacre at Wounded Knee. *Credit: Babey Elite Studios*

Nada-Yolanda, channel for the Mark-Age MetaCenter in Miami, has been given impressions which convince her that she is the reincarnation of Lobo-Tan, a princess of the ancient Tanoan tribe. She feels she has verified these impressions on her subsequent trips to the Southwest.

Tom Laughlin had his faith in the Shawnee medicine man Rolling Thunder to support his courage in the filming of the rattlesnake ceremony for *Billy Jack*. Medicine people brought Laughlin their dreams and their visions to be incorporated in *Billy Jack*, a film which has become a classic depiction of Amerindian life-style.
Courtesy Billy Jack Productions

ability to transfer some of this power to artifacts and religious icons.

On April 17, 1964, the new Anthropological Museum in Chapultepec Park in Mexico City installed a 167-ton statue of Tlaloc, Teotihuacan god of rain. The gigantic, twenty-four-foot idol had to be transported into Mexico City on a specially built trailer, and some of the streets en route had to be reinforced because of the statue's great weight. Carved from living rock about, twelve centuries ago, Tlaloc had been found years before near Coalinchan, thirty-one miles east of Mexico City. When Tlaloc arrived in the Mexican capital, he was welcomed by a cloudburst that inundated the city and rained out ball games.

Some years ago, Professor William Payne, an archaeologist, ceramicist, and art professor, found a number of likenesses of the ancient rain god Cocijo while digging at the site of the ancient Zapotec civilization in Mexico. When Professor Payne returned to his classrooms at Orange Coast College in Costa Mesa, California, he produced several ceramic copies of Cocijo and decided to try an experiment. He selected a day when the skies were cloudless and the weather forecasters had decreed that no rain was in store for Costa Mesa; then he placed the icons about the campus and convinced his students to join him in a rainmaking ceremony.

By 2:30 P.M. that afternoon, the college and the community was being drenched by rain.

Since that first experiment in 1953, Professor Payne and his students have produced rain on days when clear weather has been predicted for a total of twelve hits out of thirteen attempts. For the skeptics who were stunned enough to see an academician and his students provoking rain out of formerly cloudless skies by conducting ceremonies involving icons the size of a man's palm, four of the rainstorms came in on southerly winds from Mexico, an occurrence which is uncommon in the Costa Mesa area.

"The correct placement of the effigies involves quite a bit of work," Professor Payne commented. "That's why I don't perform the ceremony more often. Then, too, I only like to do it when rain is really needed. I won't offer theorizations as to why these ceramic figurines produce rain, except to say that they do. After all, perhaps in a few thousand years, many of the things we do today will be considered strange by future civilizations."

On June 5, 1964, the citizens of Prosser, Washington, decided to throw convention to the wind and conduct a rain ceremony in an attempt to coax rain to fall on their parched community. At first the faithful produced only a slight drizzle, but then more than a thousand of their neighbors, encouraged by the initial success, joined the ritual with noisemakers. The drizzle that had been flecking the dry soil soon became converted into a welcome downpour.

Yes, it seems entirely possible that professors and students, farmers and townspeople, can capture the essence of medicine power and utilize it to their advantage—if the need is great enough and if their belief is strong enough.

"I really believe the power of American Indian medicine comes from an attitude of acceptance," Don Wilkerson, Director of the Indian Centers in Phoenix told me.

"The traditional Indian people understand that there is both good and evil and that these things can be influenced by our actions. If you develop an attitude of acceptance toward the Unknown, you can make things happen. The Indian is not hung up with controlling nature, but he knows that he can guide it. And if he learns to understand it, he knows that he can live with Nature and have it nurture him."

In July 1970, fifty farmers from Hanska, Minnesota, most of them of Scandinavian ancestry, gathered in Amerindian costumes to perform a rain dance. They formed a circle to beseech the heavens for moisture for their dying crops, and they sought to encourage spiritual intercession by conducting their supplication in a manner indigenous to the North American continent. Adding to the physical stimulus and giving evidence of their faith and optimism, two of the farmers wore raincoats over their costumes. Their dance was received, and a thunderstorm released two inches of rain on their parched farmland.

Was the performance of a rain dance ceremony an act of cultural regression on the part of the Minnesota farmers? Or do people all over the world of all ancestral strains conduct the same kind of reaching-out rituals in their times of greatest need? Does not man, wherever he may choose to dwell, have the same common spiritual ancestry, receive the same revelations from Higher Intelligence, and express himself in similar ritual acts, whose origins may be but dim memories in the collective unconscious?

In *The World's Rim,* Hartley Burr Alexander observes:

. . . There is something that is universal in men's modes of thinking, such that, as they move onward in their courses, they repeat in kind if not in instance an identical experience—which, if it be of the mind, can be understood only as the instruction which a creative nature must everywhere give to a human endowment. The Indian gives us an understanding of life colored and adorned by his own unique familiarities with a hemisphere of Earth which for many centuries was his only; this understanding is delivered in his own imaginative guise and following the impulses of his own artistic genius. But the fact that so created—by a unique people in a unique continent—it still in substance echoes what other groups of men in other natural settings have found to be *the human* truth, so that Aryan and Dakota, Greek and Pawnee, build identical ritual patterns to express their separate discoveries of a single insight, is but the reasonable argument for a validity in that insight which cannot be lightly dismissed. . . .

While recognizing the Amerindian's uniqueness, numerous metaphysicians have drawn comparisons between many tribal rituals which would certainly appear to be "echoes" of what "other groups of men in other natural settings have found to be *the human* truth." At the same time, it may be seen that due to their hundreds of years of isolation from both East and West, the Amerindians may have preserved the essentials of the Ancient Mysteries in their purest form.

The traditional Indian makes his medicine work, and the power of his magic is usually of a higher efficiency than that of the average student of Western occultism. These men and women who seek the power of medicine must make a more total commitment and pay a higher price in self-denial to attain the *wakan,* the essence of medicine, than is required of any initiate in the schools of European White Magic.

To be a recipient of medicine power, the practitioner must live his commitment every moment of every day. The practitioner must believe in the unity and the co-operation of all forms of life, and he must cherish and value all of his little brothers and sisters.

When one must take the life of an animal in order to survive, the practitioner of medicine power kills only after uttering a prayer, as if he were performing a sacrament. The entity (the soul of the animal) and its group spirit must be told that such an act is necessary in the turning of the great Wheel of Life. It may well be that the traditional saying of "grace" before meals is the Westerner's unconscious method of duplicating this propitiatory prayer.

The vision quest, certain meditative techniques, and innumerable symbols employed in a wide variety of Amerindian ceremonies remind the student of metaphysics of so much of Tibetan mysticism. Attend any powwow, especially those in the Southwest, and one will be struck by the similarities between the masks, the headdresses, the boots, prayer wheel-like devices, and dozens of symbolic designs that are but variations on the classic Tibetan mandala. When one uses a mandala in meditation, he is to discover God in the center of the design, as He is in the center of the Universe. The four parts that surround the "eye of the Great Spirit" represent the Four Directions, the Four Seasons, the Four Ages of Man, the Four Kingdoms of Life; and as we shall learn, four is the number of power in Amerindian medicine.

Carl Jung once warned Westerners that they should be cautious of an extended practice of Yoga, as it was not a native metaphysical product of the soil on which they had been reared. Although there are basic spiritual insights which are universal, there may be unique modes of attaining extended awareness, illumination, and Cosmic Consciousness which have been given to certain peoples and places to more effectively achieve communion with the Great Spirit within the confines of cosmically determined borders. If this is true, then the Amerindian vision quest, during which the seeker goes into the wilderness alone to fast, to receive his spirit guide, and to receive his secret name, not only provides us with a prototype of the revelatory experience and the means of obtaining medicine power, but it may provide us with the peculiar mystical experience that is most efficacious for our hemisphere.

Hartley Burr Alexander saw the continued quest for wisdom of body and mind—the search for the "single essential force" at the core of every thought and deed—as the perpetually accumulating elements in medicine power. The reason the term "medicine" became applied to this life-career function is simply because those attaining stature as men and women who had acquired this special kind of wisdom were so very often great healers. The true meaning of "medicine," of course, extends beyond the arts of healing, clairvoyance, precognition, and the control of weather elements.

Medicine power enables its possessor to obtain personal contact with the invisible world of spirits and to pierce the sensory world of illusion which veils the Great Mystery. And, as the Eastern holy man intones his mantra and sings holy syllables in an effort to attune himself with the Eternal Sound, the cosmic vibration, so does the traditional Amerindian seek for magical songs which will increase the power of his medicine.

Alexander states the following in regard to the importance of the song in Amerindian medicine power (*The World's Rim*):

One cannot too strongly emphasize the fact that for the red man the discourse of song is in itself a magical, or indeed a spiritual thing. His music is his most certain means of impressing his sense of need upon the Powers, and of bringing them into communion with himself. His singing is not at all primarily for his companions in the world of men, but for the spirit beings that envelop the human realm. Cere-

monies are of greater efficacy if the songs are repeated at greater
length. . . .

With his personal songs to re-establish his position with the
mysteries about him, the traditional Amerindian regards life as an
ordeal during which he must continually prove himself and pursue
his quest for wisdom of body and soul. Although certain religious
traditions may vary from tribe to tribe, the central feature of medicine power is the reliance upon individual visions as the fundamental guiding force in the ordeal that is life upon the earth plane.

The generalities given above by way of definition of medicine
power are valid, because the dogma of tribal rituals is always secondary to the guidance one receives from personal visions. The traditional Amerindian cherishes his individuality above all things,
and he guards his personal sacred revelations with the utmost se-
crecy. Because of this emphasis upon individualism and the sacredness of personal visions, the world is far more familiar with the
mysticism of nearly any other people than it is with the teachings
of the Amerindian.

It would seem a fair statement to make that the redman has
been far more interested in personal meditation than he has been
in communicating his vision to others. Even when he sings of his
revelation, his song bears the indelible stamp of the individual
soul and that song cannot be sung by another until the creator has
either given it or sold it.

In the same manner, tribal rituals came originally to an individual visionary who transmitted the song and the dance only to
carefully approved initiates.

"Even in the great food-winning ceremonies, such as the game
and corn dances, while these are cosmically timed and set by nature, nevertheless in their mythic backgrounds is invariably recognized some personal adventure or sacrifice: some seer adventuring
the wilderness that he may bring thence the secret teachings of the
gods that will lure forth the food-animals . . . the ritual is only
the outer and incidental setting for the man's self-proof and inward

vision. Throughout, the central conception is dualistic and dramatic; the natural world and the social provide the scene and the spectacle, but in the man's soul is the action," writes Hartley Burr Alexander.

John Collier sees the Amerindian's "ancient, lost reverence and passion for human personality, joined with the ancient, lost reverence and passion for the earth and its web of life" as crucial elements which the world has lost, but must regain, lest our species die. In his *Indians of the Americas,* Collier states:

> This indivisible reverence and passion is what the American Indians almost universally had; and representative groups of them have it still.
>
> They had and have this power for living which our modern world has lost—as world-view and self-view, as tradition and institution, as practical philosophy dominating their societies and as an art supreme among all the arts.

As we have noted repeatedly, Indian medicine is fully cognizant of the nurturing Earth Mother, of one's total involvement in the web of life, and of one's inability to separate himself from the cosmic flow. Charles Alexander Eastman (Ohiyesa) observed in *The Soul of the Indian* how a nearness to Nature kept one in touch with Unseen Powers:

> I know that our people possessed remarkable powers of concentration and abstraction, and I sometimes fancy that such nearness to nature . . . keeps the spirit sensitive to impressions not commonly felt, and in touch with the unseen powers.

William Willoya and Vinson Brown (*Warriors of the Rainbow*) believe that there is a ". . . great strength in the earth and in nature that the old Indians knew about, but which is almost lost to present generations."

Willoya and Brown acknowledge the possibility that farmers who love the soil and that those who live in the wilderness for

long periods of time may experience the mysterious feeling of a
kinship with Nature that enables one's "whole being to become
sensitively attuned to both wild life and plants," but they feel the
ancient Indians were able to achieve an even greater sense of
harmony with all life:

> The Indians . . . went a step beyond this to the point where the
> human spirit in some way, possibly never measurable by scientists,
> used the animal spirit as a tool in reaching the Source of the World
> and in purifying the soul. The great, pure-hearted chiefs of the olden
> times achieved their spiritual power by the most difficult self-
> discipline, fasting and prayer, including the utter emptying of the
> heart of all earthly desires and the tuning on the inner ear to the
> whispers of the wilderness. This was not idol worship . . . but some-
> thing far deeper and more wonderful, the understanding of the
> Spirit of Being that manifests itself in all living things. . . .

In my opinion, another crucial element in the spiritual chemistry
that comprises medicine power is the ability to rise above linear
time. I have often remarked that our conventional concept of time
existing in some sort of sequential stream flowing along in one
dimension is totally inadequate to provide one with a full assess-
ment of reality. This one, two, three kind of time may be convenient
for man when he is in an ordinary, conscious, waking state, since
it will limit the input of sensory data and allow him to deal effectively with the "present." But I believe that our essential selves
can rise to a level of consciousness wherein past, present, and
future form an Eternal Now; and I believe that man may gain access to this level of consciousness in his dreams and in his visions.

In his text for Ira Moskowitz' book of drawings, *American Indian Ceremonial Dances,* John Collier comments upon the Indian's
possession of a time sense that is different, and happier, than the
whiteman's:

> . . . Once our white race had it, too, and then the mechanized
> world took it away from us. . . . We think, now, that any other time

than linear, chronological time is an escapist dream. The Indians tell us otherwise, and their message and demonstration addresses itself to one of our deepest distresses and most forlorn yearnings. . . .

. . . Did there exist—as the Indians in their whole life affirm—a dimension of time—a reality of time—not linear, not clock-measured, clock-controlled, and clock-ended for us, we would be glad; we would enter it, and expand our being there. There are human groups, normal, and efficient in difficult ways of the world, which do thus expand their being, and the tribal Indians are among them.

In solitary, mystical experience many of ourselves do enter another time dimension. But under the frown of clockwork time which claims the world, we place our experience out in an eternity beyond the years and beyond the stars. Not out there did the other time dimension originate, in racial history, but within the germ plasm and the organic rhythms and the social soul; nor is its reference only or mainly to the moveless eternity. It is life's instinct and environment, and human society's instinct and environment. To realize it or not realize it makes an enormous difference, even a decisive difference. The Indians realize it, and they can make us know.

The traditional Indian sees the work of the Great Spirit in every expression of life upon the Earth Mother. Such a reverence for his environment convinced the whiteman that the Amerindian was given to the worship of idols and graven images, a primitive man confused and frightened by a hierarchy of many gods.

The American Indian traditionalist believes that the Great Spirit may express Himself in many ways and may appear in a variety of forms during the vision quest. He also believes that the essence of the Great Spirit's power flows through all living things. But the Amerindian believes in only one Supreme Being. Regrettably, only a few of the early white Americans were able to discern the distinction between witnessing God's work in all of life and worshiping elemental nature forces.

Thomas Heriot, an erudite mathematician who became proficient in the tongues of many different tribes, reported, circa 1586:

"[The Indians] believe that there is a Supreme God who has existed for all eternity."

David Zeisberger, a Moravian missionary, translated scriptural texts for the Algonquin tribes and was proficient in several native languages. From his years of personal contact with several Amerindian nations, he wrote, circa 1779: "They believe and have from time immemorial believed that there is an Almighty Being who has created heaven and earth and man and all things else. This they have learned from their ancestors."

"You didn't try to understand our prayers," Walking Buffalo complained in *Tatana Mani, Walking Buffalo of the Stonies.* "When we sang our praises to the sun or moon or wind, you said we were worshipping idols. Without understanding, you condemned us as lost souls just because our form of worship was different from yours. We saw the Great Spirit's work in almost everything: sun, moon, trees, wind, and mountains. Sometimes we approached him through these things. Was that so bad? I think we have a true belief in the supreme being, a stronger faith than that of most whites who have called us pagans."

The inclination to condemn the Amerindian as a lost soul has not been eliminated from the contemporary scene. When I told a prominent southwestern historian the theme of my book, he snorted skeptically and told me that any shreds of religious thought that the Indian might evidence had been adapted from the whiteman.

"The Indian is a notorious borrower," he went on. "At the time of the whiteman's advent to this nation, the Indian was little more than an animal. He was totally incapable of abstract thought. After so many years of the early missionaries pounding stories of Christianity into their heads, the Indians finally caught on, called God the Great Spirit, and tried to say that they had always believed in such a supreme being. The early Indians were interested in physical survival, not spirituality. Every bit of religious philosophy you'll turn up can be traced back to the early Christian missionaries."

Prejudice is a difficult stain to remove from anyone's eyes, but the journals of the earliest whitemen on our continent tell us that the Amerindians believed in a Supreme Being long before the European set his plow in the ground and his church steeples in the air.

Edward Winslow, who accompanied the first colonists to land at Plymouth Rock and who negotiated with Chief Massasoit during the English's initial attempt to explore the interior, reported that the Indians were pleased to learn that the God of the Christians was so very much like their own Kiehtan, creator of all things, who dwelt on high in the western skies.

In a letter dated August 16, 1683, William Penn noted that the Indians in Pennsylvania believed in a Supreme Being and in immortality.

Red Jacket, a Seneca chief, made the following remarks to a group of white religionists about 1790:

> Brother! You say there is but one way to worship and serve the Great Spirit. If there is but one religion, why do you white people differ so much about it? Why not all agree, as you can all read the [Bible]?
>
> Brother! We do not understand these things. We are told that your religion was given to your forefathers and has been handed down, father to son. We also have a religion which was given to our forefathers, and has been handed down to us, their children. We worship that way. It teaches us to be thankful for all the favors we receive, to love each other, and to be united. We never quarrel about religion.
>
> Brother! The Great Spirit made us all. But he has made a great difference between his white and red children. He has given us a different complexion and different customs. To you he has given the arts; to these he has not opened our eyes. . . . Since he has

made so great a difference between us in other things, why may not we conclude that he has given us a different religion, according to our understanding?

"According to our understanding," Red Jacket said, and how many whitemen will concede even today in our era of expanding awareness that the native peoples just might have had a clearer understanding of the teachings of the Great Spirit than did the Western religionists?

The German ethnologist Ivar Lissner maintains that "there once existed a universal, primordial religion, and this primordial religion, far from gaining in strength, has become more and more atrophied." Lissner writes:

> Even in recent years, people of the West believed that mankind had moved upward in its religious beliefs, on an evolutionary spiral which began in earliest times with superstition, mingled with sorcery and magic, to the triumphant evolution of monotheism. This theory held that as man became more civilized he came to see more and more clearly that magic was false and at last reached the highest level of monotheism or belief in one God. Yet . . . a belief in a single supreme deity and creator is found among all the ancient peoples whom we in our arrogance call primitive.

Lissner contends that our continued existence and survival on this planet depend ". . . on the extent to which the world is guarded and controlled by men of spirituality." We must never cease to reflect upon existence, God, and goodness; we must never permit the arts to die; we must not forsake the heritage of spirituality that has been bequeathed to us over hundreds of thousands of years; we must not allow the materialist, the pure technologist, the rivalry in the exact sciences to dictate the fate of humanity. Mankind must be guided by "great, universal minds which are close to the secrets of the transcendental and throw more into the scales than mere weight of technological progress."

The return of medicine power and the Resurrection of the Great

Spirit may well be occurring now in an effort to balance the cosmic scales against the dross of materialism. In this chapter I have made an effort to define those transcendental elements which blend together in some spiritually indefinable way to form medicine power. It is my sincere wish that my analysis will be deemed beneficial, rather than blasphemous, and that such an attempt may prove helpful to those who seek a greater understanding of what may well be the peculiar mystical experience and the proper spiritual path for our continent.

By way of summary, I believe the most essential elements of medicine power to be the following:

1.) The vision quest, with its emphasis on self-denial and spiritual discipline being extended to a lifelong pursuit of wisdom of body and soul.

2.) A reliance upon one's personal visions and dreams to provide one's direction on the path of life.

3.) A search for personal songs to enable one to attune oneself to the primal sound, the cosmic vibration of the Great Spirit.

4.) A belief in a total partnership with the world of spirits and the ability to make personal contact with grandfathers and grandmothers who have changed planes of existence.

5.) The possession of a non-linear time sense.

6.) A receptivity to the evidence that the essence of the Great Spirit may be found in everything.

7.) A reverence and a passion for the Earth Mother, the awareness of one's place in the web of life, and one's responsibility toward all plant and animal life.

8.) A total commitment to one's beliefs that pervades every aspect of one's life and enables one truly to walk in balance.

5. Jesus' Black Robes and the Old Traditions

MORLEY, Alberta, Aug. 19 [1972]—When the Rev. John S. Hascall, an American Roman Catholic priest, says mass he prefers a teepee to a church.

Several nights ago he sat crosslegged on the ground in a large white teepee illuminated by a campfire of poplar logs. His vestments were not white but black, the traditional sacred color of American Indians, and the Lord's Prayer was in Cree.

In his homily he spoke of Jesus Christ as a "Holy Man" sent to put men in contact with the Great Spirit.

Father Hascall is an Ojibwa Indian, and like a growing number of members of his race—some Christian and some not—he has committed himself to the revival of native religious traditions.

This weekend, Father Hascall and more than 600 other Indians of similar persuasion gathered on the Stoney Indian Reserve in the foothills of the Canadian Rockies for the third annual Indian Ecumenical Conference. The conference underscored the growing interest among Indians in their religious heritage. [Edward B. Fiske, special to the New York *Times*]

When I contacted Father Hascall, a Franciscan Capuchin of the province of St. Joseph, priest of an all-Indian parish in Baraga, Michigan, he was in the midst of plastering a wall in his parish house. I apologized, offered to call again at a more convenient time, but Father Hascall said that he would be happy to take a cigarette break and answer my questions.

"Why do you believe that American Indians are beginning to commit themselves to a revival of native religious traditions at this time?"

Father Hascall: What happened is this: We have our medicine men, our holy men; we look in the past and we see the future; we look at the future and see the present. And we find that Christianity has been here since 1492 and it has not yet caught on with our people. There must be something wrong.

We had a very religious people before the whiteman came. Now our children are disobeying their parents; they are committing suicide; they are doing all kinds of evil things which they never did before when we had our own religion. Let me say, if this is the way Christianity is going to be, we will have to go back to our old ways.

"Do you feel that the religious traditions of Europe or Asia can be compatible with native American religious traditions?"

Father Hascall: If you mean European traditions with European rites, no. If you mean the Christian religion as Christ taught it, yes. I know both religions, and I see nothing incompatible.

The essential message of Christ was love. Love has always been in our people. But a lot of the dogma can be irrelevant.

"Are you going to retain your status in the Roman Catholic Church?"

Father Hascall: Yes, I will always be a priest. I will always be a Christian, an Indian Christian. Our two ways are compatible as religion, but not as rite.

"How would you prefer to conduct mass in accordance with Indian tradition?"

Father Hascall: Mass wouldn't be celebrated every week. I would schedule big days of celebration. Within those days, I would serve the Eucharist.

"You would make it a true agape, or love feast, then?"

Father Hascall: Right, as it was in the early days of the Christian Church.

"It seems to me that you are talking about the possibility of blending Apostolic Christianity with the native traditions of your people."

Father Hascall: Right, Apostolic Christianity as it was in the first century, or so. That is the true Christianity. There was not the bureaucracy that we have now.

I would say that now we are seeing the Holy Spirit bringing more relevance to the kind of nature religion that is the Indian way. This religion of the Spirit moving and working in all things was born in this country. It is the religion the Spirit gave to this country. We know that we have only one God and that His Spirit works in all creatures and all things, even the stones.

The Indian has his rites—the puberty rites, the marriage rites, the death rites. The Indian has a priesthood. I want to be able to see the Christian Church come forth and blend with the way our people have been doing things for thirty thousand years. The Lateran Council has recommended such action in other countries, but our bishop and our Church won't allow us to do it here.

"Do you in your personal life utilize dreams and visions?"

Father Hascall: Yes, I use medicine myself. I follow both religions.

"Do you have any particular techniques for inducing dreams and visions?"

Father Hascall: I would say it is through contemplation. He will speak when he wants to speak. It is not something I force. Twenty-five years ago, the young men of my tribe would go out and find our totem, our spirit vision. I never did it myself, though.

"How do you deal with the Roman Catholic tradition of saints?"

Father Hascall: I would say saints are our elders. There are always holy people in the tribes. The saints are our grandmothers and grandfathers who are in spirit and who yet pray with us in our church.

"Can American Indian traditions offer a workable faith for modern man?"

Father Hascall: I would say so for the Indians. The white people have their religion. As a whole, I do not think it is possible for a whiteman to adapt himself easily to the native traditions.

I do believe, though, that Apostolic Christianity, wherein one's faith becomes a total part of his life-style, can be made compatible with native American traditions. That is why I can be a priest. I know if the Spirit has led me this far, He has a reason for it.

Can Christianity, the religion that Manifest Destiny seized upon and distorted to help win the West, really be made compatible with the spiritual traditions of the Amerindians?

The Amerindians, together with other minority groups, have noted the great contemporary desire on the part of church leaders to make Christianity relevant by depicting "black Christs" and by distributing Christmas cards portraying the Holy Family living in a hogan on the Navajo reservation. Vine Deloria, Jr., finds such attempts to transpose the Christian mythos and archetypes into Indian, black, and Mexican terms to be "totally patronizing and unrealistic." In his *We Talk, You Listen,* he writes:

> This type of religious paternalism overlooks the fact that the original figures of religious myths were designed to communicate doctrines. It satisfies itself by presenting its basic figures as so universalized that anyone can participate at any time in history. Thus the religion that it is trying to communicate becomes ahistorical, as Mickey Mouse and Snow White are ahistorical.

As I talked to a number of native Americans, I found there were differences of opinion as to how much harm or good the "Black Robes," the Christian missionaries, had done to the early Indian and as to how well Christianity and the old traditions might blend.

Twylah, Seneca: Do I feel the religious traditions of Christianity can be compatible with native American traditions? No. No way.

The native Indian religion was not one of fear. There was no re-
taliation from a God who was punishing you.

The Indian believed that the state he lived in was his own responsibility. You can quote me on this: The American Indian's
philosophy was, you are what you eat, and you are what you think.

"So you do not believe that you were conceived in sin and born
in corruption?"

Twylah: No. To the Indian, there was only one Great Mystery,
and they saw it all around them in Nature. And they knew they
were part of it. If anyone went against the balance of Nature or
the harmony that was in his own surroundings, he was responsible
for it. Whenever there were devastations or disasters, the original
Indian believed that this was a cleansing process. Storms would
knock down trees to take out the dead, so that new ones could
grow from its decay and renew the earth from which it came. But
they did not view this natural process as the result of sin and re-
taliation.

Dallas Chief Eagle, Sioux: All religions are good. Perhaps, as in
music, we progress best by achieving combinations.

You know, Tchaikovsky's music was never appreciated until
he combined German music with Russian. Puccini wasn't appreciated until he combined oriental music with Italian. Music is the
simplest language in the world, understood by everyone.

Maybe with a combination of different beliefs, we may accom-
modate each other so that we do not destroy each other. The greatest gift Christ gave in his teachings was the element of love. I think
this is one of the greatest gaps that Christianity has overlooked
—the life-style of Christ. It is this same element of love that the
Indians have in their belief in "humanhood."

Sun Bear, Chippewa: I feel the two traditions are incompatible.
I feel that the medicine of the European Christians is for their
continent. I think that many of the visions and prophecies of our
people are for our people here.

I don't feel we need to argue about these things. If I say my ancestor was a bear and you say your ancestor was a monkey, we don't have to fight, you know. We don't have to kill each other or pour lead in each other's ears to bring about conversions. That is not the Indian way.

Rarihokwats, Mohawk: Indians have always been a great people not to make hasty judgments and to let things go their course. If they don't like something, they withdraw from it, rather than confront it. I think that the Indians have resisted to a high degree by non-participation. Indians are masterful non-participants.

I think that although there are many Indians who are devout Christians, there are many others who have dabbled in Christianity and have found it seriously lacking.

I think, more than anything, Indians right now are at a stage of history when they are saying: "Okay, we tried Christianity and it doesn't work. We can see what has happened with a Christian nation as it flowered. We now know what that flower smells like, and we just don't like it. We have decided that we don't like the sample. We are not going to participate any further."

The problem that many contemporary Indians face is that they have gone through white semi-military boarding school situations. They have accepted the Indian stereotype that non-Indians have have, in many ways, become very white in their thought patterns. They have accepted the Indian stereotype that non-Indians have foisted upon them. They think that they already are Indian and all they have to do is to find the nearest medicine man, let him do some kind of thing, and they will instantly be back into the tradition. Of course many of them become impatient when they find that the medicine people are not terribly enthusiastic. The medicine people are very hospitable, and so on, but they just are not able to give these people the instant religion for which they are looking.

You can become an instant Christian, but you can't become an instant Indian.

I am not going to criticize other people who say that they are both Christian and Indian, because, apparently, in some way, they have been able to make that synthesis. I can't, because I find too many incompatible elements that I am not able to live with.

I think there are now more Christian Indians who are able to find elements of Indian religion satisfying who are coming back to their Indian-ness, than there are practitioners of Indian religion who head toward Christianity. I think these people who are fully in the Indian religion need nothing else. They don't want anything else. They are quite satisfied emotionally and every other way, and there is no need for them to turn to Christianity. But Christians now are lacking in something, and they are turning to Indian religion to get what they are missing.

I think another problem that Western people have is their concept of time as being some sort of a progression. There are many religious beliefs which are not caught into that kind of time, beliefs that are universal and present in every era. There is really no such thing as becoming "modern" with these beliefs. They are good anytime.

The thing that Christians generally forget is that their own religion goes back two thousand years, and on the Judeo aspect, a great deal longer than that. Yet Christians somehow see themselves as holding *the* modern religion, while the Indian religion is old-fashioned and outdated. I just don't think that most Christians understand their own religious beliefs that well.

In the New York *Times* piece already referred to at the beginning of this chapter, Edward B. Fiske quoted John Snow, a chief of the Stony tribe, who hosted the third annual Indian Ecumenical Conference: "Our people are beginning to realize that we have a religious faith that is as good as any other. After many years of seeing it condemned as pagan—and accepting such judgments ourselves—we are ready again to take pride in it."

Wilfred Pelletier, a consultant to the Nishnawbe Institute, told Fiske: "Eating a meal, smoking a cigarette—these acts are all ceremonies to me. We are inseparable from the earth and the universe."

Earnest Tootoosis, a Plains Cree from Saskatchewan, a delegate to the conference, remarked to the assembly: "We were in a Garden of Eden when the white man came in 1492, but now we have been destroyed. We must go back to the way our forefathers worshipped. We must pray to the Great Spirit the way he wanted us to."

Robert Thomas, a Cherokee who had helped organize the ecumenical conferences, noted that the Indian people were searching for some kind of structure and identity, and he speculated that such a search ". . . may end up creating a new Indian religion."

Rev. Andrew Ahendkew, a Plains Cree who is an Anglican, looks for a greater integration of Christian and native American religious traditions. Although he admitted that he would like to go back to tribal tradition "100 per cent," Reverend Ahendkew said that he could not. In his view Christianity and the old traditions "must live in harmony."

Is it possible for the old traditions of the Amerindians, with their emphasis on the individual's totality with the Earth and the Universe, to be harmonious with Christianity, which, traditionally, has represented man possessed of a sinful nature, yet, at the same time, authorized man to have dominion over Nature?

In his *American Indian Religions,* John Major Hurdy writes:

Christianity claims God's laws to be above natural law, not to be its sum total. Christianity has a history of obstructing the study of nature and suppressing information about nature. It represents man's nature as sinful and this planet in its beauty as being no more than a prison house to which our parents and their progeny have been condemned. It claims sorrow and retribution for our heritage and says that life itself is unimportant except as a path to heaven. . . .

. . . [the Indians] were all oriented to the rhythm of creation. Without telescopes, the Indian visionaries felt the universe about them and dedicated themselves to keeping man's world in balance with the cosmos. All of them loved the earth and held her body and her children sacred. All of them sought to communicate with the

powers of nature. Cumulatively they developed a variety of techniques for doing so. And [their religious traditions] were an integral
part of the lives of the people. . . .

Dr. Walter Houston Clark, Professor Emeritus at Andover Newton Theological Seminary, agrees with Reverend Ahendkew about
the harmonious future which Christianity and the traditional Indian
beliefs might share.

Dr. Clark: I noted that the peyote ceremony which I attended
with the Potawatomi in Kansas was a syncretic one, which involved
both Christian and traditional Indian elements. Personally, this was
a congenial factor for me, being Christian in my general approach.

I think that as we look at the history of religion, we see that
this syncretism goes on all the time. Whenever there are two religious traditions close to one another, there is a tendency for the
two traditions to draw nearer together, even though one of the
traditions may be dominant. Certainly the Christian communion
service, the mass, and so on, owe a great deal to many of the
Eastern and Near Eastern mystery cults of two thousand or more
years ago; and I see no reason why this shouldn't be the case today.

For example, the peyote ceremony in which I participated was
the most impressive religious ceremony that I have ever attended.
For me, it would be an easy step toward using these drugs, or
similar ones, under proper supervision.

The supervision provided by the Indians in this service was
superb. The man who was in charge was experienced, and the
whole ceremony directed the experiences of the worshipers at that
service. I see no reason why that kind of religious expertise couldn't
be developed among the whites.

When you get right down to the essential elements of religious
life, as William James said, I think they are rooted in the mystical
experiences of the individual. One of the characteristics of these
drugs is their agency of releasing the mystical potentialities of men,
no matter what they are.

With this as groundwork, I think that almost any tradition could be linked with another tradition. It is when you get to the more superficial aspects of religious beliefs—the dogmas and self-righteous traditions—that you get into trouble.

I think the American Indians' concern with Nature and the environment that surrounds them is another way in which one can open up the mystical core of his nature. In this respect, I think that the two traditions are compatible, at least to some degree.

In a speech at the University of Nebraska, a Chippewa named Bellecourt commented that American Indians were not against the concept of Christianity, but they were against the way it had been used against the Indian people. "Christianity was taught to the Indian by persons who broke all Ten Commandments," he said.

"Early in the history of North American exploration," Vine Deloria, Jr., has observed, "the fundamental responsibilities of Genesis became interpreted as man's right, and basically the white-man's right, to use whatever he wanted and however he wanted to use it. Wholesale destruction of the forests, the game, and the original peoples of this continent were justified as part of God's plan to subdue and dominate an untamed wilderness. Nowhere was there any sense of stewardship between diverse elements of the new Christian settlers either collectively or individually and the continent as they found it. . . ."

M. Edward McGaa, a Sioux, Assistant Director of Minnesota Indian Education, remarked in a speech made at Navajo Community College's American Indian Seminar Series that Christian missionaries should stay off the reservations and devote more time to their own people.

"The white man's religion has destroyed our unity," McGaa said. "The white man's religion has no power. Yes, I believe in Christ. I believe he appeared to those people over there across the sea. He didn't appear to the Indians. All the tribes of North America have one God, the Great Spirit. We all have the same prophecies. All the things that are happening now were predicted.

"Indians don't argue religion; they don't try to force it on some-

one else. The white man does. . . . We've got to get back to our
values, to our religion. We must spread our values to the world.
Otherwise those people are going to blow each other up and some
of us with them."

Although a number of white judges have ruled recently that
young Indian men may receive conscientious objector status as a
result of their ascribing to the traditional beliefs of their tribe, the
vast majority of non-Indian citizens of the United States would
probably show as much respect toward practitioners of medicine
and tribal religious traditions as they would toward exponents of
the Flat Earth Society. At best, Amerindian medicine is regarded
as quaint superstition and surviving bits of folklore. In order for
the average non-Indian to consider treating medicine and the traditional Amerindian beliefs seriously, he must come to terms with
his centuries of European heritage; and he must work out some
kind of intellectual compromise with an educational background
that has conditioned him to believe that *modern* and *technological*
is good, and that *traditional* and *non-industrial* is bad.

To the Taos Indians of New Mexico, the watershed of the Sangre
de Cristo Mountains is a natural temple of meditation. They grow
no crops there. They do not harvest the trees for lumber. They
could not care less about the possibility of any valuable minerals
existing in the rocks. They have been making pilgrimages to Blue
Lake for more than seven hundred years.

In July 1970, the Taos people came under challenge and ridicule
by United States Senators who saw no reason why the Taos Pueblo
should have total control of 48,000 acres of timberland. It seemed
unfathomable to the questioning senators that the Taos could hold
a site so spiritual that they could resist the obvious financial advantage in exploiting the area.

What kind of real religion could it be that would consider trees,
flowers, grass, rocks, and soil to be sacred? These things are for
man, the apex of God's creation, to make use of as he will.

President Richard Nixon endorsed the Taos' request after meeting with their delegation and with the president of the National Congress of American Indians. In his prepared statement President Nixon said:

> . . . From the 14 century, the Taos Pueblo Indians used these areas for religious and tribal purposes. In 1906, however, the United States government appropriated these lands for the creation of a national forest. According to a recent determination of the Indian Claims Commission, the government "took said lands from petitioner without compensation."
>
> For 64 years, the Taos Pueblo has been trying to regain possession of this sacred lake and watershed area in order to preserve its natural condition and limit its non-Indian use. The Taos Indians consider such action essential to the protection and expression of their religious faith. . . .

Senator Lee Metcalf of Montana worried, though, about the danger of "medicine men springing up all over the country and asking for the same deal."

Quentin Burdick, Senator from North Dakota, asked if Taos Pueblo would agree to a "reverter clause" to return the land to the United States Government in the event that the Taos would cease utilizing it for religious purposes. Maybe, Senator Burdick speculated, the Taos might change their minds and decide to go into the lumber and mining business.

Paul J. Bernal, secretary of the Pueblo Council, indignantly retorted that it was apparent that the senators did not believe the Taos' explanation of their religion.

"We are not accepting any reverter," Bernal told the interior subcommittee. "We are not going to use this land for anything but religion. We are going to give this land back to nobody."

Interior Secretary Walter Hickel threw his lot in with the Taos, stating that while his department would not look with favor on every request of such nature, the Taos Pueblo situation was "unique" because of the established record of their having petitioned for the return of their shrine for sixty-four years.

"The administration will take a different stand for religious reasons than economic," Secretary Hickel said.

Orthodox white religions have little difficulty obtaining tax-exempt status. They may send letters of solicitation through the mails, and they may acquire land holdings and market investments, while remaining secure in their "non-profit organization" seal. The Taos Pueblo had to petition for sixty-four years in order to convince the United States Government that they should be permitted to achieve total control of a site that had been the focal point of sacred pilgrimages for seven hundred years.

It would be difficult to conceive of a Senate subcommittee convening to challenge bishops and cardinals on the matter of tax exemption on the wealth and financial holdings of the Roman Catholic Church. But think of all the tax revenue the government is losing because the Taos have these superstitions regarding 48,-000 acres of rich timberland and potentially rich mineral deposits! Why, if this were one hundred years ago, we could easily pass the proper legislation or break the appropriate treaty and see to it that the watershed of the Sangre de Christo would be correctly developed. We certainly would not permit ridiculous native beliefs about the sacredness of an area stop us. How pagan. How downright pantheistic. Trees, mountains, and lakes are not sacred. Cathedrals, churches, synagogues are sacred. Maybe all these bleeding hearts in the country have made us too damn soft.

In "An Open Letter to the Heads of the Christian Churches," Vine Deloria, Jr., had an appropriate answer to the above too familiar kind of reasoning in regard to the exploitation of natural resources and the "justification" of disregarding native traditions that might inhibit the commercial development of the Earth Mother:

> The poverty we presently endure, the confiscation of our lands, the destruction of animals we once enjoyed, the obliteration of our valleys and rivers, the exploitation of our holy places as tourist traps, all of these things might have occurred anyway. We might even have

done these things eventually, although according to our beliefs this would have been the gravest of sins.

But we would never have deliberately done these things as a religious command. . . .

It may be that we cannot change the past, but we can certainly begin to try to understand it. We have only to stand today for the things that are right, and which we know are right. If promises have been made, those promises must be kept. If mistakes are made, they must be corrected. If the lands of aboriginal peoples were wrongly taken by a Christian mandate, then what remains of those lands must not be continually taken once the mistake is known.

It remains to you as honest men to ponder what your predecessors have created, and what, by your silence, you now endorse. . . . You must renounce the errors that have led men astray from themselves, and lead the search for that understanding or that religious interpretation that can bring them to understand themselves, their fellow men, and the creation in which they live. . . .

O Great Spirit, grant us understanding!

One cannot doubt the sincerity of the early Christian missionaries, the Black Robes, who earnestly attempted to preach what they considered the authentic word of God to the Amerindians. But understanding between peoples is all but impossible if one people regard their culture, their customs, and their religion as innately superior, and all discourse is intoned in a paternal and patronizing manner.

"Lost in the dark the heathen doth languish," bemoans a familiar missionary hymn, soundly implying that there is a single source of Illumination. When the Black Robes set forth on their spiritual safaris intent upon bringing light to the lost children of Nature, they comfortably established themselves in the parental role and widened the gap of understanding between religious traditions.

In 1824, Chief Red Jacket of the Senecas clearly set forth his objections to the Christian missionaries:

. . . [the missionaries] know we do not understand their religion.
We cannot read their book—they tell us different stories about what
it contains, and we believe they make the book talk to suit themselves. If we had no money, no land . . . to be cheated out of these
black coats would not trouble themselves about our good hereafter.

The Great Spirit will not punish us for what we do not know. He
will do justice to his red children. These black coats talk to the Great
Spirit, and ask for light that we may see as they do, when they are
blind themselves and quarrel about the light that guides them. These
things we do not understand, and the light which they give us makes
the straight and plain path trod by our fathers dark and dreary.

The black coats tell us to work and raise corn; they do nothing
themselves and would starve to death if someone did not feed them.
All they do is pray to the Great Spirit; but that will not make corn
and potatoes grow; if it will why do they beg from us and from the
white people? . . . As soon as they crossed the great waters they
wanted our country, and in return have always been ready to teach
us to quarrel about their religion . . . If [the Indians] were raised
among white people, and learned to work and read as they do, it
would only make their situation worse. . . . We are few and weak,
but may for a long time be happy if we hold fast to our country and
the religion of our fathers.

The Black Coats, good Christian soldiers, marched onward as
to war against the redman's resolve to hold fast to the religion
of his fathers. The missionaries had a divine crusade to save the
Indians' souls. To leave them wallowing like animals in their pagan
beliefs would have been unthinkable, an affront to the Apostolic
commission to spread the Word to the uttermost parts of the earth.
The salvation of the Indian was but another weight to be added
to the whiteman's burden, a weight to be shouldered willingly,
since, of all races, the white had designated itself to be the keeper
of its brothers.

Any number of missionaries might have forearmed themselves
during their seminary training by reading *Information Respecting
the History, Condition and Prospects of the Indian Tribes of the*

United States: Collected and Prepared Under the Direction of the
Bureau of Indian Affairs, per Act of Congress of March 3d, 1847,
by Henry R. Schoolcraft, LL.D. In one of the papers collected
therein, Lieut. U.S.N. George Falconer Emmons characterizes the
Indian in the following manner:

> Finally, as a race, although they differ materially in language, in
> point of mental and physical development, and the color of their hair,
> eyes, and skin, I question if they differ more from each other than
> the people occupying the extremes of the United States. They are
> generally well formed, below the whites in stature, have an easy
> gait, but neither graceful nor handsome; their eyes and hair usually
> black—the latter occasionally brown, generally parted in the middle
> of the forehead, so as to hang down each side; noses broad and flat
> —some aquiline exceptions. The mouth large, lips thick, teeth fair,
> but in adults generally more or less worn.

Once the seminarian had formed a mental image of his future
children-of-Nature parishioners as squat, ugly, clumsy, black-eyed
people with worn teeth, he was presented with a summation of
their character:

> They are wily, superstitious, lazy, indolent, and dirty. With these
> traits, united to an implacable hostility which they generally enter-
> tain towards the whites, it does not, I think, require much wisdom
> to predict their fate. [At this point, Manifest Destiny seemed to be
> placing a limit on the length of time the Indian Salvation Game
> could be played. There would be a reduced number of Indian souls
> for each missionary to save.]
> Facts that have developed themselves within the last year relating
> to these tribes, must, I think, convince the observing that Indian
> agencies and treaties cannot alone save them. It is melancholy to
> see them melting away so rapidly; but it does not appear to be in-
> tended that civilization should prevent it.

In another paper included in the report, Philander Prescott,
U.S. Dacotah Interpreter, Fort Snelling Agency, Minnesota, an-

swered such specific questions about the religious life of the American Indians as the following:

"What species or degree of worship do they, *in fine,* render to the Great Spirit? Do they praise him in hymns, chants, or choruses? Do they pray to him, and if so, for what purpose?"

To analyze the worship of Indians, in our view, amounts to nothing at all. They are very tenacious and say they are right, and are very zealous and cling to their old habits like death, and will not give way to any kind of teaching. They pray, but their prayers are very short. . . .

"Is there reason to believe the Indians to be idolators? Are images of wood or stone ever worshipped? or is there any gross and palpable form of idolatry in the existing tribes, similar to that of the oriental world?"

The Dacotahs have no images of wood that they worship, nor have they any edifices for public worship. These Indians worship in their natural state. An Indian will pick up a round stone, of any kind, and paint it, and go a few rods from his lodge, and clean away the grass, say from one to two feet in diameter, and there place his stone, or god, as he would term it, and make an offering of some tobacco and some feathers, and pray to the stone to deliver him from some danger that he has probably dreamed of, or from imagination.

"Do they believe in the immortality of the soul, and the doctrine of moral accountability to the Creator? Do they believe in the resurrection of the body? Do they believe, at all, in the doctrine of reward and punishments in a future state?"

The Indians believe in the immortality of the soul, but as for accountability they have but a vague idea of it. Future rewards and punishments they have no conception of. . . . Everything appears to be dark and mysterious with them respecting the future state of both the soul and the body.

When J. Lee Humfreville published his *Twenty Years Among Our Hostile Indians* in 1899, the authorities on Amerindian life who had actually lived among many tribes—without truly understanding any of them—were already referring to the aboriginal peoples in the past tense. But the seminarian of that generation might well have added a book such as Humfreville's to his reading list, along with Bureau of Indian Affairs reports, so that he might save what few souls remained on the reservations. Even a casual perusal of *Twenty Years Among Our Hostile Indians* would cause the Christian soldier to gird his loins for a bitter fight with Satan among the redmen. Among his observations, Humfreville included these analyses:

[The Indian] depended upon his natural animal instinct more than on human judgment. Yet, granting his superiority in these and other ways, he could not compete with civilized man.

There was in the Indian nature a trait of intractability not found in any other portion of the human race. . . . He could not be enslaved. The Spaniards in the early days of discovery endeavored to enslave the Indian; the result was that he died in his chains. He was the same when I first knew him as he was then—unamenable to the law and impatient of restraint. . . . He might be brought up in the midst of civilized surroundings and educated, but at the first opportunity he would relapse into his original barbarism. . . .

He was the very impersonation of duplicity. He might enter the cabin of a frontiersman, or a military fort, or an Indian agency, and listen to all that was said, without giving the slightest evidence that he understood what he heard, or that he was taking notice of his surroundings. In his attitude and facial expressions, he might appear as taciturn as a Sphinx, and yet understand every word that was uttered and be planning a murderous raid at the same moment.

Occasionally, it is true, the Indian evinced some commendable traits of character. But these were the exception to the rule. Doubtless there are also instances of truthfulness and fidelity on his part. But granting this, it is still an indisputable fact that the Indian, of all uncivilized people, has offered the greatest degree of opposition to the influences of civilization.

In spite of the fact that the fledgling Black Coat was forewarned that the Amerindian was ugly, clumsy, lazy, dirty, superstitious, deceitful, untruthful, and stubbornly opposed to being either enslaved or civilized, the Christian Light Bearers discovered many elements within Amerindian tradition which they were hard put to explain. How, for example, had these primitive, isolated savages come to know so many of the Old Testament stories which the eager missionaries believed they were revealing to the pagan children of Nature for the first time?

The Delaware, for example, told the stories of the Creation and the Great Deluge in pictographs that their people who were wise in the old traditions translated for the Black Coats (from a translation obtained by a Professor C. S. Rafinesque in 1822, paraphrased in *Indian Myths,* Ellen Russell Emerson, 1884):

THE CREATION

At the first there were great waters above all land,
And above the waters were thick clouds, and there was God the
                                          Creator.
The first being, eternal, omnipotent, invisible, was God the Creator.
He created the sun, the moon, and stars.
He caused them all to move well.
By his power he made the winds to blow, purifying, and the deep
                                    waters to run off.
All was made bright, and the islands were brought into being.
Then again God the Creator made the great spirits.
He made also the first beings, guardians, and souls.
Then he made a man being, the father of man.
He gave him the first mother, the mother of the early born.
Fishes gave he him, turtles, beasts, and birds.
But the Evil Spirit created evil beings, snakes and monsters.
He created vermin and annoying insects.
Then were all beings friends.
There being a good god, all spirits were good—
The beings, the first men, mothers, wives, little spirits also.
Fat fruits were the food of the beings and the little spirits.
All were then happy, easy in mind, and pleased.
But then came secretly on earth the snake god, the snake-priest, and
                                    snake-worship.

Came wickedness, came unhappiness.

Came then bad weather, disease, and death.

This was all very long ago, at our early home.

THE GREAT DELUGE

Long ago came the powerful serpent, when men had become evil.

The strong serpent was the foe of the beings; and they became embroiled, hating each other.

Then they fought and despoiled each other, and were not peaceful.

And the small men fought with the keeper of the dead.

Then the strong serpent resolved all men and beings to destroy immediately.

The black serpent monster brought the snake-water rushing.

The wide waters rushing wide to the hills, everywhere spreading, everywhere destroying.

At the island of the turtle was Manabozho, of men and beings the Grand-father.

Being born creeping, at turtle-land he is ready to move and dwell.

Men and beings go forth on the flood of waters, moving afloat every way, seeking the back of the turtle.

The monsters of the sea were many, and destroyed some of them.

Then the daughter of a spirit helped them in a boat, and all joined saying, Come, help!

Manabozho, of all beings, of men and turtles, the Grand-father!

All together, on the turtle then, the men then, were all together.

Much frightened, Manabozho prayed to the turtle that he would make all well again.

Then the waters ran off, it was dry on mountain and plain, and the great evil went elsewhere by the path of the cave.

Tribe after tribe across the length and width of the continent had legends and myths which closely paralleled the accounts found in Genesis and in other books of the Old Testament. Some missionaries dealt with the problem in the same manner that the early Spanish priests had dealt with the Aztec myths: they declared that the native peoples had been told these stories by Satan.

In his study of the aboriginal peoples written during the last century, an indignant John Tanner fulminated against such accounts related by the medicine men and declared: "If the Great Spirit had communications to make, he would make them through a *white* man, not an Indian!"

Other Christian scholars and missionaries were not so certain, and a theory which held that the aboriginal peoples were the descendants of the Lost Tribes of Israel was formulated in an effort to explain the similarity between so many of the Indians' legends, rites, and word sounds and Israeli counterparts. To add a kind of intriguing credence to this theory was the enigma of the Mandan tribe—blue-eyed, fair-complexioned native peoples of the central plains. Clergymen set out with renewed vigor in an effort to reclaim the scattered Israeli tribes, lost to the fold for so long, denied the opportunity to accept Jesus as the Messiah, condemned to wander a pagan land with their holy traditions but dim memories.

Most of the early scholars, and it appears the majority of secular and clerical authorities today, hold fast to the explanation of acculturation and the early Indians having borrowed and adapted the Christian cosmology in terms of their own environment. Even in our liberal times, too many authorities see the Amerindian as spiritually retarded at the time of the whiteman's advent to this continent. At best, the aboriginal peoples are seen as superstitious, pantheistic children of Nature who prayed to every clap of thunder and every shaking bush.

"As a result of such attitudes, we have gone underground in many things," Don Wilkerson of the Indian Centers in Phoenix told me.

Don Wilkerson: The missionary influence has, in many respects, caused the Indian religions and the Indian beliefs to withdraw from their view. No one likes to be laughed at, and no one likes to be humiliated.

As far as our not having any culture or religion, I can point to the Hopi, whose religious traditions go back thousands of years.

Their ancient prophecies are being proven today. They have a pictorial and a legendary history. They have a concept of passing through a succession of worlds.

"You are suggesting that such concepts do show a capacity for abstract thinking."

Wilkerson: Yes, but sometimes abstract thought is not the answer to our needs. I think we need to do a little bit of thinking about the process of satisfying needs. But, sure, we delve into the now and the present, and we live for the present and we also live for the past. We know the future and what it holds for us. But we don't put these abstractions in the same kind of concepts that the non-Indian does.

The Hopi prophecies were made thousands of years ago. We know this takes abstract thinking to do this. We don't deal with the future in the sense that a non-Indian would, but we do consider the future. We do make suppositions about the future, but we don't allow them to become overwhelming in our lives.

Our manner of abstract thinking takes different forms, so therefore it is not recognized as such by non-Indian people. We do abstract thinking from our own frame of reference, and until you can put yourself into our frame of reference, you will never know the Indian mind. But consider the logic of this: if we had not had the capacity for abstract thought at the time of the whiteman's arrival, we never would have survived.

Our thought processes may be of a different order, but they certainly include abstract thinking and abstract reasoning. But we do not think from the materialistic viewpoint. I think this is where we get hung up with the whites. Our Circle of Life concept, for example, is certainly abstract thinking. All things interconnected, all things dependent, all things now coming full circle. People are now preaching this, but it has been with us for thousands of years.

"What of the charge that all these concepts were stolen and adapted from the whiteman?"

Wilkerson: I've heard this before also. In so many instances the whiteman puts himself in the position of the returning white god spoken of by many of our legends.

Let me put this right down to basics. We have symbolism in our beliefs wherein colors take very prominent roles. White, for example, stands for purity, cleanliness, sacredness, and all those good things. The White Painted Lady, who has been interpreted by many non-Indian people to mean, "Oh, man, here is a white Caucasian lady coming back to save the Indians," means simply this: The lady in the ceremony wears the color of white, because she has been painted with the sacred pollen and therefore appears white. Most Indian people would reject out of hand the notion of a Caucasian god coming to save all Indians.

Much of our religion was destroyed in the way that many of our tribes were destroyed. It is my own personal viewpoint—but one that I might say is shared by many Indian people—that it was the intent on the part of the Founding Fathers of this country to actually destroy native religion. There is a lot of proof around that a lot of white people fully intended to get rid of those ignorant savages and their paganism.

I reject paganism as an adjective applied to our native beliefs. I think what we had in the old traditions was a deep appreciation of the psychic forces in the world and a deep appreciation of the Supreme Being. The overwhelming evidence is that the Indian people were very deeply religious.

Mad-wa-sia-win (Joe Northrup), a Chippewa from Cloquet, Minnesota, wrote (circa 1931) that his people did most certainly have the concept of the Great Spirit before the arrival of the Christian missionaries:

In common with other primitive peoples, the Divine Spark or Spirit . . . was in the minds and hearts of these people long before the Christian religion invaded America. They knew of an all pervading force, or as they called this God, the Great Spirit, the one above all spirits; they knew of lesser spirits as well, as the Evil Spirit, whom they feared because this spirit was supposed to hate all Indians and was continually sending evil things upon them.

They worshipped in faith this Great Spirit whom they called "Ge-Ji-Munido" or Good Spirit and knew him as the author of all good, all life and embodying love and purity in its truest sense.

All life was caused by containing Spirit. Thus the Chippewa believed trees, grass, water, wind, clouds, in fact all things that grew or moved and had life or spirit were subject to the Great Spirit. Therefore, the Chippewa Indian had the utmost respect and reverence for all the forces and beauties of natural life. . . .

The Chippewa, in his native state with inborn piety left him by countless generations of natural sons of the Great Spirit, and his manner of life in nature, therefore, close to nature, imbibed the peace and quiet of the great forests, even in infancy was in closer communion with the mysterious Spirit world. So great was their faith in this unseen world, that all children were compelled at the age of reason, seven years, to fast at least one day, purifying their minds the better to get in tune with this all pervading Force. At the age of twelve came the regular fast or purifying of the mind. . . .[1]

In the 1850s James Lynd, a fur trader acquainted with the ways and the language of the Dakota, began the massive task of writing a history of his aboriginal clientele in Minnesota. He had invested several years of effort in this project when Little Crow led the Sioux War; and according to several accounts, Lynd became the first whiteman killed, on either August 17 or 18, 1862.

The Dakota entered the general store of the fur trader, killed him, and scattered the pages of his manuscript. It remains uncertain whether or not the Indians knew what was written on the pages which they threw about the store, but the manuscript pages lay scuffed, bloody, and spat upon until a soldier happened to notice what they were and considered the fact that they might have a certain value. James Fletcher Williams compiled a volume from

[1] Courtesy of the Minnesota Historical Society, Cedar Street and Central Avenue, St. Paul.

the surviving pages and made a gift of it to the Minnesota Historical Society.

Basing his opinion on many years' observation of the Dakota people, Lynd wrote the following about their belief in the Great Spirit:

No question has more puzzled—and it may be said, unnecessarily—those who have gone among the Sioux than that of, who the *Wakantanka* or Great Spirit is. Though the name is frequently heard, yet it does not appear to be well understood even by the Sioux themselves: and from the fact that they offer no praise, sacrifices, or feasts to that Divinity, many have gone so far as to imagine that the *name, even was introduced to their acquaintance by the whites!*

Nothing could be more unfounded than this. Not to mention the absurdity of the proposition that so radical an idea as that of one spirit being superior to and more powerful than all others—an idea at the bottom of and pervading all religions, even the most barbarous —should meet with an exception in the Dakota. There are internal proofs of its native origin, both in the testimony of the people, and in the use of the word itself. . . .

We have already seen that the word *Wakantanka* is of frequent occurrence in . . . Sacred Feasts: and that it is used interchangeably with the Algonquin word, *Maneto,* or Great Spirit. This, alone is proof enough; but there are other proofs. In the Medicine Dance, which though very modern as far as the Dakotas are concerned, was introduced among them long years before any Mission reached them; the *Wakantanka* is expressly declared to have been the creator of the world. . . . Further proof is not required.[2]

In his aforementioned open letter to the Christian churches, Vine Deloria, Jr., writes:

Early missionaries . . . told us the story of Adam and Eve. They went on at great length with stories of Jonah and the whale. They regaled us with the accounts of the resurrection, the Exodus, and

[2] Courtesy of the Minnesota Historical Society, Cedar Street and Central Avenue, St. Paul.

the Tower of Babel. We recognized these stories as myths by which a people explain how they came to consciousness as a national community. When we tried to explain our myths, the missionaries grew angry, and accused us of believing superstitions.

Superstition is, of course, in the dogma of the beholder. As has long been observed, the god of one spiritual expression has the potential of becoming the devil of another—especially if in the confrontation between religions, one faith has the benefit of being sponsored or cherished by the dominant, or conquering, culture.

Not every Black Coat maintained an aloof and superior stance toward the aboriginal traditions of the people whom he came to save. There were some who received the revelatory insight that the Great Spirit implants certain universal spiritual truths which are shared by all men. Bill La Gana, a marvelously informative seventy-one-year-old member of the Navajo Nation Tribal Fairs department, shared with me his memories of a missionary, whom he remembered by the name of "Shine":

Shine Smith came out to the reservation about the turn of the century. He was a Presbyterian missionary, medical. Write a book about this guy? He was too fantastic for anyone to believe. Shine? He had some song, and in it there was this part about "shine." The People picked it up and that became his name.

As a missionary, he lasted about a year, then the church turned him out as a heathen. Yessir, he had sung and danced with the Indians in their heathen dances of worship. He had become, for all intents and purposes, just plain *Dinne* [Navajo for the People]!

This did not faze old Shine. He had made Flagstaff his headquarters, and he was like all good people at passing the tin beggar's cup. He got up scratch and medicines.

When the 1918 flu epidemic hit, he gathered up his medicines and lit out for the backcountry. On the way back, the flu hit him. He took the wrong turn, the turn that led into the country of the Bad Men, the Killers and the Robbers [Navajo outlaws]. No one other than them ever went in there and was seen again.

The Bad Men took care of Shine and nursed him back to health. When they were asked why, they said, "He is a Holy Person, a Medicine Man. He keeps our People alive. What more can we do?"

Shine became the seediest-looking bum ever to come over the pike.

"Come on, Shine, I'm a gonna buy you a suit of clothes!"

"How much you gonna pay for that there suit of clothes?"

"Seventy-five bucks!"

"You are? If you have that much money to throw away on an ole bum like me, you just give me that cash. I have hungry People I can feed with that money!"

Shine would get the *majuma,* feed the People, and still be the worse-lookin' bum in all Arizona.

In his later years, Shine acquired arthritis and could not get back into the boondocks where his beloved People lived. When Shine went up the Shadow Trail, the People came out of the hills, loaded Shine's coffin into their wagons and drove away towards Tuba City. They could not let him be put in the cold ground far away from home and the People who loved him.

In the life of Heathen Shine, there were no sinners; there were only the People.

Shine was the sort of person who understood that worship of the Unknown is not something that belongs to any one group of anyone —Christian, Jewish, Buddhist, or Islam. When our People are referred to as savages or barbarians, non-Indians overlook what just happened at the '72 Summer Olympics, or some of the great killings, like at Sand Creek, led by a very Christian army colonel.

If my Indian people have sized up what is offered them in the way of the European religions, I can well understand a feeling on their part why they should return to the religion of their forebears.

Coincident with the Amerindians' return to medicine power is a growing respect for the native religious traditions on the part of the very churches that once tried to stamp them out. The ecumenical ghost of "Shine" may be touching the hearts of his contemporary living clerics.

The Reverend Dr. Benjamin Reist, dean of San Francisco Theological Seminary at San Anselmo, California, recently admitted that Christian theology is "terribly impoverished when it comes to a doctrine of nature," and prognosticated that there must soon come a day when "American Indian theology must be represented in the highest councils of Christian theology in the world."

At a January 1973 meeting of Indians and church leaders held in Estes Park, Colorado, Rev. Homer Noley, an Indian clergyman who heads United Methodist Indian work, told those assembled that the traditional Amerindian religion is "closer to original Christianity" than most orthodox church people realize. "Our ancestors believed in a spirit world of all things," Reverend Noley commented.

According to George W. Cornell of the Associated Press, the Episcopal Church, the United Church of Christ, the American Baptist Convention, and the Lutheran Council in the U.S.A. are among those denominations which have set up special Indian departments, directed by Indians, to bolster church sensitivity to Amerindian interests. If today's wearers of Jesus' black robes continue to develop a deeper reverence for Nature and a harmony with the Earth Mother, as well as a greater tolerance and communal character, then our New Age may truly apprehend that there is but one Great Spirit.

6. Magic, Witchcraft, and Medicine Power

It began in 1825, when a man of the Navajo Long Salt family became ill because of nightmares caused by the restless spirit of a slain enemy. The man's brothers sought assistance from an old, blind medicine man from the Tsegi country, and, at their request, he held a three-day *b'jene* (sing) over the tormented sleeper.

For part of his pay, the medicine man asked five butchered sheep from the Long Salts' valuable flock. But since the flock was grazing at some distance from the village (and the old man was blind, anyway), the Long Salts assigned to the task of slaughtering the animals, decided to substitute five wild antelope in their place.

The old medicine man was escorted home with the honors due his position and awarded the five carcasses. With the heads and the lower legs removed at the knees, even the Long Salts who made the presentation had been unable to detect the substitution that certain lazy and deceitful members of their family had perpetrated.

A few weeks later, an older member of the Long Salt family died. Although some deemed it strange that the old man had not suffered any illness before his death, it was not considered remarkable that an aged one should pass away. But then a robust and healthy young man fell dead for no perceivable reason; and every few weeks after that, a member of the Long Salt family would become ill, begin to waste away, then die in suffering. To the more wise and astute members of the family, it was becoming increasingly clear that someone had set a *chindi,* an evil spirit upon them. But why?

At last the lazy ones confessed their duplicity in substituting the antelope for the mutton. Family leaders of the Long Salts, who at that time numbered more than a hundred members, met in council to decide how best to deal with the frightening matter of a family curse. It was agreed that a party of Long Salts would meet with the medicine man and confront the situation without further delay.

The blind medicine man admitted that he had become angry when he discovered the deception that had been worked upon him by the Long Salts. He also admitted that he had set a chindi against the Long Salts with the instructions that the entire family should be exterminated.

The headmen of the Long Salts beseeched the medicine man to grant them a reprieve and to recall the evil demon. They had been duped as well as he by those loutish members of their family. Already several Long Salts had died. Surely he would now consider himself avenged for such a simple matter as five sheep.

The medicine man was touched by their pleas. He told them that he was not an evil man, but he had been forced to uphold his dignity and his reputation. He would remove the curse for a price, but at the moment he had no idea what to charge them for his services in recalling the chindi. He bade them return in ten days.

The delegation from the Long Salts were prompt in keeping their appointment, and on the morning of the tenth day, they arrived before the hogan of the blind medicine man. They were greeted by a sober family in mourning. The medicine man had passed to the land of the spirits during the interim.

To the Long Salts' horror, they were unable to determine whether or not the medicine man had recalled the chindi before his unexpected death. By the time they reached home, however, they had their answer. Several members of the family lay ill and dying.

John R. Winslowe wrote (*Frontier Times,* August–September 1967) that he met the last surviving member of the Long Salts, a slender teen-aged girl named Alice, in 1925.

"Despite annual additions by births," Winslowe said, "the number of Long Salts steadily declined. By 1900 only ten were living. Long since they had despaired of the family's survival.

"Alice Long Salt was born in 1912. There were then only five of the family remaining, and all were young. They were her parents, two uncles and an aunt. Curiously, anyone marrying into the family met the same fate as a blood Long Salt. Alice's mother died when the girl reached seven and while she was attending the Tuba City boarding school at the Indian agency. Alice's father became skin and bones, dying two years later. That left her an orphan. The remaining three Long Salts were ill, crippled and helpless. Friends cared for them, watching them fade into nothing before their eyes."

By 1925, Alice's uncles and aunt had succumbed to the chindi's attack, and she was the last of the Long Salts. The teen-ager had been the top student in her class at the agency school, but within a few months of the death of the last of her relatives, her teachers noticed Alice becoming dull and listless. Soon she was ill with a malady that defied the medical doctors' conventional methods of diagnosis.

An aging but determined man named Hosteen Behegade adopted Alice Long Salt and resolved that he would protect the girl from the chindi's efforts to destroy the sole surviving member of a family that had sought to deceive a blind old medicine man. Although Behegade was considered rather well off with a respectable number of sheep, horses, and cattle, medicine men conducted their sings free of charge. Each earnestly desired to be the one whose medicine could thwart the demon, but they privately admitted that they knew their attempts would come to nothing.

"By late 1927," Winslowe continued the story, "Behegade had expended all his property and was heavily in debt, fighting bravely for the girl's life.

"That year Behegade evolved a plan. To finish off the stricken girl the *chindi* had to be present. His idea was to keep moving constantly, concealing his trail. By this means he could prevent the *chindi* from locating Alice.

"One dark night an owl hooted close by. At dawn Alice Long Salt was too weak to leave her blankets. The *chindi* had found its innocent victim again. From then on Behegade always obeyed the owl's hoot, believing that it had come to his aid against the *chindi*."

In the winter of 1928, the fearful wanderers found themselves seeking refuge from a blizzard in a hogan three miles from the trading post on Red Mesa. Alice seemed to rally in health and she became cheerful. Perhaps the blizzard would protect them. Surely the chindi could not find them amidst the deep-piling snow and the howling wind.

The blizzard developed into the worst snowstorm in years. The Behegade family relaxed their guard and slept peacefully. Not even a chindi could combat such a violent working of the elements.

The next morning, Alice Long Salt was dead. The final act of propitiation had been made. At last the chindi would return to whatever realm from whence it had come, its one-hundred-year mission of vengeance completed.

When one employs any form of energy, whether it be physical or spiritual, one is dealing with both positive and negative elements. Cursing, hexing, and the manipulation of familiar spirits are as well known in Amerindian medicine as they are in the traditions of European magic. Native American practitioners of this personally exploitive and malignly directed medicine are as feared and respected as the village witch or *Hexenmeister* in European culture.

Since I recognize Wicca as a legitimate form of religious expression that has nothing whatsoever to do with dark, satanic evil, I share the dismay of my many Craft friends who object to the designation of "Witch" being applied to practitioners of magical systems which endeavor to control malignant psychic or spirit forces in order to achieve personal gain or personal vengeance.

But, alas, due to semantic limitations, I, too, in order to facilitate communication between author and reader, am often forced into using the term "Witch" to differentiate the manipulators of bad medicine from those whose medicine remains a personal, or tribally shared, vision.

It should really come as no surprise that the Witches of European tradition are most sympathetic toward Amerindian medicine in particular, and to the social plight of the Amerindian in general. The American-Sicilian Magus Dr. Leo Louis Martello told me:

> The moral leukemia practiced by the whiteman against the redman, wherein the white corpuscles eat up the red ones, can only result in the weakening and spiritual death of the whiteman. This cancer of conscience of the U.S. Government has resulted in the total demoralization and dehumanization of both its perpetrators and its victims.
>
> As a Witch, as a Pagan, as an advocate of individual rights; as a public supporter of all liberation movements (though not necessarily their motives or methods); as an American citizen; as one who lives by a three-word life philosophy (*value for value*); as one who foresaw and wrote about the rise of Red Power in 1960; as one who identifies with Nature, the natural, the rational; as a member of a minority religion; as one who has applauded man's technological achievements, but who has always identified with, and used, true magic; as one who has never claimed to be an altruist, but a practitioner of moral selfishness (i.e., everyone has the right to pursue his own best interests as long as they are not at the expense of another); my complete support of the Amerindian is not based on pity or a sense of false superiority, but on the recognition of his value as a human being, a blood brother, a fellow pagan, who has been cruelly oppressed, but who is now rediscovering his own valid lifestyle and his own creative culture. This process of rediscovery will free the Indian of trying to be a Plastic Patriot or a carbon copy of the whiteman. The American Indian will once again manifest himself in the manifold magic of the Great Spirit.
>
> The U.S. Constitution stresses freedom of religion, yet the humani-

tarian Christian missionaries crushed the spiritual heritage of the Amerindian. In place of his soul, they offered him a bowl of soup; they replaced his Happy Hunting Ground with a Christian Hell, his bow with a cross. And he has been spiritually crucified ever since. If the American Indian is to fully regain his self-identity, then he must reject conquering Christianity. He must reject the charge that he was a "pagan" or a "heathen" in need of conversion. He was/is a pagan of the country in its most profoundly positive sense.

The Amerindian must learn to uproot any sense of inferiority fostered on him by the conquering Christian whiteman. He must be certain that he has not accepted the white's evaluation of himself, even on a subconscious level. He must not judge himself by Caucasian technological progress.

The United States, unlike other countries, is not based on a geographical accident, but on an ideal. Until those in power uphold this ideal, right the wrongs, grant to the indigenous peoples the same rights it claims for itself, this country will never be at peace.

The Resurrection of the Great Spirit will succeed because it is based on justice, on unassailable rightness, on irrefutable facts. The Wheel of Fortune has turned. Mighty Manitou will replace the Mighty Machine. The ancient gods and goddesses have come out of their hibernation. The long sleep is over. Manitou and the Mighty Ones of all ancient faiths are now claiming their own.

The basics of cursing one's victim to death seem to follow general principles of application, regardless of whether the practitioner performs his grim art in Polynesia, Paris, or the plains of Kansas. The Kahuna, Witch, or Medicine Man utilizes the physical stimulus of an image or a picture of the enemy to achieve an altered state of consciousness which permits him to manifest controlled psychokinesis—the direct action of mind on matter. The "voodoo doll," the clay image, the mud ball that contains bits of the victim's hair or nail parings have no function in the malign magical transference, other than to serve as a physical stimulus upon which the practitioner may direct his conscious thoughts. Meditation upon such an artifact provides an impetus for the psyche's bursting free of the body's inhibiting three-dimensional bonds and developing the awesome power to, prismlike, focus enough psychic energy to affect the physical and mental functioning of the confused enemy.

Other researchers, who may not recognize such non-physical capacities of man, generally theorize that the intended victim gains knowledge of the curse and literally scares himself to death. Anthropologist Walter Cannon spent several years collecting examples of "voodoo death," instances in which men and women died as a result of having been the recipients of curses, alleged supernatural visitations, or societal taboos.

Since fear, one of the most powerful and deep-rooted of the emotions, has its effects mediated through the nervous system and the endocrine apparatus, the sympathetic adrenal system, Cannon hypothesized that, "if these powerful emotions prevail and the bodily forces are fully mobilized for action, and if this state of extreme perturbation continues for an uncontrolled possession of the organism for a considerable period . . . dire results may ensue."

Cannon suggested, then, that "voodoo death" may result from a state of shock due to a persistent and continuous outpouring of adrenaline and a depletion of the adrenal corticosteroid hormones. Such a constant agitation caused by an abiding sense of fear could consequently induce a fatal reduction in blood pressure. Cannon assessed "voodoo death" as a real phenomenon set in motion by "shocking emotional stress—to obvious or repressed terror."

In his collection of case histories of individuals who had willed others, or themselves, to death (*Scared to Death*), Dr. J. C. Barker assessed voodoolike death as "resulting purely from extreme fear and exhaustion . . . essentially a psychosomatic phenomenon." In his opinion, in those cases in which deaths result from premonitions, predictions, and curses, the victims died from autosuggestion. Dr. Barker states:

Initially the subject develops the notion that something is going to happen; then this idea operates through autosuggestion so as to bring about the very thing which was anticipated. We have already

On assignment from her newspaper, the Los Angeles *Herald Examiner,* reporter Wanda Sue Parrott researched a startling number of alleged haunting incidents in which the purported ghosts were those of Amerindians. In a symbolic ceremony in 1968, Len Fairchuck of the White Buffalo All-Indian Workshop in Los Angeles, made Wanda an honorary chief of the White Buffalo. The paper headdresses and neck band shown were made at the workshop established by Fairchuck to help Indians earn livings when moving from reservations to the city. Ms. Parrott has Cherokee blood in her own lineage.

Sun Bear, an influential Chippewa medicine man, is the founder of the first new tribe in this century, the Bear Tribe. Sun Bear's medicine is for both Indian and non-Indian, and much of it is built on the ancient predictions which foretold a time when the whiteman would come as a lost brother to the Indian and seek his guidance.

Russ Bernhardt, who has played Charles Dickens' "Scrooge" for thirty-one years during the Christmas season, is shown with his wife Clarisa in their Hollywood Gingerbread House home. On a recent trip to Ojai, California, the Bernhardts encountered the spirit of a departed Indian chief, who frequently gives visitors a hotfoot.

An Indian burial headstone in a wooded area near Willimantic, Connecticut. The immediate area is noted for numerous apparitions of Indians, the sound of drums during certain times of the year, and other mysterious occurrences. *Credit: Gordon Alexander*

The site of this mass Indian burial ground near Willimantic, Connecticut, has caused many visitors to complain of feelings of nausea. Psychic sensitives feel strong "vibrations" emanating from the area, and residents have long reported manifestations of Amerindian ghosts, mysterious fires, and other phenomena. *Credit: Gordon Alexander*

Ghost chasers Ed and Lorraine Warren were called to an Amerindian home on a reservation in Maine. According to Warren, the human-shaped glow in the right-hand lower window was not caused by photo flash or any other explainable causes. *Credit: Ed Warren*

This modern home in Connecticut, according to photographer Gordon Alexander, is permeated with a strong feeling of foreboding. Apparitions of Amerindians have been seen, together with ghostly children, in the field in the center of the above photograph. *Credit: Gordon Alexander*

Ed and Lorraine Warren of Monroe, Connecticut, investigated a haunted house wherein ghostly Amerindian manifestations have been reported. *Credit: Gordon Alexander*

Iron Eyes Cody and John Fire Lame Deer (subject of *Lame Deer: Seeker of Visions* by Richard Erdoes) at a recent powwow night in Los Angeles. *Credit: Iron Eyes Cody*

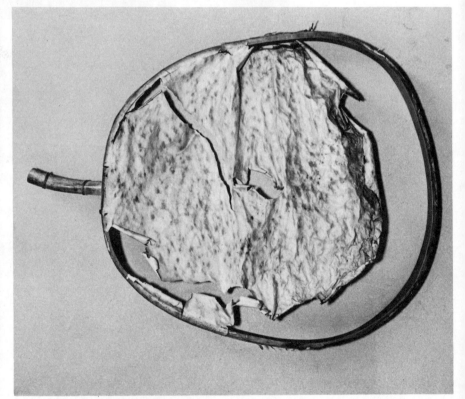

Tambourine-type drum used in ritual medicine practices by Alaskan Eskimo tribes, circa late 1800s. *Credit: Darryl Henning; courtesy Luther College Anthropology Department*

become familiar with the powerful consequences of suggestion, which can have particularly harmful effects upon the subject's state of health. It would be difficult to dismiss the death [in a particular case he cites] as being due to natural causes. If death was occasioned by other agencies, they were certainly not apparent.

My response to such hypotheses as the above is to remark that knowledge of a curse may certainly *help* bring about its unpleasant fruition, but such knowledge is by no means necessary if an accomplished practitioner has focused his psychic prism upon a victim. I am aware of too many cases wherein the suffering victims were totally unaware on a conscious level that a curse had been levied against them, and I have had too many acquaintances in the missionary and medical fields relate accounts of their utter helplessness when attempting to aid someone who was later discovered to have been cursed.

I personally have had the experience of having an external intelligence direct my selection of cards from a deck, my choice of numbers to be written on a note pad, and, in one case, even my behavior and my conversation. Fortunately, I was being controlled —not against my will, but without my knowledge—by Olof Jonsson, who is not only a master psychic sensitive, but one of the most saintlike men I have ever known.

After recounting incidents wherein Olof mentally directed a bus driver to turn around in the middle of the street, convinced a thief to return his stolen loot, and, in Australia, directed a politician to speak against himself and to endorse his opponent, I wrote in *The Psychic Feats of Olof Jonsson:*

> It is rather frightening if one really considers the implications of this strange facet of "psi," this "telepathic-psychokinesis," or whatever it may be. Perhaps there exist other masters of this awesome talent who are not as jovial and benign as Olof Jonsson. Maybe, down through the ages, this has been what black magic, voodoo, and hexing have really been all about—the genuine ability of one mind to affect the thoughts and the behavior patterns of another.

Psychokinesis, the direct action of mind upon matter or mind upon
mind, may be the real power behind what superstition and ignorance
have termed the "Black Arts."

But we have not discussed the type of cursing which involves
chindis, demons, familiar spirits. While I am more disposed toward a process of psychokinetic projection explaining curses and
"voodoo death," I will not deny that there may well be forces
or intelligences which may be harnessed—and at least partially controlled—by particularly powerful adepts. These Nature entities (for
lack of a better term) may represent another order of intelligence
which somehow shares our planet with us, or they may be but
another manifestation of the life-force, the Spirit, that pervades
every living thing. In either event, I feel confident that I may present generalized principles by which the practitioner—Witch,
Kahuna, Medicine Man—curses with spirits:

The practitioner is one who has attained a high level in his craft.
He has studied under a great master, and he has either been given,
or has acquired as a result of his own intense efforts, a familiar
spirit or spirits.

When a person is to be prayed to death (i.e., cursed) for any
one of numerous reasons, the practitioner summons his familiar
spirits and begins the ceremony of instruction. In many cases, the
spirits will be propitiated with an offering of food, for it is believed
that the entities will absorb spirit force (called *orenda* by many
Amerindian tribes, but *mana* most commonly in a kind of metaphysical consensus) from the victuals which the practitioner has
surrounded with ceremonial objects.

The familiar spirits, their strength intensified by mana, are now
provided with explicit instructions. They are commanded to catch
a scent from a bit of hair or a soiled garment belonging to the
enemy, and they are told to follow it as a hunting dog sniffs a
game track. Once they have definitely located the victim, they are
to await an opportune moment to enter his body and absorb his
vital force. The practitioner chants his instructions over and over,

not only providing the familiar spirits with an image of the victim, but supplementing their power with direct charges from his own psyche.

The Kahuna, Witch, Medicine Man believes that the spirits enter the body of the intended victim, or attach themselves to it, and vampirelike, absorb his vital force and store it in their own ghostly bodies. As the mana of the enemy is withdrawn, a numbness comes over him, which generally begins at the feet and rises slowly over a period of three days to knees, hips, and finally to the heart. Once the numbness has encircled the heart, the enemy will soon be dead.

When the victim has expired, the satiated spirits withdraw, taking with them their newly absorbed charges of mana. Upon their return to their master, the practitioner, they are commanded to play about the lodge until they have dissipated the vital force which they have stolen from the victim. Such spirit recreation finds its release in poltergeistic activities, in which objects are tossed about in violent explosions of energy.

If the intended victim should be rescued through the paranormal prowess of another practitioner, the invading spirits might be directed back to the one who chants the death prayer with fatal results. In order to prevent such a boomerang of the death curse, the skilled practitioner who looks for longevity in his craft will always observe a ritual cleansing. In certain cases, the more cautious practitioners will demand that the person who has employed them to send out a curse take an oath that the named victim is truly deserving of such drastic punishment. Should another practitioner, or the spiritual strength of the intended victim himself, thereby accomplish a reversal of the curse, the client alone will be held accountable by the enraged familiar spirits.

Universal metaphysical law seems to have it that no practitioner, no matter how skilled or adept, no matter how long he has fasted or purged himself, may direct a curse against an innocent victim without suffering a reversal of the death prayer upon himself. If the outraged spirits do not boomerang upon him at once, they

will almost assuredly return to work their ruin on him after they
have accomplished the unjust deed which they were sent to do.

Such, it is believed, was the case when Maman-ti, the Owl
Prophet, chanted the death prayer for the powerful Kiowa chief
Kicking Bird.

The Owl Prophet is not to be portrayed as a sinister practitioner
of medicine. He was esteemed by his own Kiowa people and was
so highly regarded by those tribes with which the Kiowa held al-
liances that the Comanches named him to the position of master
of all medicine men. He has been described as a tall, aristocratic
man, a warrior-priest who not only fought in the important battles but who led raids of strategic value.

Maman-ti, He-Who-Touches-the-Sky, earned the appellation of
Owl Prophet because it was the owl that became his totem-familiar
spirit and would come to tell the medicine man the outcome of
future battles. While the council chiefs sat in silence, Maman-ti
would listen to the screeching cries of an owl sounding from somewhere in the darkness. There would be the beating of wings, an
interlude of silence while Maman-ti sat in meditation, then the Owl
Prophet would interpret the message from his familiar.

By 1875 the Kiowas and their allies had been battered, scattered, and defeated by the whitemen with their inexhaustible supplies of men, weapons, and ammunition. Many of the war leaders
were dead. Five years before, the great chief Kicking Bird had
assessed their situation as futile and had urged large numbers
of Kiowa and members from the allied tribes to save their lives
and join him in the settlement outside of Fort Sill, Oklahoma. Only
Lone Wolf, the Owl Prophet, and a few others headed small bands
that continued to wage a guerrilla warfare against the numerically
superior Blue Coats. Then, in February, Kicking Bird managed
to convince even these determined defenders of their land to break
their arrows and set aside their rifles.

Quite understandably, Kicking Bird was regarded with contempt
by those of his people who had vowed to fight until the last man.
For five years he had lived with his family in a comfortable lodge

near a whiteman's fort, while his friends and allies maintained a war that was as much his responsibility to support. Even so, since Kicking Bird had his people's best interests at heart and had been compelled to make his decisions according to his medicine, some kind of union between the factions might have been accomplished if General Sherman had not decreed that certain of the recently surrendered Indians must be punished for their recalcitrance. The military authorities soon found themselves in a quandary as they attempted to decide which of their prisoners should be most eligible for imprisonment, so they turned the disagreeable affair over to Kicking Bird and told him to select twenty-six Kiowas for banishment to the dungeons of Fort Marion, Florida.

Kicking Bird complied with the orders from the military authorities. He chose Long Wolf, the Owl Prophet, Woman's Heart, and White Horse—because of their repeated raids into Texas—then rounded out the remainder of the quota with a random selection of warriors and a few Mexican captives who had been reared with the allied tribes. Although he had obeyed the whiteman's dictum with a heavy heart, now many of Kicking Bird's most loyal followers had come to regard him as a traitor and a self-aggrandizing opportunist.

On April 28, as the chained prisoners were being loaded into wagons for the long trip to Florida, Kicking Bird rode up and told the Kiowas how much he had regretted his part in their exile.

"I am sorry," he said, "but because of your stubbornness, you have not kept out of trouble. You will have to be punished by the government. It will not be for long. I love you and will work for your release."

The Kiowas in their chains, contemplating imprisonment in a foreign climate, were little impressed with Kicking Bird's sentiments and his promise to work for their parole.

Maman-ti had not lost his ability as an orator, and he delivered a scornful diatribe toward the chief he considered a traitor. He said that although Kicking Bird might be a big man among the whites and might remain free in his luxurious lodge, he should cherish his every moment of life. One day, the Owl Prophet promised, he would kill him.

Two days later on the journey, Eagle Chief, a medicine man of high ability, managed to find a seat near Maman-ti.

"You promised to kill Kicking Bird with your hands," Eagle Chief reminded him. "You have the medicine to kill him from a great distance."

"The death prayer?"

Eagle Chief nodded.

The Owl Prophet sat for several moments without speaking another word; then he said, "You know my medicine forbids me to use it against a Kiowa. It has been revealed to me that I, too, would die if I were to sing the death prayer for one of my people."

"Will there be life for you in a Florida prison?" Eagle Chief asked him.

The Owl Prophet said no more. Eagle Chief interpreted his silence as withdrawal, and he turned away from his tribesman, fearful that he had asked too much.

The wagons were quiet for many hours; then the Kiowas heard the keening wail of the death prayer.

Two mornings later, after drinking a cup of coffee, the robust, healthy forty-year-old Kicking Bird collapsed in great pain. He died just before noon, while the agency doctor stood helplessly at his bedside.

The Owl Prophet uttered a sigh of resignation when the wagonloads of prisoners received word that Kicking Bird was dead. He would endure the discomforts of travel willingly. The dungeons of Fort Marion held no threat for him. By the end of the journey, the Owl Prophet had died of "natural causes," according to the official report.

One may theorize about poison in Kicking Bird's coffee—as did the agency doctor; one may hypothesize that the Owl Prophet willed himself to death on a subconscious level; but you should not be surprised if you are unable to find a medicine adept who will accept either supposition.

"Among ourselves we are not afraid to admit that we still believe in ghosts and witches, and things of this nature, because we know that we are not going to be laughed at," Don Wilkerson told me.

"I know some people might say that we are old-fashioned, but that doesn't bother us too much. I would be reticent to tell a lot of people that ghosts and witches are very much a part of our everyday life. We have good and bad witches, and although you won't find too many Indian people admitting to this in the cities, you will find it very much a part of life at home on the reservation. There are many cleansing ceremonies to take care of evil influences. Reams of incantations have been written in the Cherokee language to deal with evil. We are talking about something real—not superstition or psychiatric problems."

Gavin Frost, Director of the School of Wicca in Salem, Missouri, is not only sympathetic toward the rebirth of Amerindian medicine power, he is convinced that the many similarities between European Witchcraft and Indian magic indicate that the aboriginal peoples of America received instruction in Wicca from early Celtic practitioners of the Craft.

Gavin Frost: In order to understand a little of the Wicca way, you have to delve somewhat into Celtic, and specifically Welsh and Irish, mythology. These mythologies all start from what is often known as the Ancient Ones, or the *Previlt*. These Ancient Ones always live in large cities, which the Welsh tradition calls *Dinasassaraon*, the place of the higher powers. The headquarters in Wales was in *Dinas Emerys* (literally, City of the Dragons of Bel) in the Mountains of Snowdon.

The first great Celtic goddess is Cerridwen, who learnt her art from the Ancient Ones in the ridge city, an exceedingly strong fortification encompassed by a circular, triple wall. The carriage of Cerridwen was drawn by dragons, and she had several magical items which always went with her.

The most important was the Cauldron of Inspiration. This has recently been equated with the Holy Grail, because it is a vessel which contains all of the life fluids—one drop of which will give you inspiration. We also have to equate the Cauldron with the Indians' Sacred Pipe, in which sweet grasses were smoked to encourage astral flight.

The second item Cerridwen had was a stone of knowledge. A stone that knew everything.

Then she had certain animals—the white sow, the young wolf, and the young eagle.

The tradition in Welsh Craft circles is that about A.D. 800 to 1000, Witches left the coast of Wales and traveled across the sea. These people were searching for mountains similar to their own where they could hide out from the onslaught and onrush of the new religion of Christianity. They navigated by fixed sights on the boat. They were excellent astronomers. They had no difficulty finding a land as large as North America.

There were, in all, a complete coven of twelve in the first group, and the Indians on the eastern coast respected their power. This first coven taught all those who would come to them. Twelve more migrations took place, the last being about 1600. The people of the last migration stayed together and became those whom we now refer to as the Robed Ones of the Ozarks. In recent times we have contacted some of these people, and we have found that their rituals are like ours in almost every detail.

The intermediate migrations—the first group and the last group stayed together, remember—traveled throughout the land giving freely of their knowledge. I would like to look at some of the Amerindian traditions and show you how they received their bases.

Most of the Indian tribes recall the White Buffalo Woman, the white Witch who came from the East to give them power and knowledge. Throughout the Indian people there is the persistent myth of the Lost White Brother, the white people who were coming and who would come later.

Of course the Witches thought that they would be followed by a large migration of people from Wales, so they were preparing their Indian friends for all these other white people who would be coming across the ocean. That the extensive immigration didn't happen is, of course, partially due to the fact that Christianity did not take on in the hills of Wales as fast as the Witches feared it would; and, secondly, at least in the early days of Christianity, there was no insistence on the Wicca giving up their pagan ways, so the people of the Craft gradually got used to their new lives, rather than the persecution that the Witches had been expecting.

The White Buffalo Woman [a Celtic High Priestess of Wicca] brought with her the pipe of inspiration, the sacred pipe. She brought with her a stone, and she told them that three animals were sacred—the white buffalo, the young coyote, and the young eagle.

The sacred pipe has on it twelve spotted eagle feathers, in remembrance that the eagle is sacred. The bowl of the pipe, of course, is stone, in remembrance of the stone of knowledge.

It seems that the White Buffalo Woman did not have a white sow with her, so she substituted the white buffalo.

If you look at a typical sweathouse ceremony of the American Indians, you will find that they sit in a circle with a fire in the center. They put up four posts in the four quadrants, or toward the four points of the compass, and they have the door to the east. This is an exact replica of the initial stages of building a Witches' circle.

We put up four candles, which have often been called the watchtowers, in the four quadrants. We have our gate in our circle to the east, where people can enter; and we always have, when we are outside at least, a simple fire in the center of the circle. I do not think there exists this similarity of arrangement by chance.

Perhaps one of the most interesting things that we have found in our research of the similarities between the Wicca way and the Amerindian tradition is the labyrinth. To a Witch, the Cretan labyrinth is a most important symbol, for it signifies the various steps you have to go through in order to reach the Cauldron of Inspiration.

The Cauldron of Inspiration can be reached only after laboriously tracing every path of a seven-tiered labyrinth. Our ancient tradition says that a child will willingly follow all of the paths and get to the center, whereas an adult will always try to find a quicker way—and discover that there *is* no quicker way. One must cover the whole of the labyrinth in order to reach the Cauldron of Inspiration in the center. ["Except one become as a child" is an oft-repeated dictum in Western mysticism and in the Christian tradition, as well as in the mystery schools.]

If you were to look in *The Book of the Hopi* by Frank Waters, Part One, Chapter Five, you will see two Earth Mother symbols; and you will see there a representation of the labyrinth. This is the same labyrinth that appears on rock carvings at Tintagel, King Arthur's castle. It is the labyrinth that is found at Glastonbury. [For the Hopi, the squared maze design represents spiritual rebirth from one world to another and is known as *Tapu'at,* Mother and Child. The circular type signifies the Road of Life which man must follow in order to reach the center and be guaranteed rebirth.]

Glastonbury is the "glass town that is buried," the other world of the Celtic religion. The spiral castle is also interestingly found in Hopi legend in the corkscrew manner in which one must go down, or come up, from the other world. When we compare the Hopi symbol we see that it is an exact representation of the Cretan labyrinth, but it is a mirror image. It is reversed.

The crooked cross, although often thought of as a Hopi symbol, is the reverse of the double S—the intertwined S. The double S was Christianized into *Sancto Spiritus,* but to us of the Wicca, the symbol means Spirit and Soul—the two being tied together so tightly as to be inseparable. We do not understand why these things were mirrored, but I find it interesting the way these things come out.

There are so many other similarities between Wicca and Amerindian traditions that it is difficult to choose which ones to discuss. The man going on his vision quest, various initiation ceremonies, the rites of purification—all of these ceremonies and observances were held at the full of the moon. All of these things are the same.

The word *wakan,* which is one of the words in the secret language used for "holy or sacred," correctly means "power." One continually comes across the word *wakan* in many Amerindian tribes, and one should think of it in terms of meaning power, rather than sacredness. This same word is also found in Islam, spelled *Waqt*—an interesting similar spelling.

Then there are the ceremonial dances. The sunwise or clockwise circumambulation is always used by the Sioux. Occasionally, however, the counterclockwise movement is used in a dance of some occasion prior to, or after, a great catastrophe. The counterclockwise movement is an imitation of the thunder beings who always act in an anti-natural way. This is precisely what the Wicca do when they want to heal or to help—they work in a clockwise, or *deosil* manner. When they want to harm or to prevent an ugly thing from happening, they work in the *witichins,* or anti-clockwise manner.

Manitou, who in the sacred language is called Skan, is an all-pervasive, ever-present, unnamed being—and, I should say, not even a being, because the concept does not take on any humanistic or animistic form. It is there. It is present. It is everywhere.

Now, the traditional Indian beliefs maintain that all things have spirit—animals, plants, rocks—everything that is separable has a spirit within. The Wicca changed away from that concept, as far as I can tell, around A.D. 500. I don't know why they changed away from it, but they turned to the belief that every *living* thing has a spirit, that inanimate objects do not have spirits. The Cauldron of Inspiration gave one the capability of contacting the spirits of all living things.

Another thing that the Wicca used to do, but changed away from about A.D. 500, was the trapping of spirits. The Wicca used to be very concerned with keeping the spirits of their ancestors around them so that they could be certain that the spirits were happy. At some point in time, around A.D. 500, they changed and they began, gradually at first, to consider that the spirit must go on and must be released to be happy. The Indian burial procedures and the manner in which they regard their ancestors all point, in my opinion, to their belief in the keeping of spirits around them. I think that the Amerindians received the earlier vision of Wicca, and that they have kept alive many Craft beliefs in their own traditions.

Have the Amerindians kept alive the ways of the Celtic Witches and incorporated the legends of immigrating Wicca covens into their own native traditions? Or do these similarities between the ways of Wicca and the ways of the Amerindian give but further evidence to the suggestion that there is something universal in man's spiritual evolution on this planet that prompts him to duplicate in substance ". . . what other groups of men in other natural settings have found to be *the human* truth, so that Aryan and Dakota, Greek and Pawnee, build identical ritual patterns to express their separate discoveries of a single insight"?

During the course of my research, I had the opportunity to speak with a delightful woman of Shawnee-Cherokee ancestry who has been a practicing rainmaker for twenty-five years. Ann Underwood of Beckley, West Virginia, underwent her training as a medicine person with her own grandfather serving as tutor. She is the only individual of whom I have knowledge who is a practitioner of both Amerindian medicine and Celtic Wicca. At the same time, Ann is very much aware of the universal aspects of her work, as well as being well informed in regard to certain parapsychological explanations for her medicine. All things considered, she was an excellent interviewee with whom to discuss magic, Witchcraft, and Indian medicine.

Ann Underwood: I got roundly chastised by my mother the first time she caught me performing rain prayers for our garden that was drying out. She wasn't aware of the fact that my grandfather had taught me the Shawnee weather ritual, which he had learned from his mother; and I wasn't old enough to know that our white neighbors would frown on us if they saw me performing the rain ritual. I got switched for my efforts.

"In your opinion, what is the power that makes rain rituals work?"

Mrs. Underwood: Oh well, it is not the dance and it is not the chant. It isn't the fire or what is offered to the fire. It is the prayers of the Great Spirit to the Mystery to send rain to prevent the crops from failing. The Indians depended for their staples on their crops. Hunting was a little chancy at the best of times, so it was their food crops that keep them alive. They prayed for rain when they needed it.

"There was a need; it was asked to be fulfilled, and the need was met."

Mrs. Underwood: The Indians painted their faces with the symbol of rain, but not of lightning. They took natural water and moistened the end of their prayer sticks and drove them into the ground with one thrust. They painted the rain symbol around the ceremonial fire. This was symbolic ritual.

The main thing was that the shamans would dance, chant, and focus their thoughts, their prayers.

"Sending an impulse to the Great Spirit."

Mrs. Underwood: Yes, for hours and hours sometimes—until it worked or the last shaman had danced himself into exhaustion.

"Do you think the sacrifice element was necessary—the offering of tobacco and food—or was this act in the nature of physical stimulus for the prayers?"

Mrs. Underwood: I think the sacrifice was just a focal point for individual thought, a concentration point, like a mandala.

I believe that Amerindian traditional beliefs are very similar to the Paleolithic religions of Europe and Asia. Ivar Lissner [*Man, God, and Magic*] brings out the theory that man has always been monotheistic. Since we are supposed to have come across the

Bering Strait, I think we brought this religion with us. When we lost contact with the other continents, we altered the religion, of course, but, basically, it is still the same religion.

For example, the ceremonial fires are kindled in the same way. The horned mask or headdress of the shaman, the medicine man, is the same (I prefer the term shaman to medicine man, having been a shaman for twenty-five years).

"As a shaman, how are you asked to serve people in your particular locale?"

Mrs. Underwood: I deal primarily with weather rituals. Weather can be a terrible problem here. We have a saying in West Virginia that we have "too weather." We either have *too* much or *too* little. Either we have had a constant downpour for the last three years, or we have had a prolonged drought for the last six years. Either we don't have enough snow to keep the soil from being weather-killed, or else we have three feet of snow all at once. So I am mainly asked to help control things in our part of the state.

"Would you care to give an estimate of your percentage of effectiveness?"

Mrs. Underwood: Oh, I think I can safely say about 70 per cent.

"Could you tell us something about your training for the role of shaman?"

Mrs. Underwood: Well, I suppose Grandpa had been instructing me in the delicate art of weather control for about two years before —at age twelve—I fasted for a week, then slept out in the woods to await my vision. Then I went back to Grandpa and told him what I had seen. We had our own private celebration, and I was able to study and to practice medicine seriously.

"One usually thinks of a shaman as being male."

Mrs. Underwood: It didn't make any difference in our tribe whether the shaman was male or female. If you had the qualifications which indicated that you could possibly be a shaman, it did not matter if you were male or female—you would be accepted for training and taught. The final test was what you saw after you had undergone the period of fasting, the ritual baths of cold water, and the time of waiting for the vision.

Grandfather had been initiated into shamanship by his mother. He had no sons, so there had to be a gap of a generation before he could initiate a granddaughter. You see, among the Shawnee medicine people, knowledge passes in the same manner as it does among the Wicca. Females can only teach males. Males can only teach females. And you must learn those rituals—which are often very complicated—letter perfect!

Another criterion appears to be that you must have had what they called the "falling sickness" sometime during your life. By this, of course, is meant a violent convulsion due to a high fever, epilepsy, or some other cause. I had one fairly violent convulsion from a food allergy—I have a vague idea it was from blackberries— that made me eligible.

"So this allergy produced convulsions, your grandfather observed you in this condition, and it gave him the first of a series of signs that you could qualify to study medicine."

Mrs. Underwood: Yes, that is correct. He never taught my older sister.

"Do you induce visions so that you might guide others and yourself?"

Mrs. Underwood: I practice meditation, which amounts to the same thing.

"Do you have any difficulties incorporating Wicca with your traditional beliefs?"

Mrs. Underwood: No, I can't see where there is any conflict with Wicca.

I have, though, tried two or three different Christian churches, and I found that I could not accept their teachings. In my opinion, their views conflicted with everything that I had been taught as a child. I grew up on the river and in the woods and received most of my traditional instruction from my grandparents. The traditional belief was always present in my mother, even though she didn't approve of my making rain rituals in front of our white neighbors.

"What are you most concerned about in your medicine work today?"

Mrs. Underwood: I am most concerned about the carelessness and greed that man is showing toward our natural resources. We Indians never fight Nature. We would rather move with Nature. I think a respect for the Earth Mother is born in nearly all of us. We are taught that the Earth belongs to the Great Spirit, to God. It doesn't belong to us. It is only ours to use for a little while. We must not mistreat it or abuse it, because it must be passed on to the next generation.

I am very deeply grieved to see men so greedy. I sometimes feel like unbraiding my hair, gashing my arms, spreading ashes on my face, and chanting a wail of sorrow.

Bevy Jaegers is a teaching psychic, director of her own school, the Psychical Research & Training Center of St. Louis, located in Maplewood, Missouri. Bevy is primarily a psychometrist in the area of psychic experience, and at one time she worked closely with an archaeologist who was investigating Amerindian burial sites. Since she is an accomplished metaphysician in the European tradition, her comments in regard to the comparisons of Western occultism and Amerindian magic would seem to present us with valuable insights.

Bevy Jaegers: The American Indians had a knowledge of man and the universe that went far beyond that which we are beginning to discover today. They were monotheistic and the mystical experience was common amongst them.

The Amerindians realized that all things were part of the whole. Man, the animals, the Earth on which they stood were a part of a great whole. Their awareness of this concept was beyond anything that we have yet been able to accomplish.

Each tribe had those who gained higher awareness through spiritual insight than the majority, and these individuals were the shamans, the medicine men.

Some tribes felt that the male, the positive aspect, was eclipsed by too much of the female, the negative aspect; and for this reason women were rarely allowed to sit in the councils and were rarely allowed to participate in religious ceremonies, except in cases wherein the two polarities were needed. This particular concept, of course, was shared by the Egyptians and the Chinese, with their concept of Yin and Yang, the balance of the Universe.

Many Amerindian tribes possess a belief that approaches reincarnation. It is thought, as did the Egyptians, that one part of the soul will remain earthbound, while another part will leave on the great spiritual journey. In order to provide for the earthbound soul segment, food and weapons and all the belongings of the person who had died are placed into the grave. (These things also carry the personality aura of the one who was gone and therefore would be best not used by another.)

The Indians did not believe that man would return as an animal; the totem animals were merely symbols of the stages through which man had evolved to reach the state of humanhood. Animals were considered little brothers of man. Something to be cared for until they, too, reached the stature of man.

Silence, solitude, and the ability to look within were the Indian methods of finding spiritual power and awareness. An elderly Indian I once knew told me that various kinds of metals and stones were used by the Amerindians to heighten their psychic perceptions and awareness. These things were bound on the forehead or worn on the chest. It could be that this was the introduction of the headband and the pendant in all civilizations.

Isn't it interesting that the youth today have returned to the headband and the heavy pendant? There is definitely a resurgence of the Great Spirit. There is a call that is being felt by the youth of this nation and of other nations—but more especially America, because of the increased awareness of the native peoples of this continent.

It seems to me that there were four main groups of Indian nations, corresponding to the four elements of astrology. There were fire people to the South and in the Southwest; water people on the West Coast and toward the North; earth people in the center of the continent and toward the East; air people in the North. I have found that this symbolism is used constantly time and again to indicate which branch or which element these tribes belong to or felt a kinship with.

Indians were always confused by the Christian idea of a devil as a separate entity, for they understood that there was no such thing as a devil, that good and evil are both present in man himself. It is choice that brings out the influence of one or the other. This is symbolized in some of the ceremonial body paintings, where the face is colored black on one side and white on the other, with the red streak of life across the forehead.

The Indians used the color red to symbolize the earth; blue for air; green for water; yellow for fire; white for spirit—which motivated and activated the other four, bringing them together into a cohesive whole. This is especially evident in Indian headdresses and ceremonial outfits, in which the colors used symbolized the required elements asked for in the rituals.

The Indian medicine people had a technique for achieving self-hypnosis in which they would rock and sway back and forth in a certain motion, while making a sound or saying a word over and over again. When they had achieved a state of altered consciousness, they would then suggest to themselves that they would receive information from the Great Spirit. Material received by one in a trance of this type was almost always regarded as infallible.

The Amerindians must have had an awareness of the human aura. I have seen petroglyph representations of humans surrounded by what appears to be an auric body. The Indians also felt that being too close to one another could be a bad thing, and they were very careful to leave living space around each other wherever it was possible to do so. They believed that permitting another human being within one's living space—the auric field—could endanger one's own state of health or mental well-being.

Most Indians believed that they could hear the voice of the Great Spirit in the rustle of the leaves, in the blowing of the wind, in the sound of the water as it trickled over the stones in a brook. They would listen to these things with the greatest attention; and because of this concentration, they would cause an altered state of consciousness and they were able to receive more easily psychic impressions.

They were also aware of the negative and positive polarities of the human body. Upon greeting another, an Indian brave would frequently extend his left hand, thus making the movement a receptive, negative, gesture—whereas extending the right hand is an aggressive, positive, gesture.

In talking to American Indians, I have found that, as a group, they understand the field of the paranormal and extrasensory perception much better than any other people I have encountered.

As further evidence of the universality of psychic, supernatural, and mythic experience, the Amerindian's cosmology is not devoid of night creatures, horrid things of darkness—all the denizens of nightmares that haunt men and women of all cultures.

"The wolfmen are not werewolves, mind you, but wolves or men or supernatural beings that take the shape of men and—at will—can travel many, many miles in the wink of an eye and appear as wolves or as men dressed in wolf's clothing, so to speak," Don Wilkerson told me. "Now, you won't tell an Indian that these things do not happen. If you get among the Navajo, you might find someone who will tell you of these things."

"One evening my brother was going to my grandmother's. It was late at night, and he was on a dirt road hitchhiking," said the attractive young Navajo woman. She was a secretary in Phoenix, a convert to Roman Catholicism.

"It was in February, and it was pretty cold. It was past midnight and he just couldn't go any farther. They have these little bus stops on the roads—you know, where they pick up schoolchildren—so he was just around there debating whether to spend the night in there or to keep walking the second half of the fifty miles to Grandmother's home.

"Then he saw this animal. He thought it was a dog. He wanted some company so he whistled at it. It came running right by him and they scared each other. The 'dog' stood up on its hind legs. My brother said it had a man's face, and the face was painted with little white dots and other kinds of signs. It had an animal's skin on. The thing ran off on four legs and my brother tried to run after it, but it was too fast.

"My brother said that it dawned on him then what he had seen. He had never really believed in things like that until then. He said, 'I guess it is true that medicine men really have the power to travel in that way.' In other words, medicine men have the power to travel long distances in no time at all in the form of a wolf. During the time that they are traveling in this fashion, they are not supposed to talk to anybody until they reach their destination.

"He did not tell my grandmother about the incident until several months later, because, if he had, my grandmother would get excited, you know, and she would say that we would have to have a *sing* to chase the evil spirits away. When he told us about his experience, it made us wonder about it."

In my opinion, true magic lies in the unlimited reach of the psyche: mind contacting mind through other than sensory means; mind influencing matter and other minds; mind elevating itself to a level of consciousness where past, present, and future become an Eternal Now. Although man may clothe these experiences according to the cultural context in which he is most functional, these evidences of man's non-physical capabilities are universal.

I believe that prestidigitation, the-hand-is-quicker-than-the-eye kind of magic, was born when man began to use his *brain* in an attempt to mimic the transcendental qualities of his *mind*.

A canny young man, jealous of a shaman's ability to move an object through psychokinesis, mind influencing matter, retreats to a darkened lodge and duplicates the feat by attaching one end of a long black hair to a pebble and the other to a finger. Since the medicine person may have spent years acquiring the discipline requisite to a semi-controlled functioning of his "psi" ability and still cannot guarantee success on every attempt, the canny young man, who can guarantee results on every attempt if one will but step into his darkened lodge, will soon be capturing more than his share of the audience and more than his share of their fees for shamanistic services rendered.

In every expression of magic, there are two basic kinds—the genuine manifestation of controlled "psi" ability and an imitative exploitation based on the essence of the authentic.

It is the wise person who learns that the "magic" of spiritual blessings has been dispensed to all men.

It is the adept practitioner who learns, in quiet moments of meditation, how best to permit a stream of the great light of the Cosmos to reach in and enrich his soul and open the borders of the Unknown.

It is the recipient of Illumination who achieves a dramatic spiritual linkup with the powers within his own psyche and the blessed Harmony that governs the Universe.

"I have had my own experiences," Don Wilkerson admitted. "I have practiced medicine, and I still do. Although I am assimilated into society, I don't accept society for what it is. I work in it, but I don't live in it. I live in my own group. When I get home, society is left behind me. I am in my own world and my own thoughts.

"This does present a problem at times. I have heard many non-Indian people say that I am anti-social, but that is not the case. This is a protective device that many of us Indians employ. I have had to use it in order to survive.

"I was raised on the reservation, speaking the language, practicing all the traditions. Then I went through a lot of traumatic experiences trying to find myself in the world. I never really found anything that answered my needs, other than with my own people and my own religion.

"Close, non-physical, ESP-types of relationships develop among many in our Indian groups. My mother and I were always in communication on this level, and I could tell when she wanted me. We always knew how the other was feeling, even when I traveled all over the world. During my twenty-three years in the Army, I never once wrote to my mother, yet we were always in contact with one another on this level of consciousness. These things are common among the Indian people.

"The fact that many Indian people have developed this ability to such a high degree can cause them some problems when they are working in white society. They may up and leave to go home without notifying anyone, because they know that something is wrong and that it requires their immediate attention. It becomes impossible to articulate these things to many non-Indian people."

We have these happenings in our non-Indian culture, as well. But we educate ourselves out of them. The Indian is not afraid to resume a more basic approach to these non-physical experiences. He does not attempt to rationalize these things, as a member of non-Indian society might.

"I think this may be true," Wilkerson said. "I don't know whether it is because of the rebirth of medicine power or not, but it seems that more and more Indians are encouraging, and responding to, these kinds of feelings. These things are not superstitions, but they exist as a very real part of our people's lives."

7. New Tribes for a New Age

When I remarked to Rarihokwats, the Mohawk editor of *Akwesasne Notes,* that non-Indian youth were demonstrating by their very choice of dress—leather jackets, beaded headbands, moccasins, etc.—that there was something about the Indian life that was attractive to them, he replied that Indian-ness required more than the adoption of certain superficial aspects of Amerindian culture.

"You know," he went on, "we meet with a lot of the young people, and we talk with them. They are very often disappointed in us because we don't live up to their expectations of what we should be like. I think that in their rejection of their own culture, they have grabbed on to the nearest convenient replacement and are trying to become 'instant Indians.'

"I think what they really have to do is to retribalize. What they are doing now is a very individualistic kind of maneuver. What is required is even deeper than living with Nature: it is living as a *part* of Nature. Indians are one with Nature in a family kind of relationship. That is why all things of Nature are expressed as brothers or sisters, grandmothers and grandfathers. It is a close family relationship."

Ann Underwood had this to say about the Amerindian's tribal relationships: "Each person, from tiny child to the oldest person in the tribe, has his own function, his own place; and he never loses touch with Nature. Emotional disturbances and insanity are almost unknown among the traditional and tribalized Indian.

"I think the Indian method of child rearing is better than Dr. Spock's. We teach each child that he is a person, that he has a respected place in his tribe, in his clan, in his family. He is told that he has certain responsibilities to face. He is taught to revere and respect his parents, his grandparents, the elder members of his clan and his tribe; and he is taught to revere the Great Spirit. From the time a child is born, he knows exactly who he is, where he is, and what he is, and exactly what is expected of him. The child is as he is, and he is accepted on those terms, without ridicule, without being put down."

In his *We Talk, You Listen,* Vine Deloria, Jr., writes of the great source of strength which every Indian finds in the tribal structure. "Being inside a tribal universe is so comfortable and reasonable that it acts like a narcotic," he informs his non-tribal readers. "When you are forced outside the tribal context you become alienated, irritable, and lonely. In desperation you long to return to the tribe if only to preserve your sanity."

Deloria sees our time as a process of retribalization, because ". . . we have become objects of a universe we do not understand and not subjects with a universe to exploit." Technological advancements disproportionate to man's humanistic growth have created an inhuman science that has displaced man from the smug master-of-his-fate role that has shaped a great deal of Western thought. The next step, as Deloria views it, is to create a new mythology and symbols to explain the new world:

> New concepts must define the questions of life, death, and society which are derived from the nature of man as a tribal animal. The individualistic rationalism that has brought Western man to the present cannot preserve his sanity for him in the future.
>
> We have come from an oral culture through a literate culture and then suddenly been thrust beyond the literate culture by our communications media into a qualitatively different oral culture

again. This generation of young people has been raised on television and has lived a continuous existence instead of the broken and alienated existence which plagued their elders. The categories of existence are different for the generations, and the older generation cannot stand the freedom which the young exhibit.

Deloria recognizes the Woodstock Nation as a new distinct minority group in our culture, a minority group that has rejected the older equality of individual mythology in favor of group tactics and group goals. He senses a desperate need for "traditional structures, concepts, and mythologies to provide a means of translating ideas and values between generations and between whites and non-whites."

If the new minority groups do not quickly translate their "harmless group feeling" into a demand for "recognition of the sovereignty of their groups," Deloria foresees their dissolution and destruction. In his opinion:

> Any future coalition of groups for change must adopt Indian formats. The desire to have spectacular demonstrations and disruptions must give way to a determination to maintain the community at all costs. This can only be possible by creation of new mythologies internal to each group in a manner similar to contemporary tribal understandings of the history of the people.

Deloria tells us that we have a chance to structure a new cosmopolitan society within the older North American society, "but it must be done by an affirmation of the component groups that have composed American society. We can no longer build upon a denial of everything that makes a person himself."

We must, in his estimation, renew various symbols in order to restore communications between generations and combine the older symbols with a "new vision of the nature of man" which has been achieved by "creating a new mythology of creation itself."

"The current fascination with ecology is one key to the new

mythology," Deloria informs us, "because it attempts to understand the real natural world as a part of us and we as a part of it. . . . We must return to and understand the land we occupy. Communications have made the continent a part of the global village. The process must be reversed. The land must now define the role communications can play to make the country fruitful again."

There are a number of communes throughout the United States and Canada that provide living substantiation for the observations Deloria makes in regard to the youth of the Woodstock Nation minority seeking to restore ancient symbols and to combine them with new mythologies and a new vision of the nature of man. Many of these New Age communes combine a dedication to the Cosmic Christ, a belief in the Brotherhood of Man, and the practice of Essenic Christianity, with an observance of the old traditions of the Amerindian. Whether these new tribal structures actually provide us with a preview of how man will live, work, and worship in the New Age or whether they represent experiments in counterculture life-styles, they are worthy of our examination and consideration.

White Bear, the Hopi prophet, is spiritual advisor to the Brotherhood of the Sun, which is located at 3,000 feet in the mountains overlooking Santa Barbara, California, and the Channel Islands, while Norman Paulson is its guiding force and strength, both its founder and its guru. Paulson has long brown hair, a full beard, and a husky build that fills out the simple work clothes that he wears. Although he is a mystic, a visionary, his hands and his physique give evidence of the years that he spent as a bricklayer, a carpenter, and, now, a tiller of the soil.

Norman Paulson: I think it is a wonderful thing that the Indians are reviving their old culture and their old ways, because the truth of the Great Spirit, or the Living God, is in every religion and in every race.

I think the Hopi are the greatest example of brotherhood and living together in harmony with the Spirit that we have today. The Hopi settled in that remote area they call home because they did not want to become spiritually lax in a fertile climate and in a fertile ground. They wanted to depend upon their attunement with the life-force to grow their food and to produce the moisture necessary.

White Bear gave us Hopi seed for squash and corn. It produced pretty good this summer on what we call Lemuria Ranch.

The Hopi tradition and our way of life is very much the same, even to our meditation. I haven't looked too extensively into the other Indian tribes, but there seems to be a similarity in religious beliefs. It appears to me, though, that the Hopi seems to have kept his traditions together more than any other tribe.

I think the White Brother is happening right now here on the West Coast. I think it is a generation of young people, as well as older people, who recognize the basic values of life and who wish to live in harmony with the world and with nature. The meaning of the White Brother and the Red Brother is already taking place. The Indians are astonished because there seems to be a generation of whites who not only want to live as the Indians have for thousands of years, but who are doing it.

Of course we do not condemn everything our society has produced. We believe in taking things that don't pollute and the good that man has created into a new environment, discarding those things that do pollute our bodies and our souls. With the guidance of White Bear, we are seeking to form our harmonious relationship with nature. We are able to show a number of these things in the movie that we produced, *Empire of the Sun.*

We selected that title for our movie because we believe that there was once a continent in the Pacific that was called Mu, which all the legends of the Hopi definitely state they migrated from. Mu was known as the Empire of the Sun, and we feel that our movie is about the resurrection of a way of life that lasted over two hundred thousand years without any wars. We are trying to show that this true brotherhood can be accomplished again.

"You mentioned that your meditation techniques were similar to those of the Hopi. Could you elaborate just a bit on these techniques, please?"

Norman Paulson: My feeling is that the pillar of fire that Moses was talking about is something that just about everyone at the Brotherhood of the Sun is aware of. We are using the ancient form of meditation, which has to do with the aperture at the crown of the head. My own experiences have shown me that this method evolved out of the continent of Lemuria, and the Hopi carried it with him when he came into North America. The Tibetans that I have met use the same type of meditation.

I experienced the raising of *kundalini* after five years of continuous effort through Yogananda's method of meditation. At the same time I experienced the descending of an inner spiritual sun. It had to do with the crown of the head and the energy that has come into the crown of the head. Both forces met in the heart. The consciousness centered in the heart and the body experienced the breathless state, the stopping of the heart, and the death trance. I experienced it for five hours the first time. My coming back into the body had to do with descending out of the burning light of inner sun, down through the crown of the head. Through this experience, I began to practice my own method of meditation, which involved receiving this life through the crown of the head.

Moses said when he led the children of Israel that there was a pillar of fire by night and a cloud by day. Everywhere we look through the ancients we find that the pillar of fire and the cloud have to do with the higher vibratory energy. My own experience was an evolution of a series of lives in Lemuria, which I remembered in my years at Yogananda's.

After becoming aware of the Hopi and their migrations, I was able to fit my own experiences to theirs; and at the right time, White Bear arrived at the Brotherhood and he gave me confirmation.

In a vision, I was shown the offshore islands around Santa Cruz Island, and I was told that these lands were going to be for the new children of the New Age. The Empire of the Sun was rising. It was stretching forth its hand from the sea to reclaim certain land for the children of the New Age. These children are white Indians or the lost White Brother, for whom they have been looking from Quetzalcoatl to the Hopi, to the Inca to the Maya. These lost white children are now reincarnated and large numbers of them have been gathering on the West Coast of the United States. Many of them are unaware of why they are here and who they are.

I was taken to our ranch, for which we have just acquired another big property in the wilderness. A standard with a full sun disk was driven in the ground on a four-cornered square. On the standard were the words *Empire of the Sun*. Spirit said these lands belonged to the children of the New Age. They will extend from here to Hopi lands, south to Mexico City, north to Mount Shasta. They will include all the Pacific islands and Hawaii.

Spirit referred to the Empire of the Sun as being the Old Garden of Eden. There were twelve tribes originally assembled there. The twelve tribes are the twelve vibrations emanating from the sun of our galaxy. These twelve vibrations of people are scattered on solar systems throughout our galaxy. When a certain solar system has reached a point nearest the higher vibration, they all reassemble. Right now we are coming out of the Dark Age, and the tribes are beginning to reassemble. This is the first indication of the return of the Garden, or the spiritual consciousness.

My meeting with White Bear is in recognition of the White Brother. White Bear has now fulfilled the prophecy that his mother told him, that in the last days he would go to the Hawaiian Islands, the last stepping-stones from Lemuria to the New World.

It all comes together. I can show you that the Tibetan prayer wheel evolved out of Lemuria exactly the same as the Hopi medicine wheel. It shows a 24,000-year cycle of our sun and planets moving around the inside of the zodiac. Every 24,000 years all these things take place.

When Lemuria existed, there were twelve tribes, basic brother-
hoods; they were different races and they looked different because
of the vibratory region of space in which they came. When the migrations from Lemuria began, some went east and some went west.
The white Indian went toward the rising sun. The White Brother
migrated into the land of the Incas and the Aztecs. From there he
went into Atlantis and from there to Greece and parts of Egypt.
The White Brother was the roots of Abraham, the Jew.

When Moses was in Egypt and said that the Garden lay east-
ward in Eden, he knew it wasn't in India, because Egypt was trading with India. He knew the Garden was further east.

The Essenes were a reincarnated group that set up the master
vortex for the coming of Christ. To set up a master vortex, you
have to have all twelve sides of the zodiac together, each illuminated in the same vibration—each one with his vortex; each one
receiving his vibrations; preferably, each one born in the center
of the zodiacal sign, not in the beginning or the end.

When the right twelve are assembled and receiving, you have
the master power. But you only have half of it. This is what Jesus
was trying to assemble out of the Essene movement. Unfortunately,
they didn't have women, which would have given them the other
half. They lost the ability to bring the whole truth, the whole realization. But now in this age we can do it.

Right now we have all twelve at Sunburst Farms, and the signs
align, as in Mary's [Mrs. Paulson] and my case. We are both
Aquarians, our moons match, both Sagittarius. We have been together from the beginning.

Now, this planet is at the threshold of the Garden. Men and
women are going to realize their true divine nature, and they are
going to ascend, instead of descend, with their energy.

We are overpopulated; there are no homes, no food; people
are dying in the street; because man went into the house of lust
with his own desires. Now we can come out. The true way to live
is by knowing the Infinite Self, the Living God.

With meditation and with the establishment of the Pillar of Fire, the life and the knowledge and the vision of your own inner sun, you will know how to enter the Aquarian Age.

The Bear Tribe, led by Sun Bear, a Chippewa medicine man, is more traditionally American Indian and has fewer Eastern and non-Indian metaphysical elements incorporated into its structure than does the Brotherhood of the Sun. The Bear Tribe is familiar with the ancient prophecies that foretold of a time when refugees from white society would come to the redman as lost brothers, and they have invited non-Indian peoples to join them and to learn to develop harmony with Nature. Sun Bear regards the Bear Tribe as the first new Indian tribe of this century, and he emphasizes its principles of returning to the land and to the traditional Amerindian way of life.

"It's time this became a national movement," Sun Bear said. "We've got to give people the word to start where they are, to get something going and start looking for land. Then we can send people around to teach our non-Indian brothers how to survive. People can become clans of the Bear Tribe if they want, but we would rather establish a network of communes than to take individuals into our own circle. We want this movement to be nothing less than a tribal alternative to the economics of America."

Sun Bear: When we first started the Bear Tribe, we held out our hands on a "bring your poor, your discontented" basis. We accepted people wholeheartedly, and we also accepted them at their word.

But a lot of people were not sincere in that theirs was a lip thing. They were rip-offs. Instead of learning that the first step toward spiritual balance is to work the land and to learn love and harmony, they just wanted to shake the rattle and sing the songs. There was no real commitment or love to anything.

"Would you say that because of their non-Indian cultural conditioning these people simply wanted spiritual blessings instantly, without having to apply any real effort?"

Sun Bear: Yes, they wanted their religion in a capsule. The other thing was that, in terms of a real relationship of living, the American society has dealt with people to the point where they aren't able to build a spiritual discipline. These are just two of the problems that I have observed in the year and a half that I have been working with the Bear Tribe.

According to the way I interpret my medicine, I must offer it to the non-Indian people as well as the Indian. This is what I will continue to do, because I see a blending, a coming together of Indian and non-Indian people. I see them walking together in harmony on the Earth Mother with a real love relationship and a responsibility for themselves and for the Earth Mother.

"I agree with you that both Indian and non-Indian peoples might benefit from the heritage our nation has in the Amerindian culture. Could you tell me what you feel the traditional ways offer to modern man in this new age of ever-rising awareness?"

Sun Bear: Well, knowledge never changes; it remains a strong and continuing thing. Indian medicine and the power behind it is very much alive today. It has not vanished; it is not antiquated. To the traditional Indian people, we see more of a strong need for it today than ever before. We see a continent being devastated by people who are stupidly trying to get rich quick by raping the Earth Mother. We feel that it is basic for the survival of this nation that people learn much of our traditions, much of the knowledge that we have to teach.

Unfortunately, too many of the non-Indian people on this continent have no real spiritual conviction. Too many practice a "Sunday religion," a mouth thing, not a heart thing. This shows in their lives. There is nothing real about this social kind of worship. We traditional Indian people feel that if your religion is a real thing, it should work for you every day.

When we make our prayers, we ask for medicine to work for us. We expect the rain to come tomorrow, not six months from now.

When the non-Indian prays for peace, he waves the sword in the other hand. They have no real commitment toward it. I make no prayers for peace for this nation, because I see its destruction by its own stupidity.

I regard myself as a humanitarian. I love my fellowman—Indian, black or white or whatever. Those whom I call brothers are those who share the same philosophy and respect for the Earth Mother and for each other as human beings.

We traditional people consider ourselves keepers and protectors of the Earth Mother. We have a responsibility not only to this generation, but to all generations to come. That is why we are concerned over the environment, concerned over the natural resources. We feel that in other lands across the world, there are other people of ancient origin who have labored in a manner similar to our work —people who are keepers and protectors.

I believe in pride and in Indian culture and in our traditional way of life. I am proud that we have been able to retain this necessary wisdom. But I don't think of this as a racist thing. I don't want to kill the whiteman or anybody else. I feel very strongly against this. I feel as strongly against the Indians who destroy as I feel sorry for the Indian people who carry a wine jug in their hands and tell me that they are traditional Indians.

A lot of people who come as seekers of Indian medicine are people who only want these powers for themselves. They don't intend to use medicine for the benefit of other people.

I had a man come to me one time who wanted me to teach him medicine ways. He was another one who was in a hurry to get hold of the rattle, you know. I asked him what he wanted medicine for. He said that he had studied Yoga and that he had studied other things. "I just want to know it for myself," he said.

I told him that I couldn't teach him. I felt that it would be a waste of time.

If the man had been willing to use medicine in harmony and to work with our people and our groups, then it would have been another thing. He was like so many people who approach their religion for selfish reasons. These people want to save their souls

from hell, or they want to be sure they get themselves to heaven.
But both reasons are for themselves alone.

Too many of these people who come to the reservations to drop
off their little boxes of old clothes are doing it to make brownie
points with the Sky God. They are not really doing it for the benefit
of someone else. They are doing it for themselves. This is the arrogance of all these people who are going along on a trip just for the
free ride. The reality of it is that if humanity is to develop and to
evolve into better balance, then somewhere along the line, we have
to put away all this arrogance crap.

In the Bear Tribe, we have three rules we ask of those who come
to join us:

First, we tell them they aren't coming to do *their* thing, they are
coming to do *our* thing.

In order to walk in balance and harmony with each other on
the Earth Mother, there is to be no liquor—because we have seen
destruction both of our own people and other people due to liquor
—and there are to be no hard drugs.

There is to be no possessiveness. That does not mean they do
not have responsibilities toward the things that are around them.
But they should look at land, vehicles, livestock, as things they
can share.

You see, the time has come when humanity walks not as men
and women, but as human beings. We don't want any of the jeal-
ousy barriers that cause the same sicknesses that build wars between nations and all the rest of it.

The medicine that I offer through the Bear Tribe and that I believe in, is not a medicine of the Sioux of yesterday or the Chippewa
of yesterday. It is a medicine of today, as well as a medicine of tradition. This is the medicine that I see is going to have to bring the
balance between the races on the Earth Mother.

Some other Indian may say, "That is not what the Sioux believe,"
or, "That is not what the Chippewa believe," or, "That is not what
I believe."

Well then, that is true. It is not. It is what I see, what my medicine has shown to me at this time.

I have had problems with some of the people who are with me, who still have not fully found the ability to comprehend what my medicine is about. But if you are to live out in the hills with a group of people, you are going to have to get it together there. You are going to have to be like the traditional Indian has always said: "They who walk with a good balance carry the law within their hearts."

We didn't need a billy club on every corner before the whiteman came, and we were able to survive on this land for thousands of years. We didn't need the corner policeman to beat our heads in.

If this nation is to grow as a true nation of brothers and sisters, then everyone must learn to walk with a good balance and to carry the law in his heart.

8. The Vision Quest

When I first asked Dallas Chief Eagle if he had undertaken the vision quest when he was a young man, he quickly replied that he had not. Then, a few moments later, he interrupted our conversation to say: "I have to be perfectly truthful with you, Brad. I forgot what your purpose is in this book you are writing. Yes, I had a vision quest, but I will not comment on it."

I thanked the Sioux chief for his honesty, then asked him: "I realize such things must be kept in secret, but could you tell me if there would still be Indian youths at Rosebud or Pine Ridge who would practice the vision quest today?"

"Yes, definitely," Dallas Chief Eagle answered. "And I wish more youth would, because the vision quest teaches one simplicity, humility, and it certainly adjusts one's attitudes in a spiritual way.

"I think all youths—non-Indian as well as Indian—who have reached puberty should go on a vision quest. Isaac, Abraham, Jacob went on vision quests. Moses went on a vision quest and obtained the Ten Commandments. Christ himself went on a vision quest of forty days. The term 'vision quest' wasn't used, but we are talking about the same thing."

As we have previously noted, the Amerindian vision quest, during which the seeker goes into the wilderness alone to receive his spirit guardian and his secret name, constitutes the very essence of medicine power. With its emphasis on individualism and the sacredness of personal visions, the vision quest supplies us with both a prototype of the revelatory experience and a demonstration of the peculiar mystical experience that is most efficacious for our hemisphere.

Don Wanatee, Mesquakie: This is the time for seeking a definite way whereby you can actually commit yourself to the tribe and to the tribe's beliefs. The tribe depends on you, and you depend on the tribe. When you become older, you must go out and fast for four days and keep on fasting until you get the power. Then it is up to you to distribute this power among your people so they can live a better life, so they can be helped, so they can achieve something and you can be strong.

I must have been about three or four years old when my great-grandfather introduced me to [the vision quest] the Mesquakie tradition. I remember him sitting their singing. I couldn't sing the songs, because they hadn't really been taught to me yet, but I could tell that they were meaningful to me. I sat there with a gourd, and I remember people dancing, the high shrill of the flute, the cadence of the drum.

I still maintain [the Mesquakie tradition], because my father followed it, my grandfather followed it, my great-grandfather taught me. That is why I believe very much in the Mesquakie religion and no other, because it was given to us to cherish as a way of life.

I believe in the [vision quest], that there is a Higher Being to tell you what to do, to tell you this is the way you must help your people, help your family, help your tribe. Yes, I believe in that.

In my *Revelation: The Divine Fire,* I quote the experience of my friend Fay Clark, who as a young boy was adopted by Chief Michael Red Cloud of the Winnebagos of Wisconsin. Fay lived among the Winnebagos for two years, and his foster father convinced him to participate in the puberty rite:

I wouldn't have been quite thirteen. We were given preliminary tutoring for several weeks on what to expect and what was expected of us. Then we were asked to go out into the woods and pick a spot where there was a stream. We were told that we must not bring food or seek out berries or any kind of food. We were also told that we must not seek shelter, but must remain exposed to the elements, to the rain or to the sun. We were to weaken our bodies and to continue praying at least three times a day for our guide.

. . . We prayed to Manitou, the Supreme Being.

The main thought behind the rite is to completely exhaust the body as quickly as possible. One of the exercises the Winnebagos suggested was to find a place where there were rocks, so that we might pick them up and run with them from one place to another. Make a pile one place, then pick them up and carry them back again, repeating the process again and again.

You see, this exercise enabled one to busy his conscious mind with a monotonous physical activity while the subconscious mind was concentrating on the attainment of one's guide.

After a while, one would begin to see wildlife that would seemingly become friendlier. After a time, some creature would approach, as if to offer itself as a totem, or guide. It could be a bird, a chipmunk, a gopher, a badger. If the boy were very hungry, and if he were afraid of staying out in the wilderness alone, he could accept the first creature that approached and say that he had found his guide. But we were taught that if we could endure, Manitou, or one of his representatives in human form, would appear and talk to us.

I spent twelve days fasting and awaiting my guide. I had many creatures, including a beautiful deer, come up to me and allow me to pet them. The deer, especially, wanted to stay. But I had been told that if I did not want to accept a form of life that offered itself to me, I should thank it for coming, tell it of its beauty, its strength, its intelligence, but tell it also that I was seeking one greater.

On the twelfth day, an illuminated form appeared before me. Although it seemed composed primarily of light, it did have features and was clothed in a long robe.

"You I have waited for," I said. And it replied: "You have sought me, and you I have sought."

Then it faded away. But it had appeared before me just as real as you are, Brad.

On the evening that each boy was required to appear before the Winnebago council to tell of his experience, my guide was accepted as genuine. And I don't think there is any way that any young boy could have fooled that tribal council. They knew when he had had a real experience and when he had used something as an excuse to get back to the reservation and get something to eat.

One thing that we were taught is that we must never call upon our guides until we had exhausted every bit of physical energy and mental resource possible. Then, after we had employed every last ounce of our own reserve, we might call upon our guide and it would appear.

The personal revelatory experience received during the vision quest becomes the fundamental guiding force in any traditional Amerindian's medicine power. The dogma of tribal rituals and the religious expressions of others become secondary to the guidance one receives from his personal visions.

The vision quest is basic to all native North American religious experience, but one may certainly see similarities between the proud Indian youth presenting himself to the Great Spirit as helpless, shelterless, and humble and the supplicants of Western occultism and Christianity fasting, flagellating, and prostrating themselves in monastic cells. In Christianity, of course, the questing mystic kneels before a personal deity and beseeches insight from the Son of God, whom he hopes to please with his example of piety and self-sacrifice. In Amerindian medicine, as in occultism, the power, the mana, granted by the vision quest comes from a vast and impersonal repository of spiritual energy; and each recipient of medicine power becomes his own priest, his own shaman, who will be guided by guardian spirits and by insights into the workings of the Cosmos granted to him by visions sent from the Great Spirit.

The vision quest is the Amerindian's first Communion. Far from being a goal achieved, the vision quest marks the beginning of the traditional Indian's lifelong search for knowledge and wisdom. Nor are the spiritual mechanics of the vision quest ignored once the youth has established contact with the guardian spirit and with the power which are to aid him in the shaping of his destiny. At any stress period of his life, the traditional Amerindian may go into the wilderness to fast and to seek insight into the particular problems that beset him.

As Hartley Burr Alexander writes (*The World's Rim*):

> The seeker goes forth solitary, if a man, carrying his pipe and with an offering of tobacco, and there in the wilderness, alone, he chants his song and utters his prayer while he waits, fasting, such revelation as the Powers may grant. Perhaps as evidence of the intensity of his need he sacrifices a dear possession or offers the blood of his own body that the Ministers of the Great Spirit may the more readily respond. The Indian prophets, men such as Tecumseh, Keokuk, Smohalla, Wovoka, have almost invariably secured their revelations in this manner; and Indian tradition is filled with tales of men and women who have undertaken the sojourn in solitude, their days in the wilderness, not alone for their individual need but for the welfare of the whole people.

Dallas Chief Eagle has already pointed out that the inspired prophets of the Jewish and Christian traditions have undertaken the wilderness sojourn in the same kind of seeking of the Great Spirit's revelations. The difference in the traditions lies in the fact that whereas the Christian or Jew accepts the idea that *special men* chosen of God have gone into the wilderness to seek illumination, the Amerindian has made the vision quest a part of the life of *everyone* who seeks medicine power. Members of nearly every Christian congregation will assume that their clerical shepherd received some kind of "call" that led him into the ministry, but the vast majority of the congregation were born into their faith and would undoubtedly be puzzled by anyone asking them if they had received a "call" to become a member of that church body. The traditional Amerindian does not wait for some cosmic signal to summon him into communion with a higher intelligence. He goes into the wilderness to await and to confront his vision and his guardian spirit.

The matter of the guardian spirit will seem but an example of primitive fairy tales to the skeptic, while to the orthodox religionist, who may cherish a belief in angels, this Amerindian belief will smack of pagan mysticism. The psychologist may tell us that men and women in isolation will often hallucinate supernatural helpers. But the concept of ultra-physical beings—call them guardian spirits, angels, etheric masters, or what you will—materializing to assist man in times of crisis appears to be universal.

I have theorized that these entities may be one of three things:

1.) Messenger entities with a more than casual interest in man, who come from the Great Spirit to perform precisely the functions which they claim.

2.) Externalized projections of man's own High Self (his Super-conscious) which appear to help man help himself.

3.) A manifestation in which the Great Spirit reveals itself to the recipient in an appropriate form which will permit him to perceive the revelation in the manner most meaningful to him.

Fay Clark told me that his guardian spirit has responded to his calls for help and that on two occasions it has appeared to warn him of approaching danger. Whether the ostensible spirit was an independent intelligent entity concerned about Fay's welfare or whether the manifestation was due to Fay's superconscious level of mind receiving information through other than sensory means and externalizing the knowledge as a warning spirit, he did not hesitate to act upon the information received.

Dr. Walter Houston Clark told me: "I have learned things about myself and the mystical consciousness from visionary experience under the influence of psychedelic chemicals, as at an Indian peyote ceremony, for example. But any figures I have seen in such states I have always assumed to have been symbols created by

my unconscious, rather than coming from an intelligence in another plane of being. Nevertheless, those who have received messages from cowled figures, angels, or venerable men in dreams and
visions and then find that these messages contain verifiable truths
should treat these figures with respect, whatever their origin."

The traditional Amerindian certainly treats his guardian spirit
with respect, and he uses the information given to him in dreams
and in visions as lessons about himself to be used in the most effective performance of his personal medicine. If one feels more
comfortable considering the guardian to be an externalized image
of the High Self which the percipient receives as a by-product of
the illumination of the vision quest, it would probably not greatly
affect one's medicine power.

To emphasize the uniqueness of the vision quest as the fundamental guiding force in Amerindian medicine is to underscore
certain universal aspects of the experience and to invite comparisons with the *samadhi* of the Yogi, the *satori* of the Zen Buddhist,
Dr. Raymond Bucke's Cosmic Consciousness, and the ecstasy of
the Christian mystic. In the chapter "Basic Mystical Experience"
in his *Watcher on the Hills,* Dr. Raynor C. Johnson named seven
characteristics of illumination which I will list together with comments directed toward our analysis of the vision quest of the
Amerindian:

1.) *The Appearance of Light.* One instantly thinks of Paul (né
Saul) on the road to Damascus being struck blind by the sudden
appearance of a bright light, but the guardian spirit also manifests
as a light being.

2.) *Ecstasy, Love, Bliss.* The traditional Amerindian, stereo-
typically regarded as stoical and unfeeling, regarded the vision
quest as a supreme emotional experience.

3.) *The Approach to Oneness.* The very essence of the traditional way of life is the awareness that one is a part of the Universe
and the Universe is a part of him.

4.) *Insights Given.* Not only did the seeker receive valuable
insights and a guardian, but he received a secret name.

5.) *Effect on Health and Vitality.* After the illumination experience, the percipient—although he may have fasted for several days and may have depleted his physical strength through monotonous tasks designed to quiet his conscious mind—would feel invigorated and would walk back to the council in full stride to recount his vision.

6.) *Sense of Time Obscured.* This seems less dramatic to the traditional Amerindian than to other recipients of illumination, since he has never permitted himself to become enslaved by linear time.

7.) *Effects on Living.* The receiving of the personal vision serves as the traditional Indian's support throughout his entire life and is incorporated into his world-view with total commitment.

"To receive visions [beyond the vision quest experience] is a great thing," Iron Eyes Cody said. "But it is not always easy to have visions. I was in the sweat lodge a couple of years ago. My son was heating the rocks. A man passed out. My son was darn near passing out. Another man was coughing so that he couldn't sing with the rest of us. Then he saw his grandmother [that is, his grandmother's spirit form] in a dark place in the sweat lodge. Now, you have to believe this, because a vision is a matter of power of the mind. Visions come. You can see them. But you have to be strong-minded.

"My wife didn't tell you this, but a couple of years ago we had a Yuwipi meeting right here in the darkroom of my photography studio. We were talking about healing a woman. There were different ones here. Eagle Feather, the medicine man, came here to conduct the Yuwipi meeting. My wife was sitting next to the woman to be healed. The drummer was going; we were chanting.

"When we stopped, something hit my wife in the lap. When we turned on the lights, we saw that it was a bundle of feathers that had been on the other side of the room. Nobody could have got there to grab those feathers. Eagle Feather was by the altar in the middle. My son, Rocky Boy, and I were singing and drumming.

Nobody could have got by us. The power of our Yuwipi happening made that bunch of feathers come and land in my wife's lap. After everyone saw what had happened, a lot of people told what they had felt and saw while we were in darkness. Magic is a strong power."

How does one best acquire the visions that lead to strong medicine power? There is the vision quest, of course; but are there other techniques which might encourage the advent of meaningful visions?

Don Wilkerson: There are certain ceremonies—and you can buy records of them—such as the Navajo *Yeibichai,* that are very hypnotic. If you listen to them, you will discover what they can do to you. Listening to a Yeibichai in a darkened, quiet room is a very, very moving experience. The tone is very high-pitched and chillingly done. It'll do it to you!"

Iron Eyes Cody: If the songs are sung properly, they can work great magic. I had been a technical advisor in films for years, but Cecil B. De Mille made an actor out of me when he filmed *The Unconquered.* "You speak the Seneca language," he said to me. "You know the Seneca songs. I want you to play Red Corn, as well as be technical advisor."

But these things must be done correctly. In *A Man Called Horse,* I was told to jump up and down and throw powder in Richard Harris' face before the Sun Dance. I said no. I am a Yuwipi man of the medicine society of the Yuwipi. It is not done that way. An old medicine man 'way up in his nineties, Richard Fools Crow, said, "I'm glad you said that, Iron Eyes. You stick to it."

I told the director that I would rather just quit than be unfaithful to my Yuwipi society. So he said, "All right, let's see you do it your way."

So I did it the very calm way and went through the ceremony, putting the eagle claws and the skewers through the whiteman's chest muscles, singing a song that defied the whiteman's magic. But the whiteman's power showed that he could do the Sun Dance, too. So at the end of the dance, I show that I admire the whiteman. I come in singing a blessing song.

I would never have sung proper ceremonial songs in some of the terrible pictures I have been in. I have been made to play hateful killers, and I would not further debase my people by permitting true ceremonial songs to be sung in these movies.

Walt Disney put me under contract for four years when he was filming the Daniel Boone television series [this early series starred Dewey Martin and should not be confused with the later series starring Fess Parker]. Walt told me that he wanted me to teach some of those Indians in North Carolina to sing an old ceremonial song. But the song I taught to them was just a common work song. I couldn't give the true ceremonial song for this series.

About five years ago I did a picture called *The Great Sioux Massacre*. I played Crazy Horse, a great man who sang strange songs, a man who saw visions. Things came to Crazy Horse that no one could explain. I read the book about him by Mari Sandoz. I talked to people up there in Rosebud, Pine Ridge, South Dakota. Nobody knew about the man, but they knew his ways and they followed them. He was a great man, and we use him now in songs. In this picture they wanted me to be Crazy Horse singing the old Sun Dance songs. I wouldn't do it.

But when *A Man Called Horse* came along, I did sing the sun vow song. At first, as I said, I would not. I did not want to ridicule my people. But when the director let me play the part in a spiritual way—the way I wanted to play it—that song came out of me as soon as I walked into the lodge. I did this great song—the *Wakan Tanka* —with feeling. I didn't see a camera. I heard nothing that was going on around me. I just went through the whole ceremonial song. The *Wakan Tanka* is not a song we sing every day. It is sung only at the Sun Dance, and this was the picture in which it was to come out for all to hear.

Black Elk, great medicine man of the Oglala Sioux, told how he began to sing his vision song when he felt that spirits from the outer world wished to speak to him. After chanting the words of his sacred song ["Behold! A sacred voice is calling you! All over the sky a sacred voice is calling!"] an uncounted number of repetitions, the two men of his great vision appeared to him with a relevant message.

In his monumental work, *Battle for the Mind,* and again in a lecture entitled "The Physiology of Faith," Dr. William Sargant discusses the two main ways in which revelatory insight may be acquired by the mystic.

The first method involves overexciting the nervous system "by means of drumming, dancing and music of various kinds, by the rhythmic repetition of stimuli and by the imposing of emotionally charged mental conflicts needing urgent resolution," and would seem to be referring to the revelations acquired by involvement in singing or dancing the Yeibichai, the Wakan Tanka, or any other particularly dramatic ceremony.

The other method inhibits most of the ordinary voluntary and even involuntary thoughts and activities of the higher nervous system: "One tries to put oneself artificially in what is now increasingly called a state of 'sensory deprivation.'"

Dr. Sargant seems to be referring to such spiritual techniques as those employed in the vision quest when he goes on to state: "In states of contemplation and mysticism . . . the individual has deliberately to learn . . . how to empty his mind of all extraneous matters, and generally to center his thoughts, if he is finally thinking actively at all, on some subject on which he desires to obtain new enlightenment . . . What then seems to happen is that, as the brain becomes more and more severely inhibited as regards its normal functions, one gets a greater and greater concentration on the one thing that matters at the time, or, as Henry Maudsley put it, 'extreme activity of one part of the brain and extreme lassitude of the rest'. . . . Suddenly the particular god . . . being concentrated on is felt actually to enter the person and become a very part of himself. . . . Impressions made on the brain at such a stage may remain lifelong in their effects, and from that time on, the individual has not the slightest doubt that the possessions or other sensations he experienced . . . were true in fact, despite all other life experiences. . . ."

Whether or not one accepts such psychological explanations for revelatory experiences, I believe that one basic question must be answered: Do rituals, drumming, dancing, chanting, fasting, or sensory deprivation induce the vision, or do these devices help enable the vision to occur?

Dr. Robert E. L. Masters and Dr. Jean Houston of the Foundation for Mind Research in New York City have concluded on the basis of hundreds of experiments with normal, healthy persons in the non-drug induction of religious-type experiences in the laboratory that "the brain-mind system has a built-in contact point with what is experienced as God, fundamental reality, or the profoundly sacred." Dr. Houston went on to comment: "The capacity for religious experience—including a deep feeling of unity with the universe—is built into human nature. It's simply a question of opening oneself up."

Twylah Nitsch teaches a course in "Seneca Wisdom" at the Human Dimensions Institute in Buffalo, New York. The course deals with "self-realization, self-control and how to live in harmony with Nature," and Twylah hopes one day to publish a book, *Wisdom of the Seneca*. According to Twylah:

The Indians did give instructions that helped one function within his highest intellectual self, which is the spiritual self. If all people would let themselves be guided by their spiritual selves, their material world would be more satisfying.

There is one technique, that of the use of the senses and going into the silence.

If you have a problem, go into the silence—which to me is not meditation. Meditation is only the door to silence, wherein you communicate with the inner self, the spiritual energy that is universal. When you have shut out the external world and are deep in the silence, you work, for instance, with sight. If you do not have success in seeing an image, try the sense of smell.

Soon you will hit on something that will be very meaningful, but you must *feel*. You cannot taste unless you feel; you cannot see unless you feel. When you are feeling and raising your emotional level, you tap into the creative self, the highest intellectual self, that which is of God and which is, to the Indian, the universal energy responsible for life.

Whenever I see or hear a prayer written by an Indian that says, "Great Spirit, grant me this or that"—a prayer of supplication—I know that it has been infiltrated with other philosophies. A traditional Indian never asks, never offers prayers of supplication—he only offers prayers of thanks. This is a true, hard fact, and one that is very important to an understanding of medicine.

My grandfather was Moses Shongo, last of the medicine doctors of the Seneca nation. He said that the people of today have not evolved sufficiently enough and intellectually enough to understand the principles of the original people of this country. He said at the end of the Fourth World—which is the world we are in now—there will be a great awakening and we may be able to talk about some of these things. That is why I am beginning to talk a little bit. I think the time is beginning to open up.

Brad, you would be doing a great service if you were to bring out the fact that the Indian woman was not a squaw, a beast of burden. There was an equality between the sexes.

It was not only the young men who sought visions. The woman would have to do what she would have to do to live with herself. She could go out and do the same things her own way. This was a personal thing. No one was ever forced to do it. When you felt you were ready, you did it. It was a communion within yourself and with Nature.

"If I am going to seek a vision or enlightenment or direction, then I usually go off by myself and find a place that is comfortable," Sun Bear said. "Sometimes I will take off all my clothing and offer myself to the Great Spirit just as I came into the world. This is the thing that I do when I seek my visions, my medicine counsel."

Winnebago dance roach, circa late 1800s. *Credit: Darryl Henning; courtesy Luther College Anthropology Department*

Chippewa eagle-feather headdress, embellished with deerskin trimmed in lynx, circa late 1800s. *Credit: Darryl Henning; courtesy Luther College Anthropology Department*

This Sioux buckskin shirt with medicine charms is purported to have been worn by the great warrior-mystic Sitting Bull. *Credit: Darryl Henning; courtesy Luther College Anthropology Department*

Winnebago otter skin medicine bag, circa mid-1800s. *Credit: Darryl Henning; courtesy Luther College Anthropology Department*

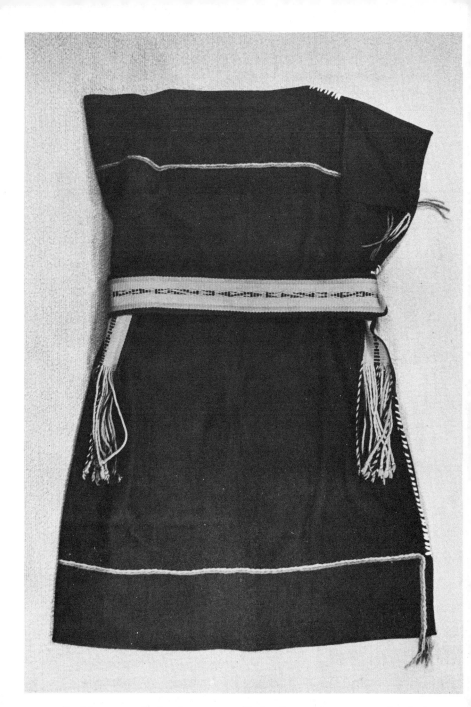

Pueblo woman's ritual manta and belt of contemporary production.
*Credit: Darryl Henning; courtesy Luther College Anthropology
Department*

Plains Indian pipe with catlinite bowl and quillwork on the stem, circa late 1800s. *Credit: Darryl Henning; courtesy Luther College Anthropology Department*

Plains Indian pipe bag with quill design, circa mid-1800s. *Credit: Darryl Henning; courtesy Luther College Anthropology Department*

Chippewa or Winnebago pipe bag with woodland beaded design, circa late 1800s. *Credit: Darryl Henning; courtesy Luther College Anthropology Department*

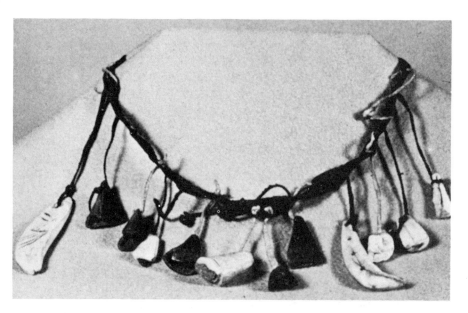

This Tlingit shaman's necklace of teeth, bones, and bear's claws was collected by G. Emmons in 1902. The Tlingits, a Northwest Coast tribe, celebrated their religious beliefs in the cedar, bone, and ivory readily available to them. This necklace is now in the possession of the Field Museum of Natural History.*

Shamans employed "soul catchers" to snare wandering spirits so that they might return them to suffering patients. These bone or ivory tubes could also be used to suck and to blow on a patient's sores or painful areas. This ivory soul catcher is in the Robert H. Lowrie Museum of Anthropology.*

This artifact was included in an exhibition entitled "The Art of the Shaman," which was sponsored by the University of Iowa Museum of Art, January 18 through February 25, 1973. Photo reproductions: John Tiffany, Iowa City.

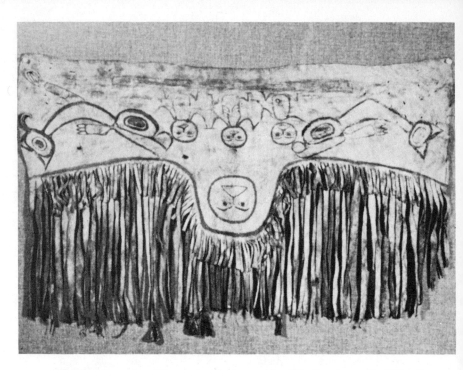

The Denver Art Museum displays this Tlingit shaman's kilt of painted elk skin.*

G. Emmons acquired this Tlingit shaman's head-dress of goat's horn and hide in 1902. It is now the property of the Field Museum of Natural History.*

This shaman's mask is of Tlingit origin and is constructed of wood and paint. It was collected by G. Newcombe, later presented to the Field Museum of Natural History.*

G. Emmons obtained this Tlingit shaman's mask of wood, goat's horn, paint, and quill from Dashed of the Chilkat tribe. The Field Museum of Natural History displays the mask.*

* This artifact was included in an exhibition entitled "The Art of the Shaman," which was sponsored by the University of Iowa Museum of Art, January 18 through February 25, 1973. Photo reproductions: John Tiffany, Iowa City.

This Tlingit shaman's doll is made of wood, hair, and paint and is 5⅞ inches high. It is now the property of the Field Museum of Natural History; it was collected by G. Emmons.*

Frank Likins collected this hawk-faced Tlingit medicine rattle in Sitka, Alaska, in 1889. It is made of red cedar and paint and is on display at the Robert H. Lowrie Museum of Anthropology.*

This artifact was included in an exhibition entitled "The Art of the Shaman," which was sponsored by the University of Iowa Museum of Art, January 18 through February 25, 1973. Photo reproductions: John Tiffany, Iowa City.

Black Elk has said, "A man who has a vision is not able to use the power of it until after he has performed the vision on earth for the people to see." He, of course, is not talking about the highly personal insight received during the vision quest, but the great vision that will enable one to become a medicine practitioner and have the strength to cure others and to counsel those who may come to him in need.

"Of course it was not I who cured," Black Elk qualifies in *Black Elk Speaks*. "It was the power from the outer world, and the visions and ceremonies had only made me like a hole through which the power could come to the two-leggeds. If I thought that I was doing it myself, the hole would close up and no power could come through."

Black Elk's qualifying remarks sound so much like the disclaimers which I have heard from sincere psychic sensitives, mediums, and healers who refuse any personal credit for their feats, but rather refer to themselves as "channels" through which the power may flow. It appears that it may be a universal law of metaphysics that those who are chosen to serve as "holes," as "channels," be ever conscious of the proper perspective in which they are to regard the stewardship of their unique abilities.

"The very fact that you can use medicine power to accomplish something is enough," Sun Bear explained. "You don't have to boast of it or pat yourself on the back. I know one brother who is a medicine person of this area [Nevada] who would boast of his medicine power. He lost his power for a period of time because of this."

Again, like so many accomplished adepts of metaphysics, the heavy practitioner of medicine believes that, from time to time, his essential self, his soul, leaves the physical shell of his body and soars free of time and space to travel other dimensions of existence and to receive spiritual insights not possible even in deep meditation or in going into the silence. Black Elk, for example, was a boy of nine when he heard voices telling him "it was time" just before he received his great vision. He fell ill, was taken

out of his body by two men who told him they were to take him
to his grandfathers. In the land of the spirits, Black Elk received
the great vision that was to sustain him all of his life. When he was
returned to his body, his parents greeted the first flutter of his eye-
lids with great joy. He had been lying as if dead for twelve days.

When he was with a Wild West show in Paris, France, the home-
sick Black Elk was partaking of a meal in the home of a family
who had befriended him, when, as he sat at the table, he looked
up at the ceiling and it seemed to be moving. Then he was soaring
through the clouds, traveling over the big water of the Atlantic,
crossing over New York City, the Missouri River, the Black Hills,
until he hovered over his home at Pine Ridge. While he viewed
the camps below him from his remarkable vantage point, he was
able to see things which he was able to verify when he returned to
the land of the Lakotas several days later. Again, he had lain as
dead—this time for three days in the home of the solicitous French
family.

In 1890, two years before the tragic Massacre at Wounded
Knee, Black Elk had an out-of-body experience while dancing,
and he returned from the land of the spirits with the design for
the holy shirts, the shirts to be used while participating in the Ghost
Dance.

The Ghost Dance was originally the vision of Wovoka, a Paiute
medicine man who was adept at sleight-of-hand magic, impressed
with the Christian stories of Jesus' Second Coming, and sorrowed
by the state of poverty and despair to which the Indian nations
had been reduced. Wovoka received a messianic charge while in
a fever-induced trance and awakened with a long-sought prophecy
of redemption for the Indian, a promise of the termination of
white domination, and a hope for the regeneration of the despoiled
earth and the return of the buffalo. Wovoka had no further use
for the magic tricks he had used to supplement his medicine. He
was imbued with power, and he would work for peace between
the Indian and the non-Indian.

Wovoka advocated a code of conduct established upon the principles of peace, brotherhood, forbearance, and non-violence. Handsome Lake, Smohalla, and John Slocum (founder of Shakerism) had preached similar principles, but they had been prophets. Wovoka told his followers that he was Jesus once again upon earth. Tragically, it would be the hypnotic manifestation of the *dance-in-a-circle* that Wovoka brought back from Spirit to permit every participant to mingle with ghosts of his loved ones that would evolve into the Sioux nation's Ghost Dance, the *wana ghi wa chipi,* that would spin the Indians away from their aspirations of a bloodless victory and lead them in confusion to the bloody Massacre at Wounded Knee.

In some cases, dancers wearing Ghost Shirts, said to be able to turn the whiteman's bullets to water, forgot that the dance was one of peace and left the circle to take full advantage of their supposed invulnerability. In other cases, fearful and suspicious whites simply could not believe that Indians could dance for peace as well as for war. This unfortunate state of tension resulted in the terrible murders at Wounded Knee. Wovoka vomited and became ill when he learned of the slaughter. He had died and gone to heaven to bring back a dance of peace, a dance which told the living that the dead would not forsake them, a dance that would make the land green and free once again. God had told him to tell his children not to fight, not to kill.

"Wovoka was a healer, a man of great magic," Iron Eyes Cody said. "We know that maybe at the beginning he fooled some of the people with tricks, but we have to say that Wovoka was a spiritual man.

"When I was a boy, I was with Tim McCoy. Tim went out to appear in Nevada and to meet a heavyset old preacher. They had a picture taken together. The old preacher—that was Wovoka—told me that he had believed what the Great Spirit had told him. He said that he didn't go into eating hallucinogenic herbs or anything like that. He had done everything through his medicine power."

I asked Iron Eyes if Wovoka still identified himself with Jesus at that time.

"Yes, he did," Iron Eyes answered. "It is too bad, but Wovoka's descendants don't even come to our powwows. It's like they don't even want to admit that they are Indians, you know."

Andrew Vidovitch, Wovoka's son-in-law, passed on in the spring of 1972, leaving, it appears, no spiritual heir to the vision that Wovoka had for his people [Wovoka died in 1932]. We have already discussed Vidovitch's active participation in the filming of *Billy Jack,* and we have heard Tom Laughlin's tribute to Vidovitch's spirituality and his willingness to commit an accurate representation of the Ghost Dance to film. It may well be that Andrew Vidovitch's own medicine told him that cinematic imagery might be an ideal method of preserving his father-in-law's vision for millions of today's youth and for those yet unborn.

I was fortunate in being able to talk with Mamie Babcock, a sister-in-law of Andrew Vidovitch, as she was clearing up the Vidovitch home in Schurz, Nevada, preparatory to leaving for her own home.

Mamie Babcock: Andy told everyone about it. He was so wrapped up in it. Every time we came down for a holiday, why, the main subject was this thing that you are talking about now.

"About the Great Spirit and the Ghost Dance vision?"

Mrs. Babcock: Yes, he always mentioned the Great Spirit. And he actually lived his belief, you know what I mean?

"He lived a completely spiritual life?"

Mrs. Babcock: Yes. He was always a good, clean-cut spiritual man. I am so sorry that you couldn't have got here before he died. It was a wonderful thing to hear him tell about it all.

"Is there anyone else in the family who will carry on Wovoka's vision?"

Mrs. Babcock: No. Among the members of the family there doesn't seem to be any interest in the old traditions. Most of them couldn't go back that far. They attend Christian churches. I go to church. It is hard getting our young people to go to church. It is like telling them to take castor oil or something.

But, oh, Andy used to speak of Wovoka all the time. Many an evening when we came down here, he told us about it. My grandchildren will always remember Grandpa Andy talking about Wovoka. Wovoka and the Great Spirit.

Although it seems rather sad that Wovoka no longer has a spiritual heir in his own bloodline, his vision is being danced time after time at innumerable Amerindian gatherings. The Ghost Dance mythos, with its melding of Christianity and the old traditions, is one of the progenitors of the contemporary Native American Church.

Some may argue that Wovoka's vision had accomplished its purpose in that it brought together the religious traditions native to this continent and combined them with the religious traditions of Europe and Asia. As certain of our interviewees have suggested, Christianity *sans* its bureaucracy may be compatible with Amerindian tradition, and a combination of the two religious strains may bring forth a truly strong religion for our New Age America.

Others may state their belief that the compromise of the Peace Messiah is no longer satisfactory in a time that is witnessing the rebirth of medicine power and the Native American's rediscovery of the validity of his religious traditions. The vision that is relevant for the New Age is that the medicine of the Great Spirit can offer modern man a workable system of spiritual guidance for those who will learn to walk in balance and to live in harmony with Nature and with the Cosmos.

9. Healing with Prayers and Herbs

Dallas, Texas—the National Institute of Mental Health, a U.S. federal agency that funds numerous projects to improve the delivery of psychiatric services, is paying six Navajo medicine men on an Arizona reservation to teach 12 young Indians the elaborate ceremonies that often cure the mental ailments of Navajos.

And, according to a conventionally-trained psychiatrist involved in the program, there is every indication that the trainees will become effective psycho-therapists, able to meet the mental health needs of a growing Navajo population that finds Anglo psychiatry ineffective.

The psychiatrist, Dr. Robert L. Bergman of the Indian Health Service in Window Rock, Arizona, described the unusual program May 4 at the annual meeting of the American Psychiatric Association here.

The program is an example of a growing awareness among Western-trained psychiatrists that the treatment for many mental illnesses must meet the cultural expectations of the patient and that virtually every culture has given rise to healers of some sort who are as effective in dealing with mental problems among their people as psychiatrists among Westerners.

Dr. Bergman said the Navajo program began when Indian reservation leaders decided something had to be done to increase the supply of medicine men. The remaining medicine men were becoming quite old and few young men were able to assume the economic hardship of several years in training, traditionally in apprenticeship to established medicine men. . . . [New York *Times,* May 6, 1972]

> O you people, be you healed;
> Life anew I bring unto you.
> O you people, be you healed;
> Life anew I bring unto you.
> Through the Great Spirit over all do I this;
> Life anew unto you!
>
> [Lakota holy song]

The unique school for medicine men is located at Rough Rock, Arizona, a community near the center of the Navajo Reservation, approximately seventy miles from its nearest border. It is a part of the Rough Rock Demonstration School, the first community-controlled Indian school. Since the very idea of a school for medicine men seems so representative of some of the things that are occurring to herald the rebirth of medicine power and the Resurrection of the Great Spirit, I considered myself extremely fortunate when Dr. Robert L. Bergman, Chief of the Mental Health Service, the psychiatrist who has been working with medicine people in Rough Rock, granted me an interview:

"Dr. Bergman, I am certain that a lot of serious-minded people must ask you this question: 'How can you be working to promote mental health when you are involved in a project that appears to be a retreat to superstition, a step backward culturally?' "

Dr. Robert L. Bergman: I usually answer that question by pointing out that the proper definition of the word superstition is, *my* knowledge, *your* belief, *his* superstition. Superstition is a word which conveys a lot of things without conveying a whole lot of information.

"You are saying, then, that superstition is a pejorative term used to express disapproval of someone else's system of beliefs."

Dr. Bergman: You could equally well refer—as I suppose some people do—to the "superstitious" belief of millions of Americans in the presence on Earth at one particular time of a person who was both human and God.

"How did the older traditionalists feel about the idea of cutting through the many years of apprenticeship and turning out medicine men in a school, à la the Western tradition of mass education?"

Dr. Bergman: Well, the school doesn't really offer any short-cuts. It is taking students a little bit longer than we had expected, probably because they are spending nearly full time on their studies. But it still takes a long time. And the ones who have graduated have only learned two ceremonies each. There is a lot of grousing right now by those graduates, who are complaining that they wanted to learn more and that they wish they had been permitted to stay in school longer. At any rate, it took them three and four years to learn just those two ceremonies, so you cannot say the school is mass production. And I should point out that the only part that is done in school proper is my work with them. The ceremonies are learned in a traditional way through apprenticeship in the homes of medicine men and in the places where they perform ceremonies.

I don't know how many ceremonies there are, but the important ones last five or nine nights; and they are difficult and elaborate to a degree approached among us conventional doctors only by open heart surgery.

A major sing, to be properly performed, demands the presence of the entire extended family, and many other of the patient's social connections. The patient's immediate family must feed all of these people for days. Many of the people present are employed in important roles in the ceremony, such as chanting, public speaking, dancing in costume, leading group discussions, and other activities which are more or less ritualized. For the singer-medicine man, the performance requires the letter-perfect performance of up to one hundred hours of ritual chant—a feat which might be compared to a perfect recitation of the New Testament from memory. In addition, the medicine man must produce a number of beautiful and ornate sand paintings, recite the myth connected with the ceremony, and manage a very large and difficult group process.

"I appreciate that clarification, Doctor. Can you tell me what would be the average age of the student and the average age of the graduate at Rough Rock's medicine school?"

Dr. Bergman: I've never figured that out. Let's see, the students who just graduated, I imagine, would average about fifty years old. The faculty currently averages about eighty-five. These studies are not usually undertaken early in life, although there are exceptions.

"Would it be fair to say that as with the holy men of other traditions—I am thinking, for example, of the Zen Buddhist priest—that these studies might be best undertaken when some of the other affairs of life, such as rearing a family, earning a livelihood, have more or less been put to one side?"

Dr. Bergman: Yes, that is quite correct in general. I think in older times the studies for the position of medicine man were really taken up in adolescence or in middle age. We had one adolescent student, but he couldn't stand the strain. Now we have another adolescent in our new bunch, and there are many men who are in their thirties. I think the average age of the present group of students is around forty.

"I have found, after interviewing medicine people from many different tribes, that one criterion for the role of shaman or medicine man is that somewhere in childhood or adolescence, the individual undergoes a seizure, an intense fever wherein he appears to die, or a high fever that brings about convulsions. Would this criterion hold for any of the medicine students at Rough Rock now?"

Dr. Bergman: No, you are talking about shamans, and these guys are not seers. Navajo practitioners generally fall into three categories. There are the herbalists, who know a variety of medicinal plants to be used primarily for symptomatic relief. Then they have the diagnosticians, who are shamans who work by inspiration and employ such techniques as hand trembling, crystal gazing, or star gazing. These diagnosticians divine the nature and the cause of an illness and make the proper referral to a member of the third and highest status group, the singers. These men—and I will use the terms "ceremonialist," "medicine man," and "singer" synonymously—do the true curative work. The school at Rough Rock seeks to train singers, medicine men.

"So the medicine people here are *medicine* in a sense approaching our Western meaning, in that they are being trained primarily to help with healing physical and mental ills, rather than developing seership."

Dr. Bergman: Yes, these fellows are learning to cure; they are not learning to divine.

[Although we have defined "medicine power" in Chapter 3, the term "medicine man" can give one a bit of a problem. Every Amerindian traditionalist has his own medicine, which gives him his own insights, strength, and spiritual power, but this medicine may not include the ability to heal. One who has developed a high degree of medicine power generally discovers that he has the ability to heal as a natural by-product of his total spiritual attunement. Some Amerindians favor the term "sacred doctor" to describe such an individual and to distinguish him from a "medicine man," who may have the ability to heal but who has not developed his full spiritual potential. Ivar Lissner defines a shaman as one "who knows how to deal with spirits and influence them. . . . The essential characteristic of the shaman is his excitement, his ecstasy and trancelike condition. . . . (The elements which constitute this ecstasy are) a form of self-severance from mundane existence, a state of heightened sensibility and spiritual awareness. The shaman loses outward consciousness and becomes inspired or enraptured. While in this state of enthusiasm he sees dreamlike apparitions, hears voices, and receives visions of truth. More than that, his soul sometimes leaves his body to go wandering."]

"You have mentioned that these students spend quite a bit of time interpreting their dreams."

Dr. Bergman: Yes, this is in relation to the curative aspects of their dreams. Again, they are not using their dreams to predict the future of the tribe or their patients. They regard their dreams as do I—as an indication of their own state of well-being. Or a patient's dreams are an important indication of how he is doing.

"This correlates with psychoanalytic procedure. Many therapists have mentioned how their dreams may give them insights into a patient's progress, and, in some cases, how their dreams may seem to intertwine with those of a patient."

Dr. Bergman: Yes. I meet with the students one full day every two weeks, and we spend a great deal of time on dreams. I admit that Navajo metapsychology still largely eludes me, but I have learned that they know about the dynamic interpretation of dreams. We have been pleased to discover that all of us follow the same custom in regard to our dreams. We all spend our first waking moments in the morning contemplating and interpreting our dreams.

"Although you have said that you have not used any of the Navajo ceremonies yourself, would you say that you have become more sympathetic toward there being a presence, an atmosphere, another order, a separate reality at work in these ceremonies?"

Dr. Bergman: Yes, I can conceive of that. I am not sure it is necessary to explain what happens, though. I am more impressed with the need of supernatural explanations for some of the things that the shaman can do; but, again, it is just one of those things where I don't think it matters a whole lot. It seems to me to be the kind of question that seems fascinating, but when you really get into it, it isn't. At least it doesn't fascinate me to try to bring together scientific principles for everything that happens in life. I think that there are some things that are better looked at from an artistic, aesthetic, religious point of view. An attempt to try to bring them into one system with a scientific analysis of natural phenomena is kind of hopeless and kind of boring.

Non-Navajo explanations of why their rituals help anyone tend to be rather offensive to the medicine men themselves. The Navajo medicine men just do not make so much of the distinctions among different levels of reality as the non-Indian. They reject as stupid and destructive any attempt to translate their words into ordinary language. Though it may seem to me that their myths and chants are symbols of human social and psychological forces and events, they would consider such statements as silly and as totally missing the point.

An one-hundred-year-old medicine man named Thomas Large-whiskers said to me: "I don't know what you learned from books, but the most important thing I learned from my grandfathers was that there is a part of the mind that we don't really know about and that it is that part that is most important in whether we become sick or remain well."

"It seems to me that you have come to accept the value of both Indian and non-Indian medicine, and like a good Yankee pragmatist, you utilize both of them. Would that be a fair statement?"

Dr. Bergman: Well, this is necessary in psychiatry. In psychiatry we use a kind of mythology of the mind. From the rigorous scientific point of view, the mind is probably a rather flimsy construct at best. We have a very elaborate dynamic model of the mind that we use constantly, but which doesn't coincide with any neuroanatomical or physiological stuff that we know. If one can stand to live with those two worlds, he can always add a few more.

"What are your plans for the future of the school for medicine men? Will you need to establish any incentive programs to keep the project running?"

Dr. Bergman: No, we don't need any incentive program, but we are going to need funds. There are already several other communities here on the Navajo reservation that are talking about setting up a similar program, and I have had letters from a number of other tribes asking me for my help in setting up a program in their areas. Indian people are getting themselves together, and sooner or later—I hope sooner—probably other communities will want to make application to the National Institute of Mental Health; and if I can, I will help them. I am not part of the NIMH, but being a psychiatrist and working for another branch of the Public Health Service, I can help them prepare applications to get source money.

"Have you ever received criticism from orthodox religious groups or from medical professional societies?"

Dr. Bergman: There is a physician who practices in Gallup, New Mexico—which is where I live—who is the son of a Baptist missionary, who wrote to his congressman, saying that we were supporting paganism. The congressman gave us a chance to reply, then used our reply to give the doctor a very firm answer. A faculty member from some small Catholic college wrote to another congressman, complaining that it wasn't right at all for Catholic elementary schoolchildren to be denied federal educational aid, when Navajo priests were being trained by federal money. After three or four days of thought, I managed to come up with a reply that federal aid does go to Catholic medical schools.

As far as criticism from my colleagues, discussions at the American Psychiatric Association called me a paternalistic racist.

"You have said that your contact with the Navajo singers has caused you to try to act like a medicine man."

Dr. Bergman: That has to do with my acquiring some of their style of communicating with patients, not in my performing any of their ceremonies. I think I picked up some of their habits of non-verbal communication and some of their attitudes toward patients. The medicine men are extremely modest. They always deny knowing anything, and they almost never make any claims for ever having any successes or having any special knowledge. At the same time, they give a lot of non-verbal clues that they expect a lot of respect. The important thing is that we have made more personal contact with one another. We have shared some of those illuminating experiences when we see what someone really meant by saying or doing something.

Actually, the major accomplishment of the school for medicine men is that we have really turned out some medicine men. And

that was the idea of our project: to replenish the supply of medicine men.

Although the Menninger Foundation of Topeka, Kansas, has
announced no plans to convert any of its facilities to a school for
medicine men, Douglas Boyd, a research assistant there, has been
assigned to follow the Shoshone medicine man Rolling Thunder
around for a year to see what he can learn about Amerindian approaches to healing.

"Rolling Thunder works on a very powerful kind of archetypal
level," said Dr. Irving Oyle, director of a health service in Bolinas,
California. "Western medicine can well afford to keep an eye on
Rolling Thunder."

"We medicine people see things that others can't see," Rolling
Thunder has said. "It's not us that does it, it is the Great Spirit."

Rolling Thunder told a group of assembled psychiatrists, psy-
chologists, and other professional people at the Menninger Foundation that every medicine man has his own medicine. He would
not define his approach for them because, "if a medicine man tells
what his medicine is, he loses his power."

It has been clear to those who have listened to Rolling Thunder
that his work with the ill cannot be separated in his mind from
his work as a close observer of the Earth Mother. Medicine people
believe that the Great Spirit would never put a disease on this
plane of existence without placing the remedy here, too. For centuries, medicine people have made sincere efforts to become
brothers with all living things so that they might discern the hidden
spirits of the plant world and be able to make remedies which
would aid their people.

The twilight-blooming Moon Flower (Jimsonweed) was used
as a soothing drug. Once the leaves had been dried, patients would
smoke them to treat such ailments as asthma, cholera, and epilepsy.
Today the chemicals in this flower are distilled for use in tran-
quilizers and eye dilations.

Medicine people found uses for mistletoe, other than as an inducement for kissing. Small amounts were found effective in treating epilepsy, and the leaves and berries, cooked with rice, formed a poultice used to draw pus from infections.

The Shoshone, Navajo, and Blackfeet chewed stone seed, a common weed of the area, for an oral contraceptive. Modern laboratory analysis has discovered that the plant contains estrogen, the same substance that is used in today's Pill.

Diarrhea was treated by the root of a cherry tree, the leaf of the horsetail weed, and the root of the blackberry.

Indians found an instant Band-Aid in the thick juice of the milkweed plant.

Toothache was dealt with by chewing the root of wild licorice and holding it in the mouth.

Salicylic acid, the basic ingredient of aspirin, can be found in willow bark, the basis of a brew medicine people would prescribe for headaches and for fevers.

Patients with stomach upsets were given swamp root, manzanilla buds, or branches of the juniper.

Soapweed may be used as a shampoo that gives a fine luster to the hair. An application of the boiled leaves of horse mint makes an excellent acne treatment.

The list of native American herbal remedies is an extensive one, but even though one may marvel at the ancient medicine people's ability to discern the curative power of roots, leaves, and barks that our modern, sanitary laboratories have since stamped with their seals of approval, an herb is, after all, an organic chemical compound and its brew is a recognizable medicine, whether it is steeped over a campfire or bottled in a pharmaceutical plant. The wonder and magic have been removed from something as familiar as a tonic, a syrup, or a chewable bromide. However, we are still curious and fascinated by acts of healing that are undoubtedly even older than the prescribing of herbs and elixirs. We want to know how faith healing, chanting, and the laying on of hands can cure.

Psychiatrist-anthropologist Dr. E. Fuller Torrey has classified what he considers to be the four common components of curing which are utilized by physician-healers all over the world.

1.) *The naming process.* Since there is nothing more frightening to a patient than the unknown, the very act of giving the illness or complaint a name that fits in with the patient's world view "may activate a series of associated ideas in the patient's mind, producing confession, emotional reaction, and general catharsis."

2.) *The personality characteristics of the healer.* The doctor-healers who possess the personal qualities of accurate empathy, non-possessive warmth, and genuineness "consistently and convincingly get better results than those who do not possess them."

3.) *The patient's expectations.* Doctor-healers all over the world use basically the same methods of raising their patients' expectations. The physical stimulus of amulet, rattle, stethoscope, or diploma are common ways in which expectations are increased. It is also a common observation that the farther a patient has to travel to visit the healer, the greater are his chances that he will be cured.

4.) *The doctor-healer's training.* Although few cultures other than the Western ones have a regular examination at the end of the training period, all genuine and sincere healers in all cultures undergo rigorous training programs that may last several years.

Dr. Torrey observes that the same techniques of therapy are used by healers regardless of whether one finds them in hogans or in Park Avenue suites. "It is this aspect of therapy that is the most difficult to see in cross-cultural perspective," he comments, "because we would like to believe that the techniques used by Western therapists are 'scientific' and those used by therapists elsewhere are 'magical.'

"In fact, this is wrong. We have failed to see this because we have confused our technology with our techniques; whatever goes on in a modern office must be science, whereas what goes on in a grass hut must be magic. We have also confused education with techniques; we assume that a Ph.D. or M.D. only does scientific things, whereas a person who is illiterate must do magical things

. . . But there is no technique used by Western therapists that is not also found in other cultures."

On November 25, 1972, Dr. Bernard Grad, an associate professor in the Department of Psychiatry at McGill University in Montreal, told a seminar on "The Mind in Search of Itself" at Washington, D.C., that the laying on of hands is an actual healing force. Because of a series of experiments which he has been conducting with a healer, Oskar Estebany, since the 1950s, Dr. Grad believes that the healing effects of such energy are real and that further research might produce substantial medical benefits.

In an interview with Tom Harpur, Religion Editor of the Toronto *Star* (December 16, 1972), Dr. Grad said that he believes the religious rite of laying on of hands releases an actual force or energy that can be tested under laboratory conditions. In addition, the Montreal biologist is also convinced that an "unseen energy or vital force" is released in all forms of human contact, from a kiss to simply shaking hands.

"It's what every mother knows," Dr. Grad told Harpur. "You comfort a child by holding it. I believe it happens when food is blessed by grace . . . or when a woman prepares her cooking with love. What is new in my work is that we have shown this energy to be something real and verifiable. It is at its peak in healers. . . .

"My personal experience is that there are different qualities of healing energy. A personal element of the healer may go along with this power and if he himself is not moved by true selflessness and concern for others, the results could be negative . . . The healer must be concerned about his own spiritual state and live a moral life."

Inspired by the work of Russian scientists with kirilian photography, wherein objects display brightly colored coronas around their edges and the hands of healers appear to have extra wide coronas, Dr. Thelma Moss, a UCLA psychologist and Dr. Marshall Barshay, a Veterans Administration kidney specialist, are investigating the powers of men and women who claim to cure illness by the "laying on of hands." Dr. Moss said in a recent interview that she strongly believed that they were making visible "something which radiates from the body of a person with healing power."

The series of experiments which Cleve Backster, the polygraph expert, has been conducting with plants is relevant to a discussion of healing, because the demonstrations of Backster Research Foundation imply that all life is one, that there is a signal linkage which exists among all living things, that there is unity to all creation. Such a belief is basic to medicine power, as well as to the essential tenets of all great metaphysicians and the inspired men and women of history. How wonderful if science's most sophisticated equipment might offer demonstratable proof of that ancient assertion.

Backster told the *Wall Street Journal* that in addition to giving evidence of a telepathic communication system, the plants monitored by his polygraphs also possess "something closely akin to feelings or emotions. . . . They appreciate being watered. They worry when a dog comes near. They faint when violence threatens their own well-being. And they sympathize when harm comes to animals and insects close to them."

On one occasion when Backster hooked an egg to the polygraph, the recording showed the heartbeat of an embryo chick. Since the egg was a non-incubated, fresh egg with no physical circulatory system to account for the appropriate 170 beats per minute, Backster has theorized that there might be an "energy field blueprint" which provides a rhythm and pattern about which matter may coalesce to form organic structures.

In an article on Backster's work in *Psychic* magazine, John W. White asks: "Does the 'idea' of an organism precede its material development? Perhaps this is evidence for what the Bible and Plato say: In the beginning was the Logos—the structuring principle of the thought-form of the entity-to-be."

Dr. Harold Saxton Burr hypothesizes in his *Blueprint for Immortality* that man, animals, and vegetables have distinctive electrical field patterns. Since all protoplasmic systems have inherent electrodynamic fields and since every living system is composed of protoplasm, a reactive tissue, every organism thereby possesses the progenitor of a nervous system because it is also composed of protoplasm. Dr. Burr told John White that there was a universality to the electrodynamic field phenomena: "It's everywhere, all through the universe and all through you and me and plants—a field that can be measured by electrical instruments."

Quetzalcoatl's promise would achieve increased fulfillment if the proliferation of the same technology which subdued the redman were to be the very instrument which would prove that the essence of the Great Spirit's power flows through all living things.

10. The Spirit World Is Always Near

We have already noted that the belief that the barrier between the world of spirit and the world of man is a very thin one is an integral part of Amerindian medicine power, but we have yet to examine the phenomenon of the "shaking tent," wherein the medicine man displays his mediumistic gift. The shaking tent ritual seems quite likely to have originated among the Eastern tribes, such as the Huron, the Algonquin, the Chippewa, and several of the Canadian tribes.

The medicine man constructs a lodge or tent in which he is to sit—sometimes naked or bound tightly with rawhide—during the ritual (one thinks of the Spiritualist minister's spirit cabinet). He lights his pipe, offers its smoke to the four directions. When the invocation has been made, the people sit in silence and watch to see the spirits come. The medicine man sings and a few chanters join. The lodge begins to shake. There is a noise and confusion thought to be the sound of spirits arriving from the four corners of the earth. The first spirit to arrive is that of an earth spirit, whose function will be to interpret for the others. Whenever a spirit arrives, a heavy blow is heard on the ground and the lodge shakes violently. When all of the spirits have arrived, the ethereal council begins. The sound of many voices is heard in the lodge, each voice distinctly different from the others. The people sit listening to the sounds in silent awe and expectation. The sacred lodge is filled with spirits of great power that have come at the bidding of the medicine man. The messages may now be given.

Those assembled may expect to receive information which will reveal the cause of certain maladies and will dictate the course of future actions. Someone wishes to know what illness besets her child. Another asks where they will find the body of an uncle who drowned in the lake. A grandmother soberly inquires if her man's spirit has been permitted to enter the Place of Departed Spirits. After each question—if the presents of tobacco are deemed acceptable—the lodge is roughly shaken and a spirit gives a direct answer.

Such tents and lodges are still used by both Amerindian medicine people and Spiritualist mediums. In the August 1969, issue of *Fate* magazine, W. D. Chesney—who describes himself as an ardent, lifelong Spiritualist—tells readers how to build "A Trick-Proof Spirit Cabinet":

> It consists of a cone-shaped tent made of opaque material with only one opening to permit entrance. Its heavy cloth floor is glued and sewed to the tent. The very peak of the cone is left open—but securely screened—for ventilation and other ventilation holes around the base of the teepee are also screened. Peepholes with hinged covers are provided, should investigators wish to look within the teepee. . . . Once constructed, the teepee is completely portable and can be taken anywhere and set up in a few minutes. It may be suspended from a tree branch or from a simple tripod made from three poles tied at the top.

Chesney, in addition to giving precise directions for the spirit teepee's construction, relates some eerie anecdotes involving its usage.

"I have witnessed genuine materializations of discarnate spirit entities," he writes. "I lived among the Indians in [Oklahoma] for many years and I saw Caucasian mediums with Indian guides [spirit controls] produce almost unbelievable phenomena."

Chesney believes, as do many Spiritualists, that American Indian spirit guides provide the strongest links between the worlds of spirit and flesh.

On the wall opposite my writing desk I have a magnificent chalk drawing of my Amerindian spirit guide, Big Arrow, which was presented to me by the Spiritualist artist Stanley Matrunick. Years ago, I made a present of an antique Amerindian bust from my study to a medium friend, who had told me that it was the exact image of her guide, Shooting Star. In essence, since the advent of modern Spiritualism in 1848, we have had a native Anglo-American religion based upon metaphysical insights of the Indian in which the alleged spirits of Amerindians serve as intermediary "saints," who channel information through mediums, guide the confused spirits of the recently deceased to higher planes of spiritual development, and make these same spirits available for communication with their loved ones.

Recently, I asked the well-known Chicago medium and former Spiritualist minister Deon Frey, why Indian spirit guides were so popular with Spiritualists:

The American Indian was close to Nature and already in the proper vibratory force when the Europeans arrived on this continent. The whole secret to metaphysics is getting in tune with the Universe. When you are in tune with the Universe, your awareness opens naturally. You become a part of all. Because the Indian was close to Nature and was in this vibratory force, the Indian spirits have a great strength and power. They come through [to the medium] much easier than other spirits do. Their great strength makes you know that they are really living and that they are really a part of this great creative force which is in existence.

In about 1948, when I had a Spiritualist church, I used to hold seances in the basement. I used to sit on the cabinet [in the manner of the medicine man in his "shaking lodge"] for materializations at least three times a week. Because of my meditations and my regular sessions, great strength was building up. One night the power was so strong in my cabinet that I left it and walked out among the people in the circle.

No sooner had I taken a seat when an Indian [spirit] walked out of the cabinet and crossed the room to stand in front of me. He was all dressed in his feathers and everything. He stood right on my toes to let me know that he had weight and substance. When he turned to walk back to the cabinet, why, it almost pulled my solar plexus out! He was using my energy to help him materialize.

This Indian spirit materialized in front of all those people to show that such things are possible. Indian spirits especially are able to get the right vibratory force built up at the right time so that they may appear. They may not stay too long, but at least they make you aware that they are really there.

One of the greatest lessons that the whiteman has to learn is that even though he did terrible things to the Indian, the Indian spirits love him and would like to try to help the whiteman. They claim that one day they will be leading the whiteman, because this is their mission. They are a forgiving race and have great spirituality.

Mrs. Vada Hill provided me with a report of a sitting with the well-known medium Charles Swann at Camp Chesterfield, Indiana, on July 30, 1972, during which his spirit guide, Crazy Horse, materialized.

Mr. Swann's basement is paneled, and this same paneling has been placed around a support which is several feet out from the four walls. Crazy Horse told us he wanted to show us his *coup* stick. He said he would pass it in front of us so we could see it. From my position, the stick moved horizontally from the darkness on the left toward the right, then left into the darkness again. About two and one half feet of the stick was visible at one time. Each feather represented a brave deed. As the stick was being passed in front of us horizontally, the feathers hung straight down.

Then Crazy Horse told us that he was going to materialize to show us that he was a handsome Indian. He appeared, life-sized, in bust form. Instead of a perfect profile, his head was turned toward us, perhaps an inch.

All these materializations were taking place, not in the very center of the room, but well away from any wall, the bottom edge of the "pictures" being approximately four and one half feet from the floor. These displays were very much like "old-time" movies, the film of which had dulled with age from black and white to a brown and white. I am saying this to explain the color, not the outline of the pictures. They were complete in themselves, and were not "run" on something used as a screen or backdrop.

Al G. Manning, a Spiritualist minister who conducts the unique ESP Lab in Los Angeles, told me that when he began seeking spirit contact in the late 1940s and early '50s, the first spirits he encountered were those of two American Indians:

It began with meditation in front of a mirror. They would project their symbols on my forehead. It was kind of frightening at first. Imagine seeing a full owl's head with all the intricate feathers appearing on the bare part of your forehead and going on up into your hair, for instance. This Indian gave me the name Wise Owl, and he became a very good friend and guide on the intellectual level.

When the other came to me, I would see one eye appear in my hairline and the other on my forehead. Then I would see the long, slender, and very hairy face of a fox. This spirit gave me the name of Cunning Fox. The two of them worked with me for several years before I had much in the way of other spirit contact.

The spirit of a medicine man named Wild Eagle comes often to assist us with our healing work. When he manifests, one can smell a peculiar kind of herbal incense. One night there were about twenty people in the room, and I looked up to see the bright spirit form of Wild Eagle in the corner. He was wearing the traditional buffalo horns of the medicine man, and everybody in that room will guarantee that they knew a spirit was there.

When we do our healing work, we ask a little mental prayer requesting the spirit people who are near to assist us in bringing the right energies to us. We work on the chakras, or psychic centers, to clean them out; and we also apply the light energy directly if there is a bad problem on the leg or the arm or somewhere.

When the medicine men participate in the healing work, things usually become a bit more dramatic. It is my experience that when they assist us, there is a good flow of energy. You feel the chakras cleaned out and you have put the trouble aside in a period of two or three days—or two or three weeks, depending on how bad the situation was.

Bess Krigel is an English teacher in the Chicago public schools, an instructor in ESP at Maine Township Adult Evening School in Des Plaines, and minister of the Church of the Divine Spirit of the Living God, 3300 West Lawrence Avenue, Chicago:

As you may know, Indians thought that they went to the "Happy Hunting Ground" after dying, and that their duty was to come back and help their fellowman. As a result of this belief, the Indian went to an astral plane close to earth, where his spirit could touch the earth plane easily. Spiritualists find it very easy, then, to use Indians as helpers and assistants on this plane.

I have a wise old medicine man, Red Arrow, who is one of the guides and helpers at my church. He is a stately old wise man, full of dignity and knowledge, a keeper of wisdom and a disseminator of universal truth.

Recently, a woman of about forty came into my church. She was very tall and erect, wore moccasin-type shoes, and styled her long straight black hair into two plaits. She had high cheekbones and a dark, olive complexion. When I got into her vibrations I received a strong Indian influence, and I "got" her working with her hands making baskets and making pictures with seeds and berries.

She laughed and told me that she had nothing to do with Indians, but she did admit that she liked to work with her hands on the projects I had mentioned. She added that she was of German descent.

German! With that peculiarly erect carriage, long black hair, and dark skin?

"I love Nature and love to do handiwork projects connected with it, but I know no Indians. I have always worn my hair like this, too, long before long hair was fashionable. My husband likes it this way, too."

She was the walking embodiment of an Indian maiden. This is
a direct past-life influence making itself known in the subject's dress,
appearance, and hobbies.

Whether one cares to explain the phenomenon by citing a collective guilt response or an idealization of a people who live a
less complicated life next to Nature, the fact remains that here
in the United States alone we have more than 250,000 members
of Spiritualist churches who have built a cosmology around the
Amerindian. Spirits of departed Amerindians are called upon for
healing, for material and spiritual guidance, and for personal support in any number of earth-plane undertakings. Just as the Roman
Catholic has his saints to serve as intercessors and intermediaries,
so has the Spiritualist his Indian guides. Icons of Indian guides
are found in nearly every Spiritualist home and are available for
sale at every Spiritualist camp, convention, and meeting place. Indian medallions are worn about the neck in the fashion of rosaries,
and Amerindian icons even take the place of dashboard saints in
Spiritualist automobiles.

"Indians can be used to find parking places," Bess Krigel told
me. "My friend Robert Quinliven told me about this several years
ago. Now when I need them to clear my way through traffic jams
or to find parking places, I call out (to myself of course!), 'Indians,
clear the way through this jam.' Or, 'Indians, get me a parking
place near this place.'

"Another medium, Fred Haase, told of one time when he circled
the block three times looking for a parking place after he had
sent his Indian out. Fred got very irritated at the failure of his
Indian to find the place and said, 'Chief Thunder Cloud, you've
certainly fallen down on the job.' With that, a car suddenly pulled
out right in front of Fred, barely missing his car. Fred said he
very sheepishly apologized to his Indian after parking his car."

Amerindian spirit guides are summoned for instruction in better
living here on the earth plane, as well as being relied upon for
guidance to Summer Land, the Spiritualist equivalent of the

"Happy Hunting Ground." Most of the guides' sermons, however, give evidence of ecumenism and liberally incorporate elements of Christian and Eastern philosophy. Great Bear, a spirit teacher, had these words on "The True Reality of Freedom" recorded in *The Golden Era,* a publication of The University of Life, 5600 South Sixth Street, Phoenix, Arizona:

> . . . There shall not be embarrassment that one shall express of love. There shall not be the barriers—the bars that shall be set in the way that there may be the expression, one for another. For it was said in the words of the man Jesus, Honor thy God and love thy God, with all thy heart and soul, and love thy neighbor as thyself. Without definition, my children, without boundary, without decree; it was not said love only a little bit. It was not said love only that which may be displayed within the jaded eyes of society. Rather was it said, Love thy neighbor as thyself.

On Thanksgiving Day, November 23, 1972, the spirit teacher Black Cloud contacted Nada-Yolanda, medium of the Mark-Age MetaCenter in Miami, with these thoughts:

> Let us collapse time and capsule all events, making this day as though it were the first true Thanksgiving Day. Our Indian astral forces are in agreement and united that we should begin anew in '72. Starting from now, we will work in true spiritual harmony and brotherhood, as we intended and tried to do on that first feast day more than three hundred years ago.
>
> Let us erase the karma that exists, burying our grievances, our mistakes and our misunderstandings of one another through love and cooperation. Let us go forward from this day onward giving thanks to our Great Spirit, sharing together the harvest of all our labors as true sisters and brothers of the One, our Father-Mother God.

And—most importantly for the Spiritualist—in addition to healing, guiding spirits of the departed to higher planes of existence, and teaching great metaphysical lessons, the Amerindian spirit guides serve as the strongest link between the two worlds of flesh and spirit and are thus able to usher the spirits of the departed back to the seance circle so that they may communicate with their loved ones on the earth plane. Just as a belief in a total partnership with the world of spirits and the ability to make personal contact with those who have changed planes of existence is a basic tenet of Amerindian medicine power, so does such a belief form the very basis of the Spiritualist doctrine.

My friend Bertie Marie Catchings, the extremely talented seeress from Dallas, Texas—although not a Spiritualist in the strict definition of the term—was kind enough to share her experiences with Amerindian spirit guides with me. In Bertie's own words, we will be able to find evidence of the strength psychic sensitives of all colors and metaphysical persuasions seem to discover in the vibratory force of the Amerindian spirit:

When I was about five years old my grandfather, Will Clampet, had a wart growing on his eyebrow. Doctors, friends, and relatives all had suggestions—from castor oil to expensive salves—which they thought would get rid of the wart. These treatments did nothing—except, perhaps, to cause the wart to grow.

One Saturday afternoon while I was with my grandfather in Rockdale, Texas, an old man approached us. "I am an Indian and my people have many ways to make people well. I can tell you how to get rid of that wart if you will promise to do exactly what I tell you to do."

My grandfather smiled and said, "I'm willing to try anything. I've tried many things already that didn't work. I might as well try your remedy."

"You take the yoke of an egg and mix it with salt until it is thick. Then you put this on the wart and cover it with a white cloth and do not remove the cloth until three days have passed. When you remove it, the wart will be on the cloth and it will never come back on your head." The Indian vanished quickly as soon as he had given the remedy.

My grandfather followed the Indian's instructions. By now many relatives and friends were very interested in grandfather's wart. It took forever for those days to pass so that we could watch the unveiling of grandfather's eyebrow. The Indian's words were true. The whole wart and its roots were stuck to the white cloth, and it never grew back again.

One afternoon about a year later I was watching my grandfather nail some boards on the side of our farmhouse. Suddenly the board and hammer fell to the ground, as my grandfather grabbed his thumb. "A splinter broke off and went in below the fingernail," he explained, as he tried to draw it out with the blade of a pocketknife.

Suddenly, we looked up and saw the same old Indian standing beside us. He was holding a prickly pear plant by the root.

"Little girl, get me a white cloth," the Indian said as he broke the root of the prickly pear and began to put the milky substance on my grandfather's thumb.

I quickly found some white cloth in my grandmother's rag box and gave it to the Indian. He tied the cloth neatly around Grandfather's thumb. Then, smiling, he said, "In the morning the splinter will be on the cloth. The soreness will be gone."

"Thank you," my grandfather said as the Indian quickly walked away.

"Where did that man come from? What did he want? How did he know what to do for your thumb?" I poured questions at my grandfather.

My grandfather had a faraway look in his eyes as he answered slowly. "I don't know." Then he pointed to the sandy path where the Indian had stood and where he had walked away.

"Look, Bertie Marie, there are no tracks here except yours and mine. It could be that you and I are the only people who have ever seen the old Indian. Remember that day in town when he appeared? Several of my friends were nearby when he came, but none of them remembered seeing a person of his description."

The next morning, when my grandfather removed the white cloth, the splinter was on it, and Grandfather said that the soreness was all gone.

Now that I'm much older, sometimes in dreams I see the old Indian and he tells me things, but not as much as I would like to know. One night in a dream he remarked, "Who ever heard of an Indian with white hair?" I did not understand the dream.

The next night a young man came for a reading. Suddenly I had an urge to tell him about my dream and ended by asking, "Does this mean anything to you?"

The young man thought for a minute. He answered, "Oh yes, I know what it means. My grandfather is a descendant of Quannah and Cynthia Parker. He had platinum blond hair, and people often remarked that it was most unusual for a person who was part Indian to have blond hair."

Sometimes when I give especially interesting readings, a spirit is standing on my right side, whispering things in my ear as pictures flash on and off on a wall before me. The spirits are different. Some are old friends, like the Indian.

Last week I was giving a difficult reading. My client asked, "What about my ninety-six-year-old mother?"

The name "Joe" was written on the wall. I said, "I see, Joe."

"That's my father, Joseph, who's dead," she remarked.

Then on the wall I saw great rolling clouds of water that looked like the ocean. "Did your mom and dad ever live near a coast?" I asked.

"No. I'm sure that they never did," she replied.

Suddenly the Indian's voice whispered, "Teepee! Storm!"

"Did your folks ever live in a teepee or tent during a storm?" I asked.

The woman thought for a moment, then said, "They sure did. They stayed in a tent while their house was being built. I was born in a tent, and the next day a storm blew it away!"

My Indian friend whispered a message which I gave to my client. "Your mother will pass over into the spirit world soon. Your father is waiting for her. He has waited a long time for this reunion. It will be all right. They will be together soon."

One day a young man with long hair said, "Mrs. Catchings, my girl friend came to see you about a year ago, and you told her that a man by the name of Max would have some trouble on a bridge. My name is Max. Shortly after that reading I did have some very serious trouble on a bridge. Can you tell me something about myself."

My Indian spirit friend seemed very interested in this young man, and he gave me much information, both with pictures and with words.

"You use drugs." I said.

"Yes. That is true," he replied. "What about past lives?"

"You were an Indian. Your father was a high chief. You displeased your father and you were cast out of the tribe. Then you gathered renegades and started your own tribe," I said, for my Indian friend was rapidly filling me in on details.

"That's cool," the young man said. "I've always had a feeling that I might have been an Indian. In this lifetime my father is a colonel, so he's still a big chief. We don't get along. He's a red-white-and-blue man, and I don't believe in violence. I don't think I should fight a war that I didn't start. My old man kicked me out of the house. He doesn't claim kinship to me anymore."

"I hope you and your father work out your differences in this lifetime," I said, "so that you won't have to go through this in another lifetime."

"How do you arrive at your conclusion that my father and I were Indians in another lifetime?" he wanted to know.

"A great many Indians are reincarnated into the world now. Some of them have Indian characteristics. They are nomadic-type people, who drift from place to place, live in the outdoors, camp here and there. They are peace-loving, and they dress in Indian attire—beads, leather suits, moccasins. The different tribes seem to find each other, and each group seems to identify with a particular tribe of Indians," I explained.

"Your answer makes sense." The young man's face lit up with a smile. "I live at the bottom of a cliff in a cave. With your theory, I could have been a cliff dweller in a past lifetime," he said, thoughtfully.

"Yes, and you will recall that it was the Indians who popularized smoking. This is why smoking seems natural for many of your friends, who are Indian reincarnated souls," I said.

"Thank you, Mrs. Catchings. Your theory of reincarnation has helped me to understand many things about myself. I know a great deal about drugs. I have seen what it has done to many of my friends. I don't smoke marijuana as much as I used to. Do you think I'll ever quit?"

"I don't know the answer to that question," I said. "If your desire is great enough, you might quit; but I really don't know."

Perhaps in this age of "man-in-outer-space" the Resurrection of the Great Spirit will find a way into the "inner spaces" of our souls with answers to our many questions.

11. The Peyote Church: Medicine and Mescalito

In a series of three remarkable books—*The Teachings of Don Juan: A Yaqui Way of Knowledge, A Separate Reality,* and *Journey to Ixtlán*—Carlos Castaneda has recorded his apprenticeship to a Yaqui sorcerer named Don Juan. In order to free Castaneda from his conventional, European world view and to permit him to look at life with new eyes, Don Juan invited the young anthropologist to join the communicants at a peyote ceremony. It was here that Castaneda met "Mescalito," the anthropomorphic representation of the protector, the teacher, the guide that many Amerindians believe may be found by ingesting peyote buttons.

Ever the inquisitive reporter-scholar, Castaneda sought to press a clearer definition of Mescalito from his tutor.

Mescalito is not a god; he is a power. Mescalito is outside us, not within. Mescalito may appear in any form, but to those who know him, he is always constant. Mescalito may appear sometimes as man, sometimes as a light.

Since Carlos Castaneda participated in the peyote ceremony and writes of his experiences with psychotropic drugs in poetic language that touches the mystical heart of his readers, *The Teachings of Don Juan* has been looked upon by exponents of drug-induced expanded consciousness as a paean to the drug experience. In recent interviews, however, Castaneda has clarified his position—and the beliefs of Don Juan—by stating explicitly that true power is not to be found through the ingestion of psychotropic drugs.

"I used to think that the psychotropic drugs were the important part," Castaneda told John Wallace (*Penthouse*, December 1972). "I no longer believe that. They were only an aid. Don Juan told me everything he taught me was a means for stopping the world."

In *Psychology Today*, December 1972, Castaneda told interviewer Sam Keen: "Don Juan used psychotropic plants only in the middle period of my apprenticeship because I was so stupid, sophisticated and cocky. I held on to my description of the world as if it were the only truth. Psychotropics created a gap in my system of glosses. They destroyed my dogmatic certainty. But I paid a tremendous price. When the glue that held my world together was dissolved, my body was weakened and it took months to recuperate. . . ."

Castaneda told Keen that Don Juan himself does not regularly use psychotropic drugs, because he has learned to "stop the world" at will. If one behaves like a warrior and assumes responsibility, he does not need aids that will only weaken the body.

Keen remarks that such a statement will come as a shock to many of Castaneda's admirers, who regard him as a patron saint of the psychedelic revolution; but Castaneda goes on to cite the elements in Don Juan's teachings which have been most important to him:

"For me the ideas of being a warrior and a man of knowledge, with the eventual hope of being able to stop the world and see, have been most applicable. They have given me peace and confidence in my ability to control my life. . . . I was always looking within and talking to myself. The inner dialogue seldom stopped. Don Juan turned my eyes outward and taught me how to see the magnificence of the world and how to accumulate personal power. . . ."

One "stops the world" by interrupting the normal flow of one's personal definition of reality. When we reassemble our personal, everyday description of the world, when we refuse to utilize the usual definition of people and things, we will see them as they really are, we will tap the flow of a separate reality.

To be a warrior, as I understand it, means to live one's life as if it were an extended vision quest, constantly accumulating knowledge, wisdom, power. The life of the traditional warrior may best be likened to that of the knight errant. The traditional Amerindian warrior in search of personal medicine power regarded life as an ordeal, the earth as a proving ground where one's courage, patience, and endurance were continually put to the test. To live a life as a warrior, as a knight errant, does not mean that one perceives his challenging dragons within his fellowman, but that one saves his sword, his lance, his arrows for the true enemies— cowardice, weakness, slavish dependence upon others, and the most relentless foe of all, death. "The art of a warrior," Castaneda has said, "is to balance the terror of being a man with the wonder of being a man."

"My apprenticeship is ended," Castaneda told John Wallace. "There is nothing more that Don Juan can teach me anymore. I have all the units of description that the sorcerer needs to proceed by myself. Don Juan, you see, was concerned with giving me another description of the world, another way of seeing, another reality. But I must do it by myself now."

Achieving medicine power, illumination, spiritual insight are, of course, very difficult goals to acquire by oneself. While it may be more admirable to embark alone on the vision quest, should one deny a special gift from the Great Spirit which, if ingested, will permit the communicant to speak to the Great Spirit face to face? Peyote was bestowed upon the Amerindians by the Great Spirit to ease the pain and sorrow they had suffered at the hands of the invading Europeans. Peyote will bring union and redemption of all Indian nations, it has been said, but peyote will not bring revenge. As in the old traditions, for those who attend the Peyote Church, religion and medicine are the same.

The age-old question of whether or not one should supplement his religious sacraments with chemical intensifiers will not be resolved in this book. Rather, it will be the author's intention to provide the reader with an examination of the Native American Church, the Peyote Church, and a discussion of its impact upon the contemporary Amerindian.

The Native American Church has members from nearly every tribe on the North American continent. It is a Christian church (the Triune God and the Great Spirit are the same) with Christian symbology and rituals, yet it incorporates the ideals of the old tradition—each individual is a part of the harmonious creation of the universe; all men are brothers and must live together in peace; the Earth Mother must be treated with respect and gratitude.

Because of the use of peyote in the sacrament, the Native American Church is most often thought of as a development of the Amerindians of the Southwest, where *Lophophora williamsii,* the peyote cactus, is indigenous; but the church's lineage may also be traced to the mystery lodges of the northern tribes. In fact, a good deal of the earliest recorded accounts of the religion are concerned with its presence among the Amerindians of the northern United States and Canada.

Because certain of its congregations have incorporated a variety of the Ghost Dance into the rituals, the Native American Church is thought to be a product of this century. Actually the church dates back at least twenty years before Wovoka, the Ghost Dance missionaries, and the Massacre at Wounded Knee, making it more than a century old.

Estimates as to its membership are difficult to obtain, but the Native American Church may have as many as 300,000 celebrants. Contrary to the general impression held by those outside the church, its trappings serve as more than an excuse to ingest a psychotropic drug; and its principles are shaped by its complex and eclectic, yet harmonious, structure of beliefs and practices.

The members of the Native American Church are universalists. They regard all religions as basically good and but variations on the same theme. They stress humility and love toward all men. They believe that man is weak and sinful and must seek God for his redemption. Peyote offers the communicant a quicker method of establishing contact with the Godhead than do the rituals, ceremonies, and services of any of the other churches.

Meetings of the Native American Church begin at sundown—it seems as though Saturday is the most common evening for meetings—and continue without interruption until sunrise. Members form a line behind the Road Man (minister/medicine man), who faces the door of the hogan, teepee, or lodge (depending upon the section of the country) and utters a short prayer. When the invocation has been completed, all members follow the Road Man into the traditional Indian dwelling.

The Road Man (sometimes called Road Chief), Drum Man, and Cedar Man sit on the west side of the dwelling. Fire Man sits by the door, which is on the east of the circle formed by the church members and by the dwelling itself. The floor is bare earth, generally covered with rugs. A fire burns in the middle of the circle.

An altar in the shape of a crescent moon, representing another traditional mother of man, has been made of wet sand. A line dawn from the center of the altar and from end to end symbolizes the Road of Life, which all men travel from birth to death. The minister, Road Chief, is to serve as a guide along this road for the members of the Native American Church.

The west wall of the dwelling supports pictures of Christ, the Last Supper, perhaps the Madonna and Child. Pictures of water scenes hang on the north and south walls.

When all the members have been seated and have sat for a few moments in meditative silence, Road Man reveals and blesses each of the symbols of the ceremony—a staff with stiff hair tassel, a rattle, an eagle or hawk feather fan, a bunch of sage, a bone whistle, cigarette papers, two beaded pouches: one with native tobacco, the other with powdered cedar bark. After these symbolic items have been blessed, an especially fine Peyote button, Chief Peyote, is placed at the center and on top of the crescent altar on four small branches of sage. The button will not be removed from its exalted position until the end of the ceremony.

Corn husks and tobacco are passed around the circle so that cigarettes might be rolled and smoked for prayers. Fire Man removes a lighted stick from the fire, and it is passed around to be touched to each cigarette. Each smoker releases his prayer with his smoke, and the wispy tendrils rise through the hole in the ceiling to the sky, taking the prayers to God. Fire Man carefully drags some coals from the fire with a curved stick, piles them inside the crescent so that Cedar Man may sprinkle the powdered cedar bark upon them as a fragrant accompaniment to the ascending prayers. Everyone fans the smoke on to himself to indicate his desire to share in the feelings being expressed by the group.

The bunch of fresh sage is passed from member to member, so that each individual might remove a few leaves and rub them on his hands. Sage has traditionally been sacred to the Amerindian, and the peyote people say this is so because sage was the first plant God gave to the Earth Mother.

Except for the tobacco, all things issuing from Road Man must be passed in a clockwise direction. Tobacco may be passed in both directions.

After each member has performed a self-blessing with the sage and the first prayers have been smoked, paper cups are passed with pitchers of peyote tea, which has been made by boiling dry peyote buds. The tea is followed by platters of dry peyote soaked in water and by dishes of fresh peyote. Each person is free to take as many buttons as he feels will be necessary for him to achieve an effective communion.

Road Man now takes the staff and the feather fan in his left hand and the rattle in his right hand. Drum Man takes the drum, which is made of an iron kettle half filled with water and four chunks of charcoal and covered with hide, and begins to beat it in a fast rhythm. Road Man sings four songs, then his staff and rattle and the Drum Man's drum are passed around the circle. The person holding the staff sings and shakes the rattle in accompaniment, while the person next to him drums. Anyone else in the circle who knows the songs joins in, as the drum, staff, and rattle are passed from one celebrant to another. The songs are in the languages of many tribes, but the lyrics express Christian ideas and symbols.

After the first round of songs, Cedar Man requests a special smoke and prayer. Road Man hands him corn husk and tobacco so that he might fashion a cigarette. Fire Man hands Cedar Man a lighted stick, and as Cedar Man smokes, he prays for healing for members of the circle who may be absent because of specific illnesses. He will ask a special blessing for the government of the United States, for the soldiers who serve the nation, for the sick and the poor, for rain so the crops will grow and the grazing animals will have food. He beseeches God to bless the Native American Church, all its members, and all other people who want peace and brotherhood.

At midnight, Fire Man leaves the dwelling and returns with a pail of water and a cup, which he places between the fire and the door. Water is a blessed thing, he says, a thing without which no one can live. He kneels in front of the water pail and asks Road Man for a special smoke so he can give a prayer of thanks for water.

Road Man passes him husk and tobacco, and after he has carefully rolled the cigarette, Fire Man lights it with a fire stick. As he smokes, he exhales the prayer of thanksgiving for the water. His prayer is a lengthy recitation, for he must detail the importance of water to man, beast, and plants.

At the completion of the special prayer, Road Man sings four songs, then blows his bone whistle (if he is fortunate, it will be the traditional eagle bone, perhaps handed down through generations) four times. The water pail and the cup are then passed around the circle, and each member is permitted to take a drink. When the pail reaches Drum Man, he pours water on his drum and shares some of the liquid with the Earth Mother beneath his feet.

After the symbolic sharing, Road Man leaves the dwelling with his staff and his bone whistle, and he sounds the whistle in each of the four directions. He utters prayers, walks about the meeting place, then returns to the circle.

When Road Man rejoins the circle, any member may request a special prayer-smoke. When this has been completed, Road Man will again pass around the staff, rattle, and drum for those in the circle who wish to sing.

After a series of prayer-smokes and the passing of the early morning hours, the Dawn Water Rite is performed in the same manner as the Midnight Water Rite, only this time the water pail and cup are presented by a woman member of the circle, since tradition has it that it was a woman who first discovered the power of peyote (a bit of a reversal on Eve, the fruit-bearing temptress who brought about Adam's fall). At the same time, Fire Man fashions the coals within the crescent into the form of the peyote bird, which carries the soul to God.

Four bowls containing water, corn, fruit, and meat are brought into the dwelling and set between the fire and the door. A special prayer-smoke of thanksgiving for the symbolic meal is said by one of the members of the circle, and the bowls are passed around so that each communicant may receive a small portion from each of the dishes.

Once the symbolic meal has been enjoyed by each of the members, Road Man leads the closing rite of prayers while he returns the peyote symbols to his case. The hide is removed from the iron kettle and the four lumps of charcoal are placed on the glowing coals of the fire. The water from the drum is poured along the upper edge of the crescent altar.

Peyote has been ingested by all present from shortly after the first smoke to an hour or so before the Dawn Water Rite.

"Peyote probably helps the worshipers to stay awake all night," Dr. Robert L. Bergman has observed. "It also seems to affect their mood. It is very difficult to assess the role of pharmacology in producing the group feeling of a meeting. Emotions are deeply felt and freely expressed. Speakers often cry and there is a great sense of communion with God and the other worshipers. It would be easier to assume that these phenomena were caused by peyote if they were not frequently observed in the part of the meeting before any medicine is eaten. It seems likely that the drug does heighten emotionality and make freedom of expression easier, and that each peyotist initially learns that kind of behavior from his drug experience and is able to repeat it without a drug effect but in the same setting."

Dr. Bergman comments that the peyotists affirm that "peyote teaches," and they often speak of learning about the depths of themselves and their problems. "This kind of insight probably is facilitated by the physiologic effect, but it would be a frightening and usually useless experience except for the help that the Road Chief and the other members give each other," he stated.

After each member has participated in the symbolic meal of corn, fruit, and meat, and the Road Man has packed the ceremonial artifacts, the circle leaves the dwelling and walks out into the sun of early morning. Individuals form groups in the manner of disbanding church congregations everywhere to discuss everything from the ceremony to the possibility of rain that weekend. In many locales, the women of the Native American Church serve a potluck meal to all members sometime during the morning, before everyone leaves for his own home.

I asked Dr. Walter Houston Clark, Emeritus Professor of the Psychology of Religion, Andover Newton Theological Seminary, what he thought of the Native American Church.

Dr. Walter Houston Clark: I think the Native American Church has been an exceedingly positive factor in the Indians developing their own sense of Indian identity. Certainly they have every right to be proud of the way they have refused to be pushed around by those who have no understanding of their culture or their religion. I think the fact that they have been willing to be arrested and to be harassed for participating in the kind of religious tradition that has meant much to them is a wholesome sign. I think the Native American Church is an exceedingly important factor in morale for the Indians. I also think that the church is almost equally important for all Americans, because our government guarantees to all inhabitants, all citizens, the right to worship in their own way, without interference from the government. Certainly if the courts do not uphold the right of the Native American Church to worship as it chooses, this will be an equally severe loss for non-Indians; because if the government can outlaw the Indians' religion, it will not be long before certain non-Indian cults will follow.

"Did you undergo any process of preparation for the peyote ceremony in which you participated?"

Dr. Clark: No, they didn't require anything. We had a few hours with them before the ceremony and we shared a meal with them, so there was a certain amount of conditioning. But we made no special effort beyond just being with them and getting to know them a bit better.

One of the things that I particularly noticed was the care that the Indians took with their ceremony as opposed to the carelessness toward so many of those values that white people might find more attractive. For example, the kind of house in which the ceremony was held and the Indians' attention to cleanliness was certainly far below the white standard. But when it came to ceremony, they were meticulous.

I think, perhaps unconsciously, this paradox may have been a rejection of the sort of values that the Indians had not been used to and was also associated with a kind of rejection that they had been given by the white people.

The members of the Native American Church have no drug problems, partly because they emphasize the positive factors in the drug. They permit young people to come to the ceremony as soon as they feel ready. They told us that they had no problem with the young people going off and using peyote outside of the ceremony.

[Dr. Robert L. Bergman has commented: "The rate of seriously negative reactions to peyote among Navajo members of the Native

American Church is probably less than one per 70,000 ingestions. The peyotists hold a positive expectation toward the experience: they place an emphasis on communion rather than withdrawal, an emphasis on adherence to the standards of society, rather than on the freeing of impulses. Though a few people use peyote religiously outside of meetings, this is an uncommon practice. The whole spirit of the religion seems best characterized as communion —with God and with other men."]

"Did you feel comfortable throughout the peyote ceremony?"

Dr. Clark: The Indians were most hospitable and cordial to us and called us their white brothers and sisters. At the same time, we were very much aware of their feeling that a wrong had been done by the whiteman to the Indian; nevertheless, none of us got the feeling that these Indians put the blame on any of us as individuals. There was no satirical or ironic factor in their calling us their white brothers and sisters. After the ceremony was over in the morning, in an amazing way, I found that they had become *my* Indian brothers and sisters. I think that the Indian and the whiteman can be a help and a blessing to one another, provided that each can empathize to some degree with the life-style and the fundamental beliefs of the other.

"The Native American Church is misunderstood by most people," Don Wilkerson said. "Most people here in Arizona seem to think that they are a bunch of drug addicts who perform orgies. This church is an outgrowth of the destruction of our traditional religion and an attempt on the part of many of our people to return to the old ways with a little bit of acceptance on the part of the non-Indian community; therefore, the Native American Church is a mixture of Christianity and older Indian religions. The peyote button is used as a kind of sacred sacrament, but one may belong to the church without taking peyote. It takes so many of the buttons to achieve the proper state that, frankly, many people reject it. It is not the best-tasting thing in the world. Your mouth is dry and you feel like you have been chewing on a piece of wood.

"These people live by commandments, rather than peyote. They neither smoke nor drink. They are generally a hard-working people. All these things that are supposed to be a part of every Christian's religion are really practiced by most Indians in the Native American Church."

"In the Native American Church, we pray," Iron Eyes Cody told me. "We pray out loud, just like at home. I told Father John that I was not a good Catholic. I told him that I belonged to a lot of religions, but especially the peyote religion. We pray more in these peyote meetings from eight o'clock in the evening to eight o'clock in the morning than they do in the Catholic Church. Father John said that he would like to attend a meeting, but at that time we had to stop the white people from coming, because the hippies were coming in and they would try to take over the ceremony.

"I have yet to eat four peyote buttons at one meeting. I have eaten two and three, and probably nibbled on one. They are very bitter. And I have never had too much to confess. We all sin, you know, but some of these people eat these buttons and it makes them confess to the Great Spirit.

"A lot of people have a misconception of peyote. They think we have these ceremonies just so we can dope ourselves, but this is no part of it. We take peyote to learn the true way to God."

Don Wanatee, a traditional Mesquakie, speaks for those Amerindians who are critical of the structure of the Native American Church: "If they want to do that scene, you know, that is their business, but I believe that the Native American Church was a product of an attempt to revive traditional religion by combining it with Christianity. I don't think this is compatible with our traditions.

"When I was younger, I criticized the Native American Church by saying that it was just like a puppy nursing on the Indian religion. When they got older, they kind of weaned themselves, but they still think that they have the old religion. In my opinion, if you took out the Indian religion, the Native American Church would be Christian, just like the white Christian churches.

"As far as peyote is concerned, I have tasted it. I have used it once, because I was asked if I wanted to try it. You know every young kid has to try everything once—like smoking cigarettes or pot. I tried pot once, too, but it didn't tickle me at all. Just like peyote: nothing. If the peyotists want to do their thing, that is fine; but they shouldn't take away from the basic Indian traditions. I will respect their ways. But they don't need to try to convert me, because I will tell them to go to hell."

Sun Bear, medicine man and spiritual leader of the Bear Tribe, accepts the Native American Church as an expression of some people's medicine, but he also advises caution in the use of psychotropic drugs:

"The Native American Church is a good thing for the people who are with it. I have attended their meetings, and I have great respect for the Peyote Brothers.

"The thing that is sad is that many young people who are attracted to the Indian way of life have a couple of peyote buttons flash in their minds, and they think that that is the whole scope of Indian religion or philosophy. This isn't what I see. I can go to the top of the mountain without any additives and get my vision.

"This whole thing was one of the conflicts I had with some of the people who wanted to join the Bear Tribe. Some of them thought that the minute I was away, they needed chemical additives in order to get their vision. I felt that if they wanted Timothy Leary's trip, then they belonged in Berkeley instead of up in the hills and mountains with the brothers who are trying to walk in balance with the Earth Mother without chemical additives."

Both medicine and Mescalito may be regarded as gifts bestowed upon the seeker by the Great Spirit. Each brother and sister must determine during the personal vision quest whether or not one needs a chemical additive to help stretch his soul to the Great Spirit's waiting strength.

12. Do the Hopis Hold the Secret of Amerindian Mysticism?

Carved on a rock near the village of Oraibi, Arizona, in the heart of Hopi land, is a petroglyphic representation that records the prophecy of the Great Spirit in regard to His return.

In the lower left-hand corner are a bow and an arrow, representing the material tools which the Great Spirit, who stands to the right of the implements, gave to the Hopi.

The Great Spirit points to his path, which is straight up. An upper path to the Great Spirit's right is the whiteman's way. Two whitemen and one Hopi—symbolizing the Hopi who forsake the old traditions and adopt other ways—walk this line. A vertical line joins the path of the whiteman with that of the Hopi, indicating their contact since the Hopi's emergence from the Lower World. The Hopi's path is lower, more spiritual, than the way of the whiteman.

A large circle represents World War I, another stands for World War II. A third circle symbolizes the Great Purification, which the Hopi feel is fast approaching, according to a timetable that was set centuries ago.

After this transitional period, the Great Spirit returns; food and water is abundant; the world is made well. The whiteman's path becomes more and more erratic until it is but a series of dots that eventually fade away.

A quartered circle in the lower right-hand corner of the petroglyph is the familiar symbol for the spiritual center of the North American continent, which the Hopi believe is the Southwestern United States, specifically the area around Oraibi.

"At one time I thought my people, the Cherokee, held *the* answer," Don Wilkerson said to me, "but now I tend to believe that the Hopis hold the secret. A lot of this is touchy ground. Much of it is conjecture, but the Hopis have done things that are unbelievable."

In the Hopi myths of their people emerging from one world to another, we may have a poetic accounting of a people's intellectual and spiritual evolution, or we may have exactly what the traditional Hopis claim: the record of major high civilizations that rose and collapsed in prehistorical times. One may call these civilizations Mu, Lemuria, Atlantis, it matters little; but the Hopi myths maintain that the human race has passed through three worlds which the Great Spirit has been forced to terminate, to purify, because of the people's corruption and materialism.

The last Great Destruction was achieved by flood, and all but a few faithful perished. The story of the Great Deluge has survived in the myths of nearly every culture, and it is said that the Hopi and all those faithful who were saved made a covenant with the Great Spirit that they would never again turn away from His path. But now, the Hopi believe, the Fourth World is coming to a close. Men have fallen away from their covenant with the Great Spirit. Once again, a Great Purification is needed.

The Hopis believe that the Great Spirit did interact with the first people and that He taught them how to live and how to worship. He breathed His teachings, prophecies, and warnings on stone tablets, before He hid Himself from the view of man. Spider Woman and her two grandsons, the Great Spirit's helpers, remained, along with other guiding spirits. These tablets were broken in half by the spirit Massau when the Hopis reached this continent. Today the traditional Hopis await the return of the Older Brother,

whose skin has since turned white, who will match his share of
the sacred stone tablets with those retained by his Younger
Brother. The rejoining of the sacred tablets will signal the advent
of Purification Day.

The Hopis were led to their present home in Arizona by a star.
As Abraham dealt with his nephew Lot, the Hopis chose desolate
and infertile land and permitted other tribes to choose the greener,
more fertile valleys. Or so it may seem to those with greedy eyes.
The Hopis settled here because it is the land of the Great Spirit.
In spite of the sparse quality of their home, the Hopis were warned,
strangers would come and try to take it away from them. The
Hopis must resist all pressures, they were told, and they must hold
on to the land and their ancient religion. If they were able to retain
control of their material and spiritual gifts of the Great Spirit and
remain true to their name ("one who follows the peaceful path"),
Hopi land would one day be the spiritual center from which all
Indians would be reawakened to the old traditions and would arise
to touch the hearts and save the souls of the invading strangers.

"There are shrines there in the spiritual center which are mark-
ers for spiritual routes which extend in all four directions to the
edge of the continent," *Clear Creek* magazine quoted an elderly
traditional Hopi. "Through our ceremonies it is possible to keep
the natural forces together. From here at the spiritual center, our
prayers go to all parts of the Earth. Our prayers are the balance
that keep all things well and healthy. This is the sacred place. It
must never be defiled. . . . Only people who know how to grow
things will survive. Through prayer, people can develop their own
way, as the Hopi have."

(That same issue of *Clear Creek, The Environmental Viewpoint*, No. 13, is largely devoted to the crisis at Black Mesa, wherein
coal is being strip-mined for a consortium of twenty-three power
companies [Western Energy Supply and Transmission Associa-
tion]. According to Ms. Melissa Savage: "This land of wide, silent

deserts and deep sky-space will soon contain six giant power plants which will make up the heart of the energy grid. . . . Together all six plants will be able to generate some 14,000 megawatts (MW), yet this is just the beginning. By 1985, the WEST consortium plans to operate plants with a generating capacity of 36,000 MW, 17 times the capacity of Egypt's famed Aswan Dam." Since Black Mesa is considered by the Hopi to be the spiritual center of this continent, one can imagine the horror the uninformed traditionalists experienced when they learned of the planned desecration. Mrs. Mina Lansa told the United States Senate: "We are holding the land for the Great Spirit . . . We heard about the Black Mesa coal mine. The land is ours and Black Mesa is on the shrine that belongs to [Hopi chiefs] and the Spirit gave it to us. We heard that the Hopi Tribal Council members and the Navajo Council members, too, are the ones leasing to the Peabody [Mining Company]. We are very sorry that they never asked permission of us. . . . I am very worried for my people. I don't want them to starve . . . I am like the mother of the earth because I am holding the land. We . . . hold the whole world all over. I am worrying about it all the time. . . ." *How long will we permit commercial interests to upset our continent's spiritual, as well as ecological, balance?*)

The Hopi traditionalists refer to their prophecies and agree that the Older Brother will soon return with his half of the Sacred Tablets. The prophecies state that the Great Purification will occur when people turn to material, rather than spiritual, things; when evil ones set out to destroy the land and the life of the Hopi and other Indian brothers; when leaders of men turn to evil instead of the Great Spirit; when man has invented something which can fall upon the ground, boil everything within a great area, and turn the land to ashes where no grass will grow. It would seem that each of these specifications has been fulfilled.

The Hopis are not alone in their anticipation of a Great Purification. Don Wanatee says the Mesquakie, a people who have proudly maintained the old traditions, see a great catastrophe happening soon to "rearrange things":

It will possibly be a great fire of some type, and it will leave pockets of men and women who will begin to people the Earth again. This is what the prophets of the Mesquakie have maintained. They have prophesied that the many people with their many languages will want to come back to their old religion. These people will want to return to the traditionalists to learn. There are traditional pockets in Mexico and in the United States. People here in Iowa have called us heathens, pagans. We shall see we are all brothers after all.

I think the end might be very near. I am not speaking as a pessimist, but as one who believes in the prophecies of the Mesquakie. A hundred years ago, the Mesquakie prophesied a box that would sit in the corner in which we would see things happening far away and hear people speaking who would not be there. They prophesied great trailways in the sky. They said that the animals would be dying. They said when many species were becoming extinct, man would begin to see unusual things. Floods, earthquakes. It would be as if the Earth were revolting against its inhumane treatment.

Other Indian tribes throughout the country are beginning to see these things coming. Many are saying in desperation, "What can we do to revive the old tradition? How can we get back to it?" Well, there is a way for them to return, of course; but time is very short. They had better start returning now, or else they are going to be left on the railway station when the train leaves. You know, it is all going to be over.

Hopi traditionalists are storing food and water for the coming Great Purification. They have been told that there will be a terrible famine sometime soon—no longer than two or three years in the future. Canned and dehydrated foods, seed, kerosene lamps, bottled water and water purification tablets are being put aside in carefully concealed caches.

The Chicago medium Deon Frey related an interesting experience which she shared with a delegation of Hopi who were traveling to Washington and the United Nations to declare a warning of the coming Time of Purification:

> We went to what they called a Council of Mankind. It was held in the city of Chicago at the university. There were spiritual leaders representing each country in the world. This meeting was unknown to me. I had seen nothing on television, nor had I heard anything about it on radio, or read about it in the newspaper. Someone said that W. Clement Stone, the insurance man, had paid large sums of money to keep it going.
>
> The odd part of it was that we had to be known by someone in attendance before we could be admitted. Without my even knowing I would attend—one of the Hopis, who said he was 103 years old, had invited me—I was ushered in to a seat that had been reserved for me. We were placed in what seemed like separate boxes arranged in a circle. Each representative from these individual countries was to stand and give his view of what he thought the world was coming to and what could be done to save mankind and what we could do to help the people understand what is happening. Each representative wore his own dress and stated the views of his own faith.
>
> We were not allowed outside of the building once the sessions had begun. Lunch was served there and everything was free. After breaks, we would return to the sessions and the individual statements would resume. We were there in session for three days. The Hopis told us about the Older White Brother and the secret of what was to happen in our world.
>
> When the meetings were over, I accompanied the Hopis to a place where they told us more things and said how they would meditate and receive these things directly from Spirit. At that time they already had three years of food stored away. One of the men claimed to have half of the original stone which would fit with the White Brother's other half.
>
> The elderly man explained to me how they traveled at night, by what I would call astral travel. The Hopis visualize themselves in a boat moving on a stream. He said that if I ever wanted to get in

touch with them, I should just visualize myself in a boat coming toward them, and they would be able to pick me up.

I have tried this and it has worked. I have visualized the blue water, the canoe, and myself in the canoe paddling toward them. The Hopi seem to be able to pick up that vibration quite easily. This seems to be one of their ways of attuning themselves to the white-man.

I was given a spiritual name by the Hopis, a name which meant something to them and to me. I was honored that they considered me spiritual enough to accept their ideas and to understand them. Very often we could just look at each other and tell what the other was thinking. We did not always have to use words to communicate. The Hopis are very aware.

The Hopis told about the Great Purification that is coming sooner than we think. This is why they store up food. There will be a great catastrophe, and they believe that their home in the Southwest is the safest place to be.

When non-Indian Paul Solem told the media that he had been sent to the Hopi reservation to "call down" UFOs to present the Hopis with a sign, then produced what the waiting, skeptical press called "a flying saucer" ("It looked like a star—almost. It rose in the sky, stopped, hovered, wavered to one side and then continued across the sky repeating the maneuvers" [Joe Kraus, Managing Editor, Prescott *Courier,* August 9, 1970]), he provoked yet another split among the traditional Hopi. But 109-year-old Chief Dan Katchongva said that both the division and the UFOs are in fulfillment of the old prophecies foretelling the Great Purification:

"A petroglyph near Mishongnovi on Second Mesa shows flying saucers and travel through space. The arrow on which the dome-shaped object rests, stands for travel through space. The Hopi maiden on the dome shape represents purity. Those Hopi who survive Purification Day will be taken to other planets. We, the faithful Hopi, have seen the ships and know they are true. We have watched nearly all our brethren lose faith in the original teachings and go off on their own course. Near Oraibi was closely shown the Plan of Life, and we are gathered here to await our True White Brother."

Paul Solem claims that the UFOs are piloted by a people descended from the Ten Lost Tribes of Israel. The Hopi share this lineage, and the Great Star which led them to Oraibi was a guiding UFO. Certain Hopis state that the ships are manned by Kachinas, entities which are portrayed in traditional Hopi dances.

"I doubt very much if you will find another Indian who will tell you this," I was told by an Amerindian who has made a study of the origins of his people, "but I don't believe that there is any doubt whatsoever that there are Indian people on the face of this Earth who did not originate on this planet. I tend to think that once the Hopi prophecies are carried out and their revelations are made known, they will bear this out. The Hopis came from *out there.*"

"Many people have said that our picture-craft is nothing but primitive doodling," White Bear, a Hopi historian and traditionalist remarked, "but centuries and centuries ago, the Hopi drew a jet airplane on a rock which depicted our people arriving from the birthplace of our fathers. Yes, centuries ago, we had a picture-craft of a flying saucer."

White Bear provided the drawings and source material for the classic Frank Waters volume *The Book of the Hopi.* Since I am honored to count White Bear and his charming wife Naomi as friends, I have the privilege of including an interview with White Bear in this book.

"Do you agree with me that the power, richness, and relevance of Amerindian magic are being reborn in our decade?"

White Bear: That is a positive truth. As far as our side of knowledge is concerned, this is due to the planetary system which is forcing man to come to full realization and to see that this may be obtained from our tribal religious order.

There are certain events that are taking place now which we know give evidence that the old traditions are regaining strength.

These activities are going on in the atmosphere, as well as in human affairs. This is why, as a Hopi, I am very concerned that people are coming to full realization now.

"What special insights might you, as a wise man of your people, share that will help us all come to full realization?"

White Bear: As far as the events that are occurring in our nation today, this is an important part of our prophecies. There is so much evidence here [Oraibi] that I can give, but I am concerned how many people will get to realize it and acknowledge it. In the first place, I will have to get rid of my skin before everyone will accept my knowledge. Prejudice is a great barrier.

"Skin color offers no barrier between brothers of the soul; but, unfortunately, for some, pigmentation does present a problem."

White Bear: Well, that has been the greatest opposition to the white people accepting our knowledge and recognizing what we can bring to them. My uncle made a trip to Washington back in 1890 and tried to warn the government about the events in time that would take place.

"You feel that a message of great importance has been presented to contemporary man in your ancient Hopi prophecies, but that this message has been continually ignored."

White Bear: Exactly. But who are we? We are not an aggressive people. We are not going to make any kind of aggressive movement against someone who is doing wrong to us. We leave all things to our Divine Creator to straighten up.

"We see now more Amerindians reviving interest in their native traditions and in their native religious philosophies."

White Bear: Yes, but you see two types of Indian movements. There are two types of forces that are now active. One is the aggressive, and the other is a spiritual movement. The spiritual movement will prevail and become stronger, because the aggressive force will get caught up in national affairs and lose sight of important issues.

"What is your opinion of the use of psychotropic drugs as an aid to spiritual development?"

White Bear: To tell you the truth, for those who truly wish to advance in spiritual ways, to resort to marijuana, peyote, and these other things is wrong. Completely wrong. I cannot go along with these things. My people cannot.

"You are saying that there are no shortcuts to true spirtuality?"

White Bear: That is right. You have to start from within. You cannot receive your upliftment from chemicals. Meditate. Receive important messages from your dreams.

"Do you feel that the religious traditions of Europe and Asia—Christianity, Buddhism, Judaism, etc.—may be compatible with your ancient traditions?"

White Bear: According to that part of the prophecy, there will be a spiritual awakening in the continents you mention, but they must come to America. This is where the freedom was. This is where the true spirit of the Brotherhood was established. Regardless of how many religious orders they may have set up thousands of years ago, we are the people who have not contaminated the true spiritual knowledge.

"White Bear, can you speak frankly about our future survival as a species?"

White Bear: If you want me to say that we are going to clean up this mess that has been made, I cannot. The pollution of our atmosphere is the worst thing that man has done. This pollution will get into our soil and into the physical parts of our people, as a whole race of mankind. Worse, not only will people's bodies be contaminated, but their spirits. The Hopi are trying their best to awaken all the nations of the world to this part of our prophecy.

"Do you see any particular areas that will be healthier after the Great Purification?"

White Bear: As far as our knowledge is concerned, the area within one hundred miles of Oraibi is the best. Scientists have found no evidence of contamination of our soil. There is no radioactive fallout. That is why we are here. That is why we came here centuries ago. We had full knowledge of this before we came.

"What is so mystical about that area around Oraibi?"

White Bear: If you had been here with us and with our guests from Europe, from India, from Japan, from Korea, you would have felt this strong feeling. [White Bear was mildly put out with me at the time of this interview, because I had been unable to witness a special ceremony due to a personal complication which prevented me from being in attendance.]

"When do you look for the return of the Older White Brother?"

White Bear: Some people think, you know, that this refers to the modern whiteman, but this is not so. We refer to the spiritual brother who has understanding of all kinds. He is not of human flesh at the moment, but he will come. Certain aggressive actions by nations, who call themselves the Great Powers, will set in motion a certain event that will lead to the coming of the True White Brother.

"Do you see this happening before the end of our century?"

White Bear: Not quite. All has been arranged. There is nothing new. There has been a great program laid out. Everybody has to go by the schedule of the weeks. The weeks run from Sunday to Sunday. There are certain things that people may do in between, but they must arrive at the next Sunday. There are things on the great program that may take years and years to be fulfilled, but all things are laid down on the schedule.

"And everything is going according to schedule?"

White Bear: That is right. In fact, we are now delaying the schedule by fifteen years.

"The schedule is now fifteen years behind?"

White Bear: That is right. I wish you would have been here to witness the ceremonies, and you would have known exactly what is going on.

"What do you think is happening now with non-Indian youth who are seeking to emulate the Indian life-style and religious philosophy?"

White Bear: There are great universal powers which are making young people get into these activities without their having full knowledge. Unfortunately, not all of these young people are motivated by spiritual things, and they are destructive.

"Can their energies be made constructive, rather than destructive?"

White Bear: I wish it could be that way. As far as their adopting our tribal ways and customs, we are trying to keep ourselves clean. The opposite force is being used among these young people. It is the wrong kind.

"What guidance can you give young people to make their lives more positive?"

White Bear: Many of these young people come from wonderful people, but until they learn the true way of getting on the right course of the spiritual life through meditation, this opposite force will continue to motivate them. Some speak of having lived before as Hopis. I am positive this is not so. They are more aggressive in their way of conduct than I would be if I were being reborn again.

"So when young people come to you, you look at their spiritual attitude; and you find that it is more aggressive than it should be."

White Bear: That is right. When you deal with the human action on the opposite side, well, then you know their spiritual attitude just isn't right. They are too rebellious. But I am trying my best to do what I can to try to help our nation's young people.

We Hopis have our doctrine and complete, full knowledge in our sacred tablets. You know that Naomi and I are going to present this evidence in our new book that we are working on. What we have can offer true spiritual guidance for modern man. This has to be brought out in the type of work that you are doing. We Hopis are the only people who have this knowledge within our souls. We have kept ourselves uncontaminated.

If the Hopis hold the secret of Amerindian mysticism, then it is a secret that has to do with the Amerindians'—and perhaps all peoples'—true place of origin and the true nature of man's spiritual inheritance. The Hopis claim that mankind has been engaged in

its struggle for spiritual perfection for aeons longer than our orthodox science can either conceive or acknowledge. If the Hopis'
tablets record more than a symbolic representation of man's social,
intellectual, and metaphysical evolution and do actually carry an
account of the progression of sophisticated civilizations that have
risen and fallen as the victims of their own materialistic technolo-
gies, then the Hopi prophecies indicate a time spiral, a calendar
of time, that warns us that our own days are numbered and that a
Great Purification is overdue. Now, more than ever before, mankind needs to walk in balance and become receptive channels to
the Great Spirit.

13. Walk in Balance

O Great Spirit, bring to our white brothers the wisdom of Nature and the knowledge that if her laws are obeyed this land will again flourish and grasses and trees will grow as before. Guide those that through their councils seek to spread the wisdom of their leaders to all people. Heal the raw wounds in the earth and restore to our soil the richness which strengthens men's bodies and makes them wise in their councils. Bring to all the knowledge that great cities live only through the bounty of the good earth beyond their paved streets and towers of stone and steel. [Jasper Saunkeah, Cherokee]

It was from Sun Bear, the Chippewa medicine man, that I first heard the expression "Walk in Balance." That brief prayer-admonition presents the crux, the essence, the ideal, not only of Amerindian medicine power, but of all positive metaphysical doctrines.

"Regrettably, Sun Bear, not everyone can go out into the hills and go to the mountaintop. Is it possible to walk in balance, to practice the ideals of Amerindian medicine if one lives in the concrete canyons of some large city?"

Sun Bear: You can practice medicine in the city or in any other place. I strive to practice it right here. Sometimes, you know, I have to stand aside for a while and just keep within my heart what I believe. A lot of people still can't comprehend medicine, but I don't put it out of my mind or out of my life just because there are people who are not yet capable of understanding it.

"I am fortunate enough to live out with the nature forces—the hills, the trees, the trout streams—here in northeast Iowa. I need this for my balance. But we must recognize that many of our brothers and sisters live crowded together in the cities. Some of the traditionalists have told me that they have to get back to Pine Ridge, to the Black Hills, to the mountains before medicine will work most effectively."

Sun Bear: This is true within the hearts of many of those people. Right now I am working—between work on *Many Smokes* magazine and other things—to find ways to help keep some of my Indian brothers and sisters on the reservations so they don't have to come to the city and pay a hundred and fifty dollars a month rent, utilities, and the rest of the crap. I am trying to work it out so that by marketing their arts and crafts and other items, they might earn a hundred dollars extra to supplement their income and allow them to continue to live comfortably where they are.

"You would agree with me that the psycho-religious system of the Amerindian may offer relevant spiritual guidance and a workable structure of applied metaphysics for modern man?"

Sun Bear: I would agree with you. I think we offer a pattern of balance. We may not have all the answers that pat. Or maybe we have *all* the answers, but we don't have them in a manner that can be interpreted in a manner to be everything for everybody.

You know, I accept a lot of the teachings of Gandhi. I think he was a great man. I find a lot of harmony with what he taught. I find no disharmony with the teachings of the Carpenter of Nazareth, either. But I mean the *real* things he spoke of.

"*Christ*ianity, then, not *Church*ianity."

Sun Bear: Yes, I find that some of the double-mouthed bastards who go around claiming to rep for him and who put their blessings on the various military regimes of whatever country they inhabit are not my species of man.

"But you do feel that medicine power can be used in any environment?"

Sun Bear: Yes. I have to deal with the world every day. I don't feel that I have to retreat into a cave with my rattle like some of my people want me to do. I don't feel that I have to be the kind of holy man who gets out of contact with the world. I feel that a good portion of my medicine is a battle with the world as it is now, trying to rectify, trying to build things that are beneficial both for my Indian people and my non-Indian people.

"I personally applaud such a position. I have always felt that the holy man must be with the people, struggling with contemporary society as it exists, not sitting somewhere as a recluse, contemplating his navel."

Sun Bear: Yes, I have used that same "contemplating the navel" reference. Maybe I quote it too often, because I don't feel that just crying "OM" and so forth is the total sum of humanity. If you aren't in the battle with life, doing something worthwhile for humanity, then it just isn't there. Cesar Chavez is a holy man in his way.

The other thing of it is that you have to watch so that you don't misuse power. I have known both Indian and non-Indian leaders who have used power as a whip to take things for their own gain. Power is something you have to watch. You must maintain a balance.

I try to ingrain in the Bear Tribe that we don't have to be a breechcloth-dragging outfit. Eating regularly is not immoral, either. One of my very close associates wanted me to set up a hierarchy, where nobody could talk to me except by special interview and so forth, but I couldn't see that.

"I think we have enough hierarchies, secret societies, and exclusivities as it is."

Sun Bear: Everyone must learn to walk with a good balance. They must learn that I can't just give them a daily transfusion of medicine power. This has been the problem of a lot of people who come to us saying they don't want the Establishment anymore, but they don't have the ability to balance themselves yet. This is where the big struggle is. It is a hard thing for the man who has not yet learned to carry the law within himself and to walk as a brother.

"This is a hard thing. It is a contest for which one must constantly train. One must stay in good spiritual condition, as well as good physical condition. We have never been told it is going to be easy."

Sun Bear: My medicine is for every day. It is not a thing for a Sunday treatment. Sometimes the Nez Perce or the Klamath or some other tribe call on me to come up. If my knowledge of economic development or how to create something will be satisfying to them on that level, I am happy to make it that way. I am capable of surviving successfully on that level. Because I have these talents, some people think that I am a promotor and so forth. But I can also take my jackknife out and skin three deer, or I can hoe a couple of acres of corn, if I have to. That is all part of the thing of it.

The sad thing about this society is the fact that they have tried to put everything into little boxes. Religion is in this box, and religion doesn't have anything to do with the growing of corn or the making of love or anything else in those boxes over there. All things can come together in harmony. This is a natural thing, a balance thing. You can be a natural human being, blending in with the balance of everything, and you can be a medicine person, too.

There are a lot of medicine men on the reservations across the country whose work is more with the herbs and with healing. There are different degrees of medicine men. Some work with healing and some work with things of a higher nature, where they call in spirit powers to work with them.

They say that knowledge is also healing. If I can take my medicine and use my knowledge to heal the heads of people who are screwed up and going in six different directions . . . if I can bring a balance to them so that they can walk with a good balance on the

Earth Mother, well, that is medicine and that is where the medicine power lies at this time—in teaching.

If I wanted to go up and spend a month by myself on top of a mountain, I could perhaps generate the power to do some of the things our ancient medicine men did, like teleporting myself or like raising the lodge. This is real power, and it is something that a person can get if he really needs it. Maybe that is the medicine that will be there for me; maybe that is a part of it, but to me, the doing, the teaching, the helping is where my medicine is right now.

Some of the things I must do are just dull, everyday things. We must figure out how to get better distribution for our books and for *Many Smokes,* our magazine. We feel this is good knowledge, and it should be getting out to more people. We must plan how to move our people out on the land where we may have a permanent land basis. This is all part of living.

"You may not be of the world, but you are in it, and you are going to have to survive."

Sun Bear: Right. And it is a good thing. I don't feel restless or agitated, like a lot of other people feel, because they don't have their goals of tomorrow yet today. I feel content in what I am doing. I feel happy.

Don Wanatee is rather dubious about one's ability to practice medicine effectively while living in a large city.

Don Wanatee: I feel that you have to go back to where the "action" is, as they say. I don't think medicine can be practiced as effectively in the cities. I think that many of these Indians have lost their medicine, their religion, and they are trying to find another way to get it back. I would say that their journey, their search, is going to be difficult. I say that they must go back to their religious men to be taught, then they might have a chance.

But, like in our religion, there are so many ways that we must follow. For instance, when women menstruate, they cannot eat with you, they cannot enter a holy area, they cannot take part in the ceremonies. But if you go to a whiteman's church, how many women are menstruating? If you try to practice effective medicine in, say, Los Angeles, *good grief,* how many women are menstruating in the whole city? It would just kill your effectiveness!

Like once when I was going to Iowa State, I decided to play a joke on my holy man, who came to visit me. I said, Let's go riding around and talk. So I bought a six-pack of beer, because holy men are just like other human beings; they like to drink beer sometimes. They are not gods. So I said to my wife, I wonder if I should play a trick on him? I wonder if I should take him through that big women's dormitory? Just give him a tour through that whole dormitory. Just think of all the women who are menstruating. Think how that would destroy his effectiveness! It would be the same in any large city. That is why I leave my medicine tobacco in my room [Don was in Denver when I interviewed him, eager to return to the Mesquakie settlement near Tama, Iowa]. If I carried it with me, it would be killed.

"Do you feel that we may rediscover medicine power today and adapt it for modern man?"

Wanatee: I think in so far as the Indian tribes are concerned, they have been given a way of life, a religion, a belief, a philosophy, or whatever it is; and if they have lost it, then certainly they will have some difficulty getting it back. If they are shown the way by somebody who has fasted and found the path again, I think they can revive it. But as far as white people are concerned, I think they are going to have to do more than just look. They are going to have to exert themselves, not only in the Indian ways, but in their own ways, whatever they may be. Their beliefs will have to be engraved right into their souls.

Most whites believe in some form of Christianity. I hear that the "freaks" [hippies] know the presence of a single God, but they are looking for a means of communication. The Mesquakies have no problem with communication. They have a direct line. They can still do the same things they did three or four hundred years ago.

Some pockets of native belief are still present among the Sioux, but there are a great many areas where they have been converted to some other religion. The Sioux who want to go back to the old traditions have a far better chance of re-creating that religion than do the whites, who wish to acquire this tradition for the first time.

I think that if the whites went back to the type of religion that was first given to them and really practiced it, they would be happier. Indian traditions and non-Indian traditions are not incompatible; but at the present time, I don't think they can really come together. We have maintained our beliefs and they are sacred to us. They demand an intense participation that becomes life itself, a total thing.

Rarihokwats, Editor of *Akwesasne Notes,* recognizes that people other than Amerindians may develop a natural life-style and strive to live in total harmony with the Earth Mother and with the Cosmos, but he issues certain cautions:

The way too many people approach Christianity is to learn a certain number of formulas and rituals, believing that in the words there is some magic. What they don't understand is that those rituals and those words merge and become manifestations of certain feelings and certain attitudes, and that one who recites the Lord's Prayer or something without these feelings and attitudes really isn't achieving anything at all.

There have been a lot of anthropologists who have criticized Indian medicine practitioners today by saying that their words are not accurate. They say they have a recording that was done in 1902 and that the practitioner has changed the words and the ritual isn't correct. Well, of course, the practitioners have changed the words. The feelings and attitudes are the important ingredients.

I think that what is essential for those non-Indian people who are wanting to get something out of medicine power and find something in there for their own lives is that they make sure that they get this not by imitating and copying the Indian, but by developing their medicine in the same way that Indian people have developed this power.

Go to the waters and listen. Try to hear what it is that the waters have to say. What is the essence of the spirit of the waters?

The only formula is to go and sit and listen. This is what the non-Indian should do, rather than trying to take over what has already been developed by the Indians, because I don't think the non-Indian can do it.

On the other hand, we also recognize in other people who are living a natural life-style and who are living in harmony with all things, a high degree of brotherhood and unity. We recognize those people for who they are. I don't think they need to become Indians in the stereotyped meaning of that word. I think that where many people make their mistake is that they are trying to take on an Indian identity, rather than becoming a real person.

I would hope that people would just seek to become real people, whoever they are, and not attempt to be Indian.

I asked Dr. Walter Houston Clark if he considered it a step backward, intellectually and spiritually, to embrace a tradition that was in this continent before the whiteman came:

I think that the Indians have enormous contributions in their religious traditions and in their attitude toward the environment to make to the kind of dried-up, desiccated sort of civilization that typical America represents. I don't think we can turn back the clock to two or three hundred years ago, when there were great spaces all over the continent, but I do believe that in our metaphysics we have much to learn from the Indians.

At the same time, I think that the Indians have a great deal to learn from us. But we must start on a basis of mutual trust, mutual understanding. Profound mystical experiences have been shared between the whites and the Indians. I think that Carlos Castaneda's book *A Separate Reality* is a kind of indication of a community of interest and values at a very profound level. The separate reality of Don Juan is very similar to the enlightenment of Plato, when he uses his Allegory of the Cave. I think the essential message here is really the same, and here is just one example of a compatibility of a Western philosopher, who lived in another country and at a different age, with Don Juan, an Amerindian sorcerer. The essential beliefs and values are very similar, if not identical. It is at this level that I think there is a possibility that oil and water may mix. I hope that the Indians keep themselves at this level, then persuade the white people to meet them in this same area.

About a year ago, I came across a statement from William James in which he says, "The mother sea and fountainhead of all religions lie in the mystical experiences of the individual. All theologies, all ecclesiasticisms are secondary growths, super-imposed." I seem to see an enlightenment coming into our young people so that those who come into contact with the Indian culture will find a much readier empathy and understanding than the typical orthodox churchgoer or church leader could ever understand.

For many years now, my own personal metaphysics have been based upon Amerindian medicine. I am careful to say, "based upon," for I am a non-Indian and I wish only to be deemed respectful, not presumptuous.

I agree with William James's statement that the very essence of all religions lies in the mystical experiences of the individual, and I agree with Rarihokwats, who has told us that we should not imitate the Amerindian's spiritual achievements, but that we should develop our own medicine in the same ways that the Indian developed his medicine power, by going into the silence and listening. And I seek always to follow Sun Bear's admonition to walk in balance, to remain the spiritual warrior, struggling with contemporary society as it exists, devoting my strength to a disciplined and lifelong vision quest for knowledge.

I offer the following as examples of procedures employed in my personal medicine. They are not to be construed as guidelines, for, if pressed for advice, I will only echo the words of Rarihokwats: "The only formula is to go and sit and listen."

It is imperative in Amerindian medicine or in any practice of metaphysics to set a time apart to enable one to enter the silence.

In my own practice, I have a daily exercise routine in which I work vigorously with barbells and dumbbells, ride a stationary bicycle, in order to exert my physical body and distract my conscious self. I find that just as one on a vision quest may deplete his physical self with monotonous and strenuous tasks in order to free the subconscious, so, for me, does a workout with weights accomplish this same goal.

After my period of purgative exercise, I enter a hot shower—in one sense, I suppose, the counterpart of the sweat lodge. After I have toweled dry, I lie down flat on my back in a quiet place, apart from everyone and all distractions, and permit whatever is to come to me from the silence easy access to my heightened state of awareness.

For an added physical stimulus, I might wrap myself in a blanket, even covering my head. Such a withdrawal and sealing off increases the sensation of being totally isolated and permits one to become even less aware of his physical body and his surrounding environment.

One may also smoke as an aid to meditation. The Amerindian smoked by way of religious observance, not for personal pleasure. I recommend such a moderate usage of tobacco. Again, as a physical stimulus, offer the pipe (cigarettes or cigars are less preferable) to the four directions, upward to the Great Spirit, downward to the Earth Mother.

The puffs of smoke being carried toward the ceiling or the sky should represent one's thoughts or prayers being wafted to the Great Spirit. One should use these rhythmically released clouds of smoke as focal points for concentration. If one has achieved an attitude of calm before smoking, he should find that thoughts and images will begin to come to him almost at once. If one wishes, he might obtain *Kinnikinnick,* Indian bark for smoking, and use it straight or mixed with tobacco in his pipe.

Traditional Amerindians carry a medicine bag which is filled with objects regarded as personally sacred to the bearer. If one should wish to emulate this practice, he should remember to include objects symbolic of the four elements—fire, water, air, and earth. For example, a bit of obsidian, representative of fiery lava, or a bit of flint, the stone used to strike a fire; a small earthen water bowl or a dried water plant; a talon or feather from a bird; an unusual stone that for some reason caught the eye on a walk. One should remember that these objects, and any other items that may have personal significance to the bearer, serve as physical stimuli upon which the bearer might meditate in order to open the channel of his subconscious.

I believe that my dreams are telling me something about myself that I do not already know or that they are revealing patterns—future or present—of which it would be to my advantage to be made aware. Dream control is difficult, though hardly impossible, to learn, but anyone can keep dream diaries and maintain a permanent record of the assistance he is being given nightly by his unconscious —or, if you will, by the Great Spirit. Dream symbols are personal, and while there seem to be universal images which bear consistently similar messages to dreamers in several cultures, one must come to know himself during his vision quest so that he may be able to sort out glimpses of the future and items of knowledge, from bits and pieces of psychological garbage which are being vented by other levels of consciousness.

One may acquire his personal song, or he may have learned a mantra which he sounds in order to facilitate his meditation. Again, these songs are often given in dreams or in visions. Do not overlook certain pieces of music which contain personally nostalgic triggers. From time to time, I may employ a record of a song that is loaded with sentimental images for me. I find that the melody immediately sends me back to that particular experience; but after that moment in time has been relived, my unconscious is soaring here and there and often returning with valuable insights.

Do not neglect the Navajo Yeibichai or other recordings of native American music.

A contemporary composer-artist I find particularly effective in assisting me to transcend the ordinary is Wilburn Burchette, who with his Impro guitar, literally plays emotions, rather than notes. I have utilized both his *Occult Concert* and his *Seven Gates of Transcendental Consciousness* with excellent results.

In our modern American society, one may become rather uneasy in stating his belief in a total partnership with the world of spirits, especially when we have learned so much about the limitless reach of the human psyche. One might begin by at least keeping the door open to the possibility that one may establish contact with those who have graduated to other planes of existence. With a small group of like-minded friends, one may begin to sit in development circles, remaining receptive to whatever communication might be channeled to any one of the circle. Under no circumstances should the situation be forced. A relaxed and tranquil state of mind will best permit the psyche to soar free of time and space and return with images, impressions, messages, perhaps even an accompanying guide or a concerned entity. Each session should begin with each member of the circle asking a prayer for guidance and protection.

It is extremely difficult for those who live in a society so completely and pervasively governed by man-made markings of linear time to "stop the world" and develop a "magic" or spiral time sense. Meditation affords the most effective method I know for allowing one to break free of the boundaries of conventional time. For a level of the unconscious, linear time does not exist. All is an Eternal Now. By utilizing any one of the meditative techniques discussed above, one may achieve an altered state of consciousness which will permit him to enter that time-free, uncharted, measureless kingdom of the psyche.

One must learn to really see and to appreciate the adornments and trappings of the lovely Earth Mother. One must come to know that he is a part of the Universe and that the Universe is a part of him. One must recognize that the essence of the Great Spirit is to be found in all things, and all things are linked in ways that are as yet too subtle for man's comprehension. One must bear his responsibility toward all plant and animal life with dignity, not with condescension.

In my opinion, a total commitment to such medicine power is in complete harmony with the basic tenets of all schools of positive metaphysical teachings and should be considered complementary to those bodies of philosophical thought which consider themselves to be orthodox religions.

Although I have long since abandoned anthropomorphic concepts of a Supreme Being, in moments of intense prayer I find myself speaking to the Great Spirit as if I were truly His child. Intellectually, I know the truth of the relationship must be something very different and that to speak to All That Is as a Father is but a psychological device that is based upon my filial affection for childhood's image of my father, but the unconscious mechanism that is established enables one, I believe, to have an emotional sense of devotion and humility which will permit him to achieve the proper psychic attunement with that Supreme Intelligence that exists beyond one's conscious self. If one has attained the proper spiritual linkup and not simply rattled off his prayer as if it were a religious nursery rhyme, he can come to feel in touch with an energy source outside of himself and he will come to feel a new power within his own being.

With thanks to my friend Iron Eyes Cody, here is a prayer that may be used by all who seek to walk in balance:

Great Spirit, whose voice I hear in the winds and whose breath gives life to the whole world, hearken!

I come before you as one of your many children. See, I am small and weak; I need your strength and wisdom.

Permit me to walk in beauty. May my heart treat with respect the things which you have created; may my ears hear your voice!

Make me wise that I may understand the things which you have taught, which you have hidden in every leaf and rock.

I long for strength, not in order that I may overcome my brother, but to fight my greatest enemy, myself.

Make me ever ready to come to you with pure hands and straight eyes, so that my spirit, when life disappears like the setting sun, may stand unashamed before you.